25
CBSE

Class 10
English Language & Literature

Chapter-wise, Topic-wise & Skill-wise

Previous Year Solved Papers (2013 - 2023)
with Value Added Notes

DISHA™
Publication Inc

DISHA Publication Inc.

A - 23, FIEE Comples,
Okhla Industrial Area Phase-II, New Delhi-110020
Tel: 49842349/ 49842350

Edited by : Ananta Ahuja

Typeset By
DISHA DTP Team

Buying books from DISHA

Just Got A Lot More Rewarding!!!

We at DISHA Publication, value your feedback immensely and to show our apperciation of our reviewers, we have launched a review contest.

To participate in this reward scheme, just follow these quick and simple steps:
- Write a review of the product you purchase on Amazon/Flipkart.
- Take a screenshot/photo of your review.
- Mail it to *disha-rewards@aiets.co.in*, along with all your details.

Each month, selected reviewers will win exciting gifts from DISHA Publication. Note that the rewards for each month will be declared in the first week of next month on our website.

https://bit.ly/review-reward-disha.

Write To
Us At

feedback_disha@aiets.co.in

CONTENTS

> **3rd Level of Division : Skillwise Division**
> Each Question in the topic has been further divided skillwise using following codes:
> **K** Knowledge
> **U** Understanding
> **Ap** Application
> **A** Analysis

Bhagvad Gita

The Story Way

for Students & Parents

- 21 Lessons of Gita explained with Stories & Anecdotes
- Specially written for students & parents

70+ 5 star ratings

by Avinash Agarwal

Author of
- How to raise a Topper
- Topper s' Study Hacks
- The Secret code of UPSC Toppers

amazon.in

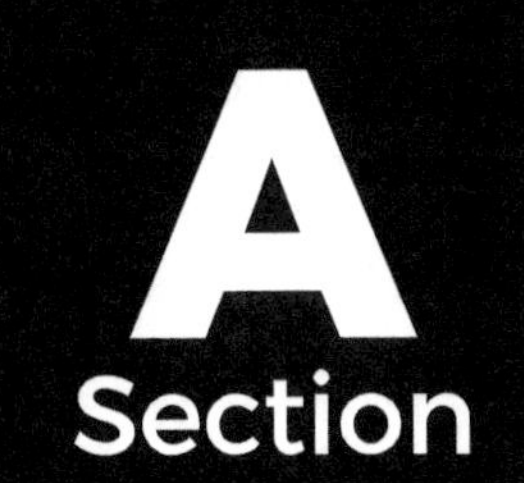

Topic-a: *Discursive Passages* ....O

1. Read the following passage text.

[CBSE Sample 2023-24 U]

1. As a high school student, studying poetry can be a rollercoaster ride. This journey is punctuated by moments of profound appreciation for simpler pieces and intermittent frustration with more complex works. Let's be real here - some poems are just plain confusing and no amount of re-reading seems to help decipher the intended meaning. The puzzlement that results from such instances can be both vexing and demotivating. If solving a riddle is what was intended, then playing Sudoku is a better option. One is led to ponder if obscurity was the goal.

2. Conversely, some pieces resonate with the reader's soul. stirring feelings of warmth, happiness, and connection to the world. Often, these compositions centre on themes that are universally understood, such as love, nature, or faith. Being able to actually understand what the poet is trying to say can feel like a little victory and is a welcome relief after grappling with more perplexing poetry.

3. Then there are poems that are emotionally charged; the ones that make the reader curl up in a ball and cry or jump up and down with joy. One is left in awe of the poet's ability to convey emotion through words. Let's not forget the downright weird poems. These are the ones that defy categorization and leave the reader to their own devices in attempting to interpret meaning. The author's use of figurative language and unconventional imagery can create a sense of bewilderment that is either intriguing or off-putting. Regardless, the reader can appreciate the uniqueness of the work.

4. Despite the wide range of emotions and reactions that come with studying poetry, it can be a rewarding pursuit. Not only does reading poetry allow one to appreciate the artistic beauty of the written word but also enables one to develop crucial critical thinking and analytical skills. The process of unlocking a

poem's meaning can feel like cracking a code or solving a puzzle but the sense of accomplishment derived from mastering a challenging piece can be deeply gratifying. Finally, impressing an English teacher with a well-analysed poem can be a source of pride and validation.

5. Overall, studying poetry is like a box of mixed chocolates, you never know what you're going to get. But whether it's complex, emotional, simple, or just downright weird, there's always something to be gained from the experience. So, let's applaud all the poets out there, for making us laugh, cry, scratch our heads, and occasionally feel like a genius.

Answer the following questions, based on the passage above.   **10×1 = 10**

(i) Which of the following statements best describes the author's attitude towards studying poetry?

(a) Finds poetry to be a frustrating and meaningless endeavor.

(b) Believes that the emotional rollercoaster of studying poetry is not worth the effort.

(c) Recognizes the challenges of studying poetry but also acknowledges the rewards it offers.

(d) Feels that poetry is too obscure and abstract for the average person to appreciate.

(ii) What is the tone of the writer in the given lines from paragraph (1)? Rationalise your response in about 40 words.

If solving a riddle is what was intended, then playing Sudoku is a better option. One is led to ponder if obscurity was the goal.

(iii) Complete the sentence appropriately.

The author's use of vivid imagery in the paragraph (3), such as "curl up in a ball and cry" and "jump up and down with joy", greatly affects the reader because ____________.

(iv) The passage includes some words that are opposites of each other. From the sets (a)-(e) below, identify two sets of antonyms:

(a) intriguing and off-putting

(b) deciphering and interpreting

(c) appreciate and applaud

(d) simple and challenging

(e) emotions and feelings

(v) Complete the sentence appropriately.

We can say that the author's tone becomes more neutral and objective when discussing weird poems, compared to other types of poetry because ____________.

(vi) Based on the reading of the passage, examine, in about 40 words, how studying poetry can be like exploring a new city.

(vii) What is the message conveyed by Hina's experience, in the following case?

Hina spends hours trying to analyze a poem for her assignment and finally feels a sense of accomplishment and pride, once she understands.

   (a) Only those with natural talent for poetry should engage with it.

   (b) Persistence makes studying poetry a rewarding pursuit.

   (c) Study of poetry is guaranteed to impress others.

   (d) The efforts of studying poetry is inversely proportional to the rewards gained.

(viii) State whether the following lines display an example of a simple / complex / emotionally charged / downright weird , poem.

> The sun rises in the east,
>
> A new day begins, a fresh start.
>
> Birds chirp, nature wakes up,
>
> A peaceful feeling in my heart.

(ix) Supply one method of how we can control the contamination of organic and non-organic food.

(x) List one factor that certifies food to be organic.

2.   Read the following passage carefully:

[All India, 2023 Ⓤ]

1. Organic food is very popular these days. It can also be very expensive. Some organic food costs twice as much as non-organic food. Parents of young children and even some pet owners, will pay high prices for organic food if they think it is healthier. But many others think organic food is just a waste of money.

2. There is one main difference between organic and non-organic food. Organic farms do not use agricultural chemicals such as pesticides that stop insects from damaging crops. In many countries, foods that claim to be organic must have special labels that guarantee they're grown organically.

3. Some people think organic also means 'locally grown' and originally it was indeed true. But over a period of time organic farming has become a big business, with many organic foods now being grown by large agricultural companies that sell their products far from where they're grown. Processed food made with organic ingredients has also become more popular. At first, only small companies produced these products. But as demand overtook supply, big food companies that had been selling non-organic products for many years also began selling organic products.

4. Is organic food safer and more nutritious? This is an important part of the debate. Many farmers and consumers believe it is safer and more nutritious. They think agricultural chemicals can cause serious illnesses such as cancer, but there isn't much evidence proving this is true. However, recent studies have shown that eating organically-grown produce reduces your chances of developing heart diseases. Many doctors think it is more important to stop dangerous bacteria from contaminating foods. These bacteria can contaminate both organic and non-organic fruits and vegetables, and doctors recommend washing produce carefully before eating it. Meat, fish and chicken can also become contaminated so washing your hands before handling these foods is also very important.

Based on your understanding of the passage, answer the questions given below:

(i) People are willing to pay high prices for organic food because

    (a) it is not easily available.

    (b) it helps in weight loss.

    (c) it is produced by small companies.

    (d) it does not contain agricultural chemicals.

(ii) Select the option that displays what the writer projects with reference to the following:

Is organic food safer and more nutritious? This is an important part of the debate.

    (a) denial   (b) confirmation

    (c) caution   (d) acceptance

(iii) Complete the following with a phrase from paragraph 3.

Opinion	Reason
Big food companies have started selling organic food products.	

(iv) The writer contrasts organic food to non-organic food. State one point of comparison between the two.

(v) Based on your reading of the text, list one benefit of eating organic food.

(vi) What connect does the writer draw between contamination of food and washing hands?

(vii) The writer says that people believe that it is safer and more nutritious to eat organic food. Select the reason for his sceptical view.

    (a) the price decides the popularity

    (b) there is no confirmed evidence

    (c) it is tastier

    (d) it is marketed by big food companies

(vii) Supply one point to justify the following:

Some people think organic also means 'locally grown'.

(ix) Supply one method of how we can control the contamination of organic and non-organic food.

(x) List one factor that certifies food to be organic.

3.   Read the following passage carefully:

[Delhi, 2023 U]

1. Hiking is a great source of pleasure to us besides being beneficial for health. Once we leave the crowded streets of a city and go out for a walking tour away from the mad world, we really feel free. The open air has a bracing effect on the mind. The congestion of the city, the uproar and tumult, the intolerable noise of traffic, the hectic daily routine, all these are forgotten and the mind is at ease. We then feel like running, leaping, singing and laughing. We travel merrily mile after mile in the company of friends and associates.

2. Hiking takes us in the midst of nature. The sight of waterfalls, flowers, streams, trees and bushes is pleasing. A connect is established between us and nature. Various sounds of nature, like the murmur of a brook or the song of a bird, acquire a new meaning and significance to us.

3. You enjoy the beauty of nature. Minute observations like a snake casting its slough, a mouse peeping out of its hole, a squirrel leaping about on the branches of a tree, a bird flying past us, all these are noticed and they arouse our interest. We have no business worries, no fear of the examination, no anxiety about the home. We have leisure to stand, to walk and talk. It is more thrilling and pleasurable to hike in a mountainous region than in the plains. The excitement of climbing up to the top of a hill, the adventure of coming down a slope, the grandeur of sunset behind a mountain-All these sights lend a rare charm and interest to our journey.

4. We walk along a zigzag motor road or cut across a mountain path in search of adventure. We may have bright sunny weather or might get caught in a shower of rain. We may look below us into the yawning chasm or up at the mountain peak. The feeling of unlimited freedom makes our hearts leap with joy.

5. Hiking is one of the healthiest sports. It ensures a complete escape from the urgent and busy activities of life and therefore gives solace to our brain. It regains its lost energy and is able to do twice as much work as before.

6. The fresh air, beautiful mountains, majestic trees, chirping sound of birds make one's mind and soul at peace with nature.

Based on your understanding of the passage, answer the questions below: **10 × 1 = 10**

(i)   To go out for a walking tour is

   (a)   to stroll.   (b)   to ramble.

   (c)   to hike.   (d)   to saunter.

(ii) Why does the writer say that the mind is at ease when you hike?

(a)　because hiking is an inexpensive activity.

(b)　because it brings families together.

(c)　because of intolerable noise of traffic.

(d)　because the depressing daily routine is forgotten.

(iii) Complete the following with a phrase:

The various sounds of nature acquire...............

(iv) Infer one reason for the following based on information in paragraph 2.

A contact is established between us and nature.

(v) Complete the following analogy correctly with a word from paragraph 2.

aroma: cooking; fragrance:.........................

(vi) Give one reason why it is a pleasure to hike in the mountains than in the plains.

(a)　because observation is sharpened.

(b)　because of the excitement of climbing up and adventure of coming down.

(c)　because it is leisure to stand, to walk.

(d)　because there are no worries.

(vii) Hiking gives the brain, the rest it needs because

(a)　it is a short time activity.

(b)　it is one of the healthiest sports.

(c)　it makes us sleep peacefully.

(d)　it is an escape from our busy schedule.

(viii) List any two examples of minute observations you make while on a hike.

(ix) Supply one point to justify the following:

Hiking gives us a feeling of unlimited joy.

(x) Substitute the word 'leap with joy' with one word similar in meaning in the following sentence from the passage.

The feeling of unlimited freedom makes our hearts leap with joy.

I.　**Read the passage given below :**

[CBSE Sample 2022-23 **U**]

1　Mountains have always been held in great awe by mankind. They have been a challenge to humans. Those brave among us have always wanted to conquer them. You see, the more incredible the mountains, the greater the thrill – a challenge to the bravery of the human race. Climbing mountains is an experience that is hard to put into words. You are in a beautiful environment and, when you reach the top, you feel incredible. But you also have to climb down, which is when most accidents happen – people are tired, it gets dark, it's harder. So, mountain climbing is undoubtedly one of the most popular adventure sports along with being challenging and risky for the climber.

2　Without any perceived risk, there can't be a feeling that any significant challenge has been surmounted. Fair, but we have to bear in mind that mountaineering is not a sport that can be embraced without preparation.

The enthusiasts must develop in themselves the spirit of adventure, willingness to undertake hardships and risks, extraordinary powers of perseverance, endurance, and keenness of purpose before climbing a mountain. They should also know how to handle the mountaineering equipment. Then comes the penance of the rigorous training. This could very well be the lifeline up there. It helps inculcate and hone survival instincts that allow the climber to negotiate perilous situations. There are numerous institutes in India and abroad that offer such training.

3   Mountain climbers are unanimous in agreeing that the unpredictable weather is what they fear the most. There may be sunshine one moment and a snowstorm the other. At higher altitudes, snow is a regular feature and being decisive about setting up camps or proceeding further is crucial. The icy sheets after ice storms make walking treacherous, while the powdery snow makes a mountaineer sink deep into the snow. Up there, where the intention is to embrace Nature's wonder, one realises that it cannot be done without facing its formidable glory. A true mountaineer may challenge the mountain, yet is always respectful to the powerful forces of nature.

4   Summiting mountains carries its own health risks such as oxygen and altitude sickness problems, frost bites, swelling of hands and feet, fluid collection in brain or lungs and exhaustion. Yet, the gratification mountaineers feel from mastering something that is so frightening, urges them to undertake these endeavours. We may think that the mountaineers are fearless, experts say, "Not at all. It's fear that keeps them so intrigued with such arduous journeys." Impulse and brazenness can be deadly foes. In the words of the Indian mountaineer, Bachendri Pal, "The biggest risk ... is to not to take the risk at all. Remember that."   (444 words) Adapted

Based on your understanding of the passage, answer the questions given below.

1.   Why does the writer say that mountains inspire 'awe' in humans? (Paragraph 1).

    (a) They present us with opportunities for exciting sports.

    (b) They evoke the wish in us, to master them.

    (c) They inspire in us, deeds of valour.

    (d) They represent peace and calm, to us.

2.   Select the option that corresponds to the following relation below:

    The more incredible the mountains—the greater the thrill (Paragraph 1)

    (a) The higher the stamina—the lower the food intake

    (b) The more you laugh—the lesser your illness

    (c) The smaller the car—the bigger the advantage

    (d) The heavier the luggage—the higher the penalty

3. Select the option that displays what the writer projects, with reference to the following:

So, mountain climbing is undoubtedly one of the most popular adventure sports (Paragraph 1)

(a) doubt

(b) caution

(c) conviction

(d) denial

4. Complete the following with a phrase from paragraph 1.

Opinion	Reason
_____________	Best experienced rather than described

5. The writer compares training to penance in the line

--Then comes the penance of the rigorous training. (Paragraph 2)

State 1 point of similarity between training and penance.

6. Based on your reading of the text, list 2 reasons why the writer says that "mountaineering is not a sport that can be embraced without preparation". (Paragraph 2)

1. _____________________

2. _____________________

7. What connect does the writer draw out between unpredictable weather and setting up of camps? (Paragraph 3)

8. The writer says, "A true mountaineer may challenge the mountain, yet is always respectful to the powerful forces of nature." (Paragraph 3)

Select the reason the mountaineer is respectful to the forces of nature, up in the mountains.

(a) survival

(b) experience

(c) tradition

(d) directive

9. Supply 1 point to justify the following:

While mountain climbing, an impulsive mountaineer is either disaster-prone or as good as dead.

10. Evaluate the INAPPROPRIATE reason for the feeling of exhilaration on reaching a summit, that the mountain-climbers experience.

(a) Achievement of a seemingly impossible feat

(b) Spectacular panoramic view

(c) Application of the inculcated survival instincts

(d) Opportunity to use sophisticated mountaineering equipment

5. **Read the passage given below:**

[All Indian 2022, T-II [U]]

(1) Milkha Singh, also known as The Flying Sikh, was an Indian track and field sprinter who was introduced

to the sport while serving in the Indian Army. He is the only athlete to win gold in 400 metres at the Asian Games as well as the Commonwealth Games. He also won gold medals in the 1958 and 1962 Asian Games. He represented India in the 1956 Summer Olympics in Melbourne, the 1960 Summer Olympics in Rome and the 1964 Summer Olympics in Tokyo. He was awarded the Padma Shri, India's fourth-highest civilian honour, in recognition of his sporting achievements.

(2) The race for which Singh is best remembered in his fourth-place finish in the 400 metres final at the 1960 Olympic Games. He led the race till the 200 m mark before easing off, allowing others to pase him, Singh's fourth-place time of 45.73 seconds was the Indian national record for almost 40 years.

(3) From beginnings that saw him orphaned and displaced during the partition of India, Singh became a sporting icon in the country. In 2008, journalist Rohit Brijnath described Singh as "the finest athlete India has ever produced".

(4) He was disappointed with his debut performance at the 1956 Melbourne Olympics. "I returned to India, chastened by my poor performance in Melbourne. I had been so excited by the prospects of being part of the Indian Olympics team, but, hadn't realized how strong and professional the competition would be. My success in India has filled me with a false sense of pride and it was only when I was on the track that I saw how inconsequential my talents were when pitted against superbly fit and seasoned athletes. It was then that I understood what competition actually meant, and that if I wanted to succeed on the international arena, I must be prepared to test my mettle against the best athletes in the world."

(5) Then he decided to make sprinting the sole focus of his life.

"Running had thus become my God, my religion and my beloved."

"My life during those two years was governed by strict rules and regulations and a self-imposed penance. Every morning I would rise at the crack of dawn, get into my sports kit and dash off to the track, where I would run two or three miles cross-country in the company of my coach."

(6) On how he pushed himself through the tough days of vigorous training. "I practiced so strenuously that often I was drained of all energy, and there were times when I would vomit blood or drop down unconscious through sheer exercise. My doctors and coaches warned me, asked me to slow down to maintain my health and equilibrium but my determination was too strong to give up. My only focus was to become the best athlete in the

world. But then images of a packed stadium filled with cheering spectators, wildly applauding me as I crossed the finishing line, would flash across my mind and I would start again, encouraged by visions of victory."

Based on your reading answer any five questions from the six given below :   **(1 × 5 = 5 Marks)**

(i) What is Milkha Singh known as ? What realization did Milkha Singh have when he was on the track during the melbourne Olympics ?

(ii) List any two Milkah Singh's achievements.

(iii) What strict rules and regulations did Milkha Singh follow ?

(iv) State two consequences of his hard and strenuous practice.

(v) What motivated Milkha Singh to become the best athlete in the world ?

(vi) Explain the phrase 'I would start again' in the last sentence.

6. **Read the passage given below and answer the questions/complete the statements that follow by choosing the most appropriate options from the given ones : (any eight)**

In most societies that have any glimmering of civilization, a person accused of wrong doing is given at least a nominal chance of proving his innocence. The Romans had a highly sophisticated / comprehensive system of courts and the members of their legal profession were well educated but the Saxons who followed them to rule Britain used rougher methods.

From about the sixth century A.D. to the eleventh the majority of the trials were in the form of cruel physical torture (carrying a piece of red hot iron, stepping barefoot and blindfold across a floor covered with red hot coals or sometimes by a gentler method of oath – swearing.

The accused was ordered to bring to the Saxon authorities, a police officer or a priest : could be persuaded to swear on oth or still a number of persons who would say that the accused was of good character and thus innocent. The number of persons who swore depended on the crime. A noble / a landlord or a priest counted for up to half a dozen ordinary peasants. As almost everyone lived in small villages, where almost everyone knew everyone else, and very few would risk telling a lie on oath (the people were mostly religious), the truth was generally told. If the accused could not produce enough oath helpers, he was found guilty and punished.

In the eleventh century the Normans introduced trial by battle in certain cases. The accused and the accuser fought with special weapons until one was dead or surrendered. It was believed that God would know the guilty and give the innocent the power to win. The whole idea became ridiculous when both the parties were allowed to hire champions who would fight on their behalf. It seemed likely whoever could pay the more for a stronger professional fighter stood a good chance of winning and judged innocent. This may sound unfair to us but there is a parallel with a wealthy person today who can hire a costly and brilliant barrister to defend him.

In the early middle ages when England was a land of small villages remote from each other, crime tended to be basic and direct : beating up, theft, sex and murder being the main offences. But as towns and manufacturing and commerce grew, the possibilities for cheating and fraud soared. The whole organisation of society become more complex and opened the door to a world of more sophisticated wickedness. With no regular police force, spies and informers were offered rewards when they brought in criminals.

1. England (or Britain) turn by turn came under the rule of :   **[All Indian 2022, T-I U]**

    (a) Saxons ; Romans ; Normans

    (b) Normans ; Saxons ; Romans

    (c) Romans ; Saxons ; Normans

    (d) Normans : Romans ; Saxons

2. The article describes :   **[All Indian 2022, T-I U]**

    (a) The development of the system of justice in England

    (b) Civilized societies and justice

    (c) Justice v/s Civilisation

    (d) Rule of Justice in England

3. Study the following statements:

    [All Indian 2022, T-I U]

    (A) Romans were proud of their judicial system.

    (B) There is not much difference between the Norman modern system of justice.

    (a) (A) is right and (B) is wrong

    (b) (B) is right and (A) is wrong

    (c) Both (A) and (B) are right

    (d) Both (A) and (B) are wrong

4. Match the following   **[All Indian 2022, T-I]**

(A) Romans	i.	A priest to swear for the accused
(B) Saxons	ii.	Highly paid lawyers can win a case
(C) Modern	iii.	Educated judges and lawyers
(D) Normans	iv.	The winner in a battle declared innocent

    (a) (A) iv ;   (B) ii;   (C) i;   (D) iii;

    (b) (A) iii ;   (B) i;   (C) ii;   (D) iv ;

    (c) (A) i ;   (B) iii ; (C) iv ; (D) ii ;

    (d) (A) ii ;   (B) i ;   (C) iii ; (D) iv ;

5. Study the following statements:

[All Indian 2022, T-I **U**]

(A) In a trial by battle, money played a main role.

(B) God helped the innocent win the battle.

(a) (A) is right and (B) is wrong

(b) (B) is right and (A) is wrong

(c) Both (A) and (B) are right and (A) was the conclusion

(d) Both (A) and (B) are right and (A) was not the conclusion

6. Study the following statements:

[All Indian 2022, T-I **U**]

(A) Saxon system of trial was nobler than that of the Romans.

(B) Saxon system had two aspects - rough and noble.

(C) The rich Saxons could hire champions to argue their case

(D) Even an innocent person would be held guilty if enough people did not swear for him.

The following are correct

(a) (A) and (B)

(b) (B) and (C)

(c) (C) and (A)

(d) (B) and (D)

7. Study the following statements

[All Indian 2022, T-I **U**]

(A) Earlier England comprised small villages each with a small population.

(B) Crimes like cheating and fraud were rare.

(a) (A) is an assertion and (B) is the response

(b) (B) is an assertion and (A) is the response

(c) Both (A) and (B) are unrelated assertions

(d) Both (A) and (B) are responses to some other assertions

8. Which of the following statements are true ?

[All Indian 2022, T-I **U**]

The rich have always enjoyed an advantage in the judicial system because

(A) they were physically strong, so would win the trial by fighting

(B) they could hire the strongest champion.

(C) they can hire the best lawyers.

(D) they could persuade the priest to swear on their behalf.

(a) (A) and (B)

(b) (B) and (C)

(c) (C) and (D)

(d) (A) and (D)

9. Which of the following statements are <u>not</u> true? **[All Indian 2022, T-I U]**

(A) In the quest for justice the guilty often went unpunished.

(B) For seven hundred years from the sixth century trial was mostly rough.

(C) Swearing value of a priest was equal to a dozen ordinary peasants.

(D) Use of champions in a trial by battle finds an equivalent in the modern times.

(a) (A) and (C)

(b) (B) and (C)

(c) (C) and (D)

(d) (A) and (B)

10. 'any glimmering of civilisation'

[All Indian 2022, T-I U]

'Glimmering' in the above expression has been used as a metaphor.

Glimmering stand for

(a) a slight suggestion

(b) a great hope

(c) some fear

(d) a little confidence

7. **Read the passage given below. [CBSE Sample 2021-22] U**

5 Technology is making advancements at a rapid rate but at the cost of a valued tradition—the crafts industry. The traditional crafts industry is losing a lot of its trained and skilled craftsmen. With that, the art of embellishing brass and copper utensils with fine engravings is also disappearing. The government has identified around 35 crafts as languishing craft.

10 The speciality of handcrafted items is its design, an association with long traditions belonging to a specific region. The word 'handcrafted' does not imply the involvement of dexterous human fingers or an agile mind with a moving spirit anymore. Lessening drudgery, increasing production and promoting efficiency have taken precedence. The labour-saving devices are taking the place of handcrafted tools and this has jeopardized the skills of these artisans.

15 Mechanisation has made its way into everything - cutting, polishing, edging, designing etc. Ideally, the use of machinery should be negligible and the handicrafts should be made purely by hand with a distinguishable artistic appeal. However, with the exception of small-scale industries, the export units are mostly operated by machines. The heavily computerised designs contribute to a faster production at lower costs.

20 Although mechanization of crafts poses a challenge to safeguarding traditional crafts, the artisans are lured with incentives in order to impart handicrafts training. Some makers do see machines as a time-saving blessing since they are now able to

accomplish difficult and demanding tasks with relative ease. These machines might give a better finesse to

25 these products but they don't stand out as handcrafted. Quantity has overtaken quality in this industry.

30. A need to highlight the importance of the handmade aspect is required by both the government and private sectors, in order to amplify awareness and also support the culture of making handicrafts. A few artisans are still trying their best to rejuvenate and revive their culture and heritage but it's an uphill task competing with the machine-made goods. A multitude of artisans have changed their professions and are encouraging their progeny to follow suit. There are others who have stayed their ground but are clearly inclined towards buying machines.

35 Nearly two decades ago, there were around 65 lakh artisans in the country. Three years ago, when the government started the process of granting a unique number to the artisans based on the Aadhaar card, 25 lakhs were identified. Loss of traditional crafts is clearly a worrying issue, but it stands to reason that forcing any artisan to follow old ways when concerns of livelihood overrule other considerations, is unfair.

Based on your understanding of the passage, answer ANY FIVE questions from the six given below.

(i) What does the writer mean by calling handicrafts a 'valued tradition'?

(ii) Rewrite the following sentence by replacing the underlined phrase with a word that means the same from lines 5– 15.

If it continues, the workcation (work + vacation) trend will be a powerful boost to domestic tourism operators failing to make progress in the economic slump caused due to the pandemic.

(iii) State any two reasons why artisans are choosing to work via machines rather than handcrafted tools.

(iv) Why do the artisans need to be 'lured with incentives' to impart handicrafts training?

(v) List one likely impact of the support of government and private sectors towards the culture of making handicrafts.

(vi) How does the writer justify an artist's act of abandoning her/his traditional craft for a more lucrative option?

8. **Read the following passage carefully.**

[All India 2020, Delhi 2023 U]

Caged behind thick glass, the most famous dancer in the world can easily be missed in the National Museum, Delhi. The Dancing Girl of Mohenjo-daro is that rare artefact that even school children are familiar with. Our school textbooks also communicate the wealth of our 5000-year heritage of art. You have to be alert to her existence there, amid terraootta animals to rediscover this bronze image.

Most of us have seen her only in photographs or sketches, therefore the impact of actually holding her is magnified a million times over. One discovers that the dancing girls has no feet. She is small, a little over 10 cm tall __ the length of a human palm __ but she surprises us with the power of great art __ the ability to communicate across centuries.

A series of bangles __ of shell or ivory or thin metal __ clothe her left upper arm all the way down to her fingers. A necklace with three pendants bunched together and a few bangles above the elbow and wrist on the right hand display an almost modern art.

She speaks of the undaunted over hopeful human spirit. She reminds us that it is important to visit museums in our country to experiences the impact that a work of art leaves on our senses, to find among all the riches one particular vision of beauty that speaks to us alone.

On the basis of your reading of the above passage, answer the following questions.

(a) The Dancing Girl belongs to

    (i)   Mohenjo-daro

    (ii) Greek culture

    (iii) Homosapiens

    (iv) Tibet

(b) In the museum she's kept among

    (i)   dancing figures

    (ii) bronze statues

    (iii) terracotta animals

    (iv) books

(c) Which information is not given in the passage?

    (i)   The girl is caged behind glass

    (ii) She is a rare artefact

    (iii) School books communicate the wealth of our heritage

    (iv) She cannot be rediscovered as she's bronze

(d) 'Great Art' has power because:

    (i)   it appeals to us despite a passage of time

    (ii) it is small and can be understood

    (iii) it's seen in pictures and sketches

    (iv) it's magnified a million times

(e) The jewellery she wears:

    (i)   consists of bangles of shell, ivory or thin metal

    (ii) is a necklace with two pendants

    (iii) both (i) and (ii) are correct

    (iv) neither (i) nor (ii) is correct

(f) She reminds us

    (i) of the never say-die attitude of humans

    (ii) why museums in our country are exciting

    (iii) why she will make us come into money

    (iv) of dancing figures

(g) The synonym of the word "among" in para 1 is

    __________ .

(h) The size of the dancing girl is equal to the length of human palm. (True/False)

9. Read the following passage carefully.

[Delhi 2020, All India 2020 **U**]

As the family finally sets off from home after many arguments there is a moment of lull as the car takes off. "Alright, so where are we going for dinner now?" asks the one at the driving wheel. What follows is a chaos as multiple voices make as many suggestions.

By the time order is restored and a decision is arrived at, tempers have risen, feelings injured and there is at least one person grumbling.

Twenty years ago, you would step out of home, decision of meal and venue already made with no arguments or opposition and everybody looked forward to the meal with equal enthusiasm. The decision was made by the head of the family and the others fell in line. Today every member of the family has a say in every decision which also promotes a sense of togetherness and bonding.

We empower our kids to take their own decisions from a very early age. We ask them the cuisine they prefer, the movies they want to see, the holiday they wish to go on and the subjects they wish to study.

It's a closely connected world out there where children consult and guide each other. A parent's well meaning advice can sound like nothing more than unnecessary preaching. How then do we reach our children through all the conflicting views and make the voice of reason be heard? Children today question choices and prefer to go with the flow.

What then is the best path to take? I would say the most important thing one can do is to listen. Listen to your children and their silences. Ensure that you keep some time aside for them, insist that they share their stories with you. Step into their world. It is not as complicated as it sounds; just a daily half an hour of quality time would do the trick.

9.1. On the basis of your reading of the above passage, answer the following questions in 30-40 words each.

(a) Write one advantage and one disadvantage of allowing every family member to be part of the decision making process.

(b) In today's world, what are parents asking their kids?

(c) Which two pieces of advice does the writer give to the parents?

(d) The passage supports the parents. How far do you agree with the author's views? Support your views with a reason.

9.2. On the basis of your reading of the above passage, answer the following:

(a) The synonym of 'hurt' as given in paragraph 2 is

_______________ .

(b) The word which means the same as 'a style or method of cooking' in paragraph 4 is:

    (i) Cuisine

    (ii) Gourmet

    (iii) Gastric

    (iv) Science

(c) The antonym of 'agreeable' as given in paragraph 5 is ______________ .

(d) The antonym of 'simple' as given in paragraph 6 is

    (i) difficult

    (ii) complicated

    (iii) easy

    (iv) tricky

10. **Read the following passage carefully.**

1. Few guessed that this quiet, parentless girl growing up in New York city would one day become the First Lady of the United States. Even fewer thought she would become an author and lecturer and a woman much admired and loved by people throughout the world.

2. Born Anna Eleanor Roosevelt in 1884 to wealthy, but troubled parents who both died while she was young, Roosevelt was cared for by her grandmother and sent to school in England. In 1905, she married her distant cousin, Franklin Delano Roosevelt. She and her husband had six children. Although they were wealthy, her life was not easy and she suffered several personal tragedies. Her second son died when he was a baby. In 1921, her strong athletic husband was stricken with polio, which left him physically disabled for life.'

3. Eleanor Roosevelt was a remarkable woman who had great intelligence and tremendous strength of character. She never let things get her down. She nursed her husband back to good health and encouraged him to remain in politics. She then helped him to become Governor of New York, and in 1933, President of the United States.

4. While her husband was President, she took a great interest in all the affairs of the country. She became her husband's legs and eyes; she visited prisons and hospitals; she went down into mines, up scaffoldings and into factories. Roosevelt was tireless and daring. During the depression, she travelled all over

the country bringing goodwill, reassurance and help to people without food and jobs. During World War II, she visited American soldiers in camps all over the world. The United States had never known a First Lady like her.

5. Roosevelt also kept in touch with the American people through a daily newspaper column called 'My Day'. She broadcast on the radio and delivered lectures, all first for a First Lady.

On the basis of your understanding of the above passage, answer the following questions: (**any eight**)

(a) How was Eleanor Roosevelt's personality in contrast to what she became? **[All India 2019 U]**

(b) Apart from being the First Lady what else did she have to her credit? **[All India 2019 U]**

(c) What challenges did she face in her personal life but remained unfazed? **[All India 2019 U]**

(d) Eleanor was a strong woman who helped her husband become the President of America. How?

[All India 2019 U]

(e) What does the statement: 'She became her husband's legs and eyes' mean? **[All India 2019 U]**

(f) What was her special contribution during the depression? **[All India 2019 U]**

(g) How did she motivate soldiers during World War II? **[All India 2019 U]**

(h) What did she do for the first time for a First Lady?

[All India 2019 U]

(i) What side of her personality is reflected in this passage? **[All India 2019 U]**

20. **Read the passage given below carefully and answer the questions that follow.**

1. Overpowering prey is a challenge for creatures that do not have limbs. Some species like Russell's viper inject poison.

Some others opt for an alternative non-chemical method – rat snakes, for instance, catch and push their prey against the ground, while pythons use their muscle power to crush their prey to death. But snakes can't be neatly divided into poisonous and non-poisonous categories.

2. Even species listed as non-poisonous aren't completely free of poison. The common Sand Boa, for instance, produces secretions particularly poisonous to birds. So the species doesn't take any chance – it crushes its prey and injects poison as an extra step.

3. Do vipers need poison powerful enough to kill hundreds of rats with just one drop? After all , they eat only one or two at a time.

4. While hunting animals try their worst to kill most efficiently, their prey use any trick to avoid becoming a meal, such as developing immunity to

poison. For instance, Californian ground squirrels are resistant to Northern Pacific rattlesnake poison.

5. Competition with prey is not the only thing driving snakes to evolve more and more deadly poison. Snakes also struggle to avoid becoming prey themselves.

6. Some snake killers have partial immunity to poison. Famously, mongooses are highly resistant to cobra poison, and with their speed and agility, kill snakes fearlessly. It would be the death of cobras as a species if they didn't evolve a more deadly poison to stop mongooses.

7. Poison has another important role. It's an extreme meat softener; specific enzymes break up the insides of the prey. Normally, a reptile depends on the sun's warm rays to aid digestion.

8. But I wonder why we cannot use venom in our favour. In remote parts of India, local hospitality often involves leather-tough meal. I chew and chew until my jaws ache. If I spit it out or refuse, our hosts would be offended, I swallow like a python stuffing a deer down its throat and hope I don't choke. If only 1 had poison.

11.1. Read the questions given below and answer **any four** in 30-40 words each.

(a) Russell's viper and rat snake have different methods to attack prey. How? **[All India 2019 U]**

(b) How does Sand Boa kill its prey?

[All India 2019 U]

(c) There is a constant tussle between the hunting animal and its prey? Why? **[All India 2019 U]**

(d) What makes mongoose a snake predator?

[All India 2019 U]

(e) What difficulty does the writer face when he is entertained in the remote parts of India?

[All India 2019 U]

11.2. On the basis of your reading of the above passage fill in **any two** of the following blanks.

(i) Overpowering __________ is a challenge for creatures that do not have limbs. **[All India 2019 U]**

(a) a killer

(b) humans

(c) a python

(d) prey

(ii) Poison ______ meat. **[All India 2019 U]**

(a) enhances taste of

(c) hardens

(b) softens

(d) breaks down

(iii) Californian squirrels are ______ rattlesnake poison.

[All India 2019 U]

(a) afraid of (b) helpless against

(c) resistant to (d) indifferent to

11.3. Find words from the passage which mean the same as:

(any two)   **[All India 2019 U]**

(a)   Another (para I)

(b)   Liquid substances released from glands (para 2)

(c)   Particular (para 7)

12.   Read the passage given below and answer the questions that follow :

1.   Keep your watch accurate. For some people, moving up the time on their watch will help them to get up early. For others, they will remember that the time on the watch is wrong and will disregard it altogether. It may be helpful to set your watch just two minutes ahead instead of five or ten.

2.   Keep a clock, phone, computer or anything that displays time in each room of your house. One of the easiest ways to run late is simply by not realising that the time is passing as quickly as it is.

3.   Set all your clocks and watches to the same time. Don't be an optimist. Things usually take longer than what you'd expect, even without major delays. If you have a dinner appointment at 7·30 p.m., don't think you can work till 7 p.m., then take a bath, dress and reach on time. Realistically, calculate the time you will take at each step and then add 10 minutes more to allow for unexpected delays, or you cannot get to your job in time.

4.   Wake up when you are supposed to wake up. Don't hit the snooze button, keep on lying in bed, and watch TV at the very start of your day. Maybe try even setting your clock 10 minutes earlier than you need. If you have difficulty with this, move your alarm clock to somewhere away from your bed; that way, you have to get up to turn it off. Commit yourself to being 15 minutes early for everything. If you have to reach your place of work at 8·00, don't even tell yourself this. Just tell yourself (and everyone else who listens — but don't annoy them or make them think that they are late or early!) "I have to be at work at 7·45." If you do this, you will be on time even with little unforeseen delays. You will be on time even with a traffic jam.

12.1 Complete the following statements using words/phrases from the passage. Attempt any eight.

(a)   Some people believe that if _______ it will help them be earlier.   **[Delhi 2019 U]**

(b)   Many others know ___________ they disregard it altogether.   **[Delhi 2019 U]**

(c)   Keep ___________ in each room.   **[Delhi 2019 U]**

(d)   One of the things that can be done is ________ of five or ten minutes.   **[Delhi 2019 U]**

(e)   Many a time we do not realise that ___________ .

                                    [Delhi 2019 U]

(f) Instead of pressing the snooze button ____________ .

[Delhi 2019 U]

(g) If you have difficulty in getting up ___________.

[Delhi 2019 U]

(h) It is a good habit to ________ somewhere away from your bed. **[Delhi 2019 U]**

(i) It is good to commit yourself __________ for everything. **[Delhi 2019 U]**

13. Read the passage given below and answer the questions that follow :

1. Music is perhaps the most popular and widely practised form of Fine Arts, transcending all kinds of cultural and linguistic barriers. Any form of fine art is difficult to master and almost impossible to perfect and music is no exception.

2. Nature, it is learnt, has blessed almost two-thirds of the human race with musical ability of some sort. Music has the power to bring out the deepest emotions. It can make one cry or bring a smile on one's face. In fact it is a magic medicine and many seek refuge in it when they are depressed or stressed. It is this intimacy that makes us listen to music or even hum or sing sometimes. This singing, or realistically speaking, expressing one's emotion musically sometimes takes a serious turn. This desire to show musical expression in public then becomes a serious business profession. And from here the musical journey begins.

3. This desire to sing before an audience is innocent and beautiful and indeed it is perfectly alright to have such a genuine desire. But it is also important to understand that singing is an intricate art — a highly refined one at that, which requires systematic, prolonged and strict training, to be acceptable. This is an aspect we forget in our keen desire to reach the stage and perform. It is almost like preparing a formal meal for some specially invited guests, without even having learnt and trained in the basics of cooking. This is why we have more noise and less music nowadays.

4. These days almost everyone sings and it does not stop here. Most of us want to become professional singers. Result : a complete disregard for and ignorance of the training part, as the need is never felt to go through one and the urge to get to the stage and perform overcomes even a little desire to learn, if any. If at all, somewhere along the way one feels the need to gain some knowledge and training, it leads to hurried shortcuts and half-hearted attempts, best described as 'Crash Courses'.

5. It is observed that those who have attained the so called partial success, suddenly feel that they lack the required knowledge and are not learned enough. But it is too late by then. It should be understood here that the stage or a performance brings in a different

mindset within the artist. It is always recommended and rightly said, that while on stage, cover the mistakes and weaknesses if any, and get along. But the contrary is true when it comes to acquiring knowledge and during the learning process. While under training, the student is expected to make mistakes but then rectify those mistakes under the supervision and guidance of the teacher. Therefore, it is good to make mistakes and then be corrected during the process of learning as this subsequently makes one flawless and educated. This is a different mindset. And these two mindsets discussed above, (those of a performer and that of a student) cannot co-exist.

13.1 On the basis of your understanding of the above passage, answer any four of the following questions in 30 – 40 words each :

(a) The desire to sing in public overcomes the need to train. Elaborate. **[Delhi 2019 U]**

(b) How can we say that music is a magic medicine ?

[Delhi 2019 U]

(c) What is best described as 'Crash Courses'?

[Delhi 2019 U]

(d) What should be the mindset of a student of music ?

[Delhi 2019 U]

(e) Why is singing a refined and intricate art?

[Delhi 2019 U]

13.2 On the basis of your understanding of the above passage, answer any four of the following :

(a) Almost _________ of human population is blessed with musical ability of some sort. **[Delhi 2019 U]**

   (i)   two-thirds

   (ii) one-third

   (iii) half

   (iv) one-fifth

(b) Any form of _______ ________ is difficult to master. **[Delhi 2019 U]**

   (i)   visual art

   (ii) audio-visual art

   (iii) fine arts

   (iv) design art

(c) 'Transcending' in para 1 means **[Delhi 2019 U]**

   (i)   drown under

   (ii) rise above

   (iii) surrender

   (iv) fail

(d) 'Refuge' in para 2 means **[Delhi 2019 U]**

   (i)   shelter from rain

   (ii) shelter from storm

   (iii) shelter from unhappiness

   (iv) shelter from sun

(e) 'Partial' in para 5 means **[Delhi 2019 U]**

   (i)   unfair   (ii) incomplete

   (iii) whole   (iv) total

14.   Read the passage given below:

(a) Tourists to Jammu and Kashmir have another attraction – a floating post office on the Dal Lake in Srinagar, the first in the country. 'Floating Post Office, Dal Lake' – claimed to be the only one such post office in the world – is built on an intricately carved maroon houseboat, fastened on the western edge of the Dal Lake.

(b) This post office lets you avail of all the regular postal services available in the country while being afloat. The seal used on everything posted from Floating Post Office is unique – along with the date and address, it bears the design of a boatman rowing a shikara on the Dal Lake. The special feature of this post office is that letters posted from here carry a special design which has the picturesque scenery of Dal Lake and Srinagar city. These pictures reach wherever these letters are posted to and hence promote Kashmir as a tourist destination across the world.

(c) This is actually a heritage post office that has existed since British times. It was called Nehru Park Post Office before 2011. But then the chief postmaster John Samuel renamed it as 'Floating Post Office'.

(d) The post office's houseboat has two small rooms – one serves as the office and the other a small museum that traces the philatelic history of the state postal department. It has a shop that sells postage stamps and other products.

(e) But for the locals, Floating Post office is more than an object of fascination ₹ 1-2 crore is deposited per month in Floating Post Office by communities living in and around the Dal Lake. The lake has several islets that are home to more than 50,000 people.

(f) The greatest fear is the recurrence of 2014 like floods in which the houseboat had gone for a toss uncontrollably pushed by the flood. Rescue teams had to anchor it using special mechanism in a nearby highland. Then it was brought back on the Dal after the water receded. The biggest boon is that at no time of the year do you need a fan in this post-office!

1.1   Attempt any **eight** of the following questions on the basis of the passage you have read:

(a) What is the location of the Floating Post Office in Srinagar?   **[All Indian 2018 U]**

(b) What is special about the seal used in the post office?
                                                                           [All Indian 2018 U]

(c) How is the post office helpful in promoting tourism?
                                                                           [All Indian 2018 U]

(d) Who renamed the post office as 'Floating Post Office'?   **[All Indian 2018 U]**

(e) What are the two rooms of the post office used for?
                                                                           [All Indian 2018 U]

(f) How is the post office beneficial to the locals?
                                                                           [All Indian 2018 U]

(g) What is the greatest fear that the post office has?

[All Indian 2018 U]

(h) How is the post office a big boon to the people?

[All Indian 2018 U]

(i) Find the word from the passage which means the same as 'attraction'. (para 5)   **[All Indian 2018 U]**

15. Read the passage given below.

(1) It is an indisputable fact that the world has gone too far with the innovation of new technologies such as mobile phones, the internet and so on, due to which people are able to tour the cosmos virtually sitting at one place using their smart devices or other technological gadgets. Though mobile internet access is oftentimes hurried and short, it can still provide common internet features like alerts, weather data, emails, search engines, instant messages, and game and music downloading.

(2) Due to the easy access of smart phones, communication has been very effective and instant. People are able to convey their message all around the globe to their loved ones without spending hefty sums of money. Adults are always fond of such gadgets and they always welcome and adopt such new technology readily. Further, young people have been able to broaden their minds and improve their skills by doing research on the Internet. For instance, they use smart phones to look up any new word they come across. As we know that most of the universities have online teaching provision and smart phones assist the students to complete their assignments on time.

(3) The mobile phone has been a lifesaver for a lot of people in case of an emergency. Likewise, use of smart phones can be of vital importance in preventing crimes in the society by providing information to the security forces in time.

(4) Nonetheless, for the young the use of mobile phone can be like an addiction and they can misuse it. Young people are also prone to getting involved in undesirable activities on the Internet. This might have adverse effect on their academic performance. Therefore, young people should always be monitored and made aware of its bad outcomes.

(5) Also a major contributor to its popularity is the availability of prepaid or pay as you go services from a phone shop or an online store. This allows subscribers to load text or airtime credits to their handsets by the use of their credit cards, debit cards or by buying a prepaid card from the network they subscribe to. This plan also doesn't commit a particular customer to a contract. If prepaid card is not that appealing to you, then you can opt to subscribe using the pay by month plan.

15.1 On the basis of your reading of the passage, answer any **four** of the following questions in 30-40 words each :

(a) How are smart phones helpful in communication?

[All Indian 2018 U]

(b) What are the benefits of mobile phones for the young generation?   **[All Indian 2018 U]**

(c) How can mobile phones be considered 'lifesavers'?

[All Indian 2018 U]

(d) Mention any two demerits of mobile phones.

[All Indian 2018 U]

(e) How is a prepaid card useful to mobile phone users?

[All Indian 2018 U]

15.2 On the basis of your reading of the passage, answer any four of the following:

(a) In para 1, synonym of 'innovation' is __________.

[All Indian 2018 U]

   (i)   production

   (ii) sincerity

   (iii) invention

   (iv) prevention

(b) Mobile internet can provide access to :

[All Indian 2018 U]

   (i)   telegram

   (ii) emails

   (iii) schools

   (iv) university

(c) Grown-ups should __________ the use of new technology by the young people.

[All Indian 2018 U]

   (i)   reject

   (ii) criticize

   (iii) monitor

   (iv) accept

(d) Meaning of the word 'adverse' in para 4 is :

[All Indian 2018 U]

   (i)   positive

   (ii) negative

   (iii) admirable

   (iv) unguided

(e) According to the passage, one can opt for __________ plan if prepaid plan doesn't suit.

[All Indian 2018 U]

   (i)   yearly

   (ii) weekly

   (iii) monthly

   (iv) daily

16.   Read the passage given below :

Then all the windows of the grey wooden house (Miss Hilton used to live here. She expired last week), were thrown open, a thing I had never seen before.

At the end of the day a sign was nailed on the mango tree :

FOR SALE.

Nobody in the street knew Miss Hilton. While she lived, her front gate was always locked and no one ever saw her leave or saw anybody go in. So, even if you wanted to, you couldn't feel sorry and say that you missed Miss Hilton.

When I think of her house I see just two colours. Grey and green. The green of the mango tree, the grey of the house and the grey of the high iron fence that prevented you from getting at the mangoes.

If your cricket ball fell in Miss Hilton's courtyard you never got it back. It wasn't the mango season when Miss Hilton died. But we got back about ten or twelve of our cricket balls.

The house was sold and we were prepared to dislike the new owners even before they came. I think we were a little worried. Already we had one resident of the street who kept on complaining about us to our parents. He complained that we played cricket on the pavement; and if we were not playing cricket, he complained that we were making too much noise anyway.

One afternoon when I came back from school Pal said, "Is a man and a woman. She pretty pretty, but he ugly like hell." I didn't see much. The front gate was open, but the windows were shut again. I heard a dog barking in an angry way.

One thing was settled pretty quickly. Whoever these people were they would never be the sort of people to complain that we were making noise and disturbing their sleep.

A lot of noise came from the house that night. The radio was going at full volume until midnight when the radio station closed down. The dog was barking and the man was shouting. I didn't hear the woman.

On the basis of your understanding of the above passage, complete the statements that follow:

(a) Nobody went into Miss Hilton's house because her front __________ .   **[All Indian 2017 U]**

(b) Her house had only two colours, (i) ______, and (ii) ________ .   **[All Indian 2017 U]**

(c) The high iron fence did not let the boys get __________ .   **[All Indian 2017 U]**

(d) They never got it back if their __________ fell into her courtyard.   **[All Indian 2017 U]**

(e) The boys were ready to dislike the __________ .   **[All Indian 2017 U]**

(f) One resident of the street always __________ .   **[All Indian 2017 U]**

(g) The new owners of Miss Hilton's house were (i) ________, and (ii) ________ .   **[All Indian 2017 U]**

(h) The man was shouting, the dog was barking, only __________ .   **[All Indian 2017 U]**

17.   Read the passage given below :

1.   During our growing up years we as children were taught — both at home and school — to worship the photos and idols of the Gods of our respective religions. When we grew a little older, we were to read holy books like the Bhagwad Gita, Bible and Quran; we were told that there are a lot of life lessons to be learnt from these holy books. We were then introduced to stories from our mythologies which taught us about ethics and morality — what is good and what is bad. I also learnt to be respectful towards my parents who made my life comfortable with their hard work and love and care, and my teachers who guided me to become a good student and a responsible citizen.

2.   Much later in life, I realised that though we learn much from our respective holy books, there is a lot to learn from our surroundings. This realisation dawned upon me when I learnt to enquire and explore. Everything around us — the sun, the moon, the stars, rain, rivers, stones, rocks, birds, plants and animals — teach us many valuable life lessons.

3.   No wonder that besides the scriptures, in many cultures nature is also worshipped. The message that we get is to save our environment and maintain ecological balance. People are taught to live in harmony with nature and recognise that there is God in all aspects of nature.

4.   Nature is a great teacher. A river never stops flowing. If it finds an obstacle in its way in the form of a heavy rock, the river water fights to remove it from its path or finds an alternative path to move ahead. This teaches us to be progressive in life, and keep the fighting spirit alive.

5.   Snakes are worshipped as they eat insects in the field that can hurt our crops, thus protecting the grains for us. In fact, whatever we worship is our helper and makes our lives easy for us. There are many such examples in nature, but we are not ready to learn a lesson. Overcome with greed, we are destroying nature. As a result, we face natural disasters like droughts, floods and landslides. We don't know that nature is angry with us.

6.   However, it is never too late to learn. If we learn to respect nature, the quality of our life will improve.

17.1 Answer briefly the following questions :

(a)   What are we taught in our childhood and growing up years?   **[All Indian 2017 U]**

(b)   Why should we respect our parents and teachers?   **[All Indian 2017 U]**

(c)   What message do we get when we worship nature?   **[All Indian 2017 U]**

(d) How does a river face an obstacle that comes in its way? **[All Indian 2017 U]**

17.2 Give the meanings of the words given below, as used in the passage, with the help of the options that follow :

(e) guided (Para 1) **[All Indian 2017 U]**

 (i) answered

 (ii) advised

 (iii) fought

 (iv) polished

(f) explore (Para 2) **[All Indian 2017 U]**

 (i) search

 (ii) frequent

 (iii) describe

 (iv) request

(g) valuable (Para 2) **[All Indian 2017 U]**

 (i) proper

 (ii) desirable

 (iii) available

 (iv) useful

(h) harmony (Para 3) **[All Indian 2017 U]**

 (i) beauty

 (ii) friendship

 (iii) discomfort

 (iv) honesty

18. Read the passage given below and answer the questions that follow :

If you are addicted to coffee, and doctors warn you to quit the habit, don't worry and just keep relishing the beverage, because it's not that bad after all ! In fact, according to a new study, the steaming cup of Java can beat fruits and vegetables as the primary source of antioxidants. Some studies state that coffee is the number one source of antioxidants in American diet and both caffeinated and decaf versions appear to provide similar antioxidant levels.

Antioxidants in general have been linked to a number of potential health benefits, including protection against heart diseases and cancer, but Sandra Vinson, a dietitian said that their benefits ultimately depend on how they are absorbed and utilized in the body. The research says that coffee outranks popular antioxidant sources like tea, milk, chocolate and cranberries. Of all the foods and beverages studies, dates actually have the most antioxidants based solely on serving size, but since dates are not consumed anywhere near the level of coffee, the drink comes as the top source of antioxidants, Vinson said.

Besides keeping you alert and awake, coffee has been linked to an increasing number of potential health benefits, including protection against liver and colon cancer, type 2 diabetes, and Parkinson's disease, according to some recently published studies.

The researchers, however, advise that one should consume coffee in moderation, because it can make you jittery and cause stomach pains.

(a) Why do doctors advise us about the habit of drinking coffee? **[All India 2016 U]**

(b) What are the two versions of coffee that are drunk in America? **[All India 2016 U]**

(c) State any two benefits of antioxidants. **[All India 2016 U]**

(d) What does Vinson say about the consumption of antioxidants? **[All India 2016 U]**

(e) Name any two popular sources of antioxidants. **[All India 2016 U]**

(f) How does coffee outrank dates in the level of antioxidants? **[All India 2016 U]**

(g) Mention any two benefits of coffee. **[All India 2016 U]**

(h) What do researchers warn us about the excessive use of coffee? **[All India 2016 U]**

19. Read the following passage carefully :

Gandhiji As a Fund Raiser

1. Gandhiji was an **incurable** and irresistible fund raiser. He found special relish in getting jewellery from women. Ranibala of Burdwan was ten years old. One day she was playing with Gandhiji. He explained to her that her bangles were too heavy for her delicate little wrists. She removed the bangles and gave them away to Gandhiji.

2. He used to talk jokingly to small girls and created distaste for ornaments and created a desire in them to part with the jewellery for the sake of the poor. He **motivated** them to donate their jewellery for social usage.

3. Kasturbai didn't appreciate this habit of Gandhiji. Once she stated calmly, 'You don't wear jewels, it is easy for you to get around the boys. But what about our daughters-in-law. They would surely want them.

4. "Well!" Gandhiji put in mildly, "our children are young and when they grow up they will not surely choose wives who are fond of wearing jewellery". Kasturbai was very **upset** with the answer.

5. Gandhiji was determined to keep the jewels to raise community fund. He was of the opinion that a public worker should accept no costly gifts. He believed that he should not own anything costly, whether given or earned. Kasturbai was a female with a desire to adorn. But Gandhiji moved towards **renunciation** and donated every penny earned in South Africa to the trustees for the service of South African Indians.

19.1 Answer the questions given below :

(a) How did Gandhiji create a distaste for jewellery in Ranibala? **[All India 2016 U]**

(b) What was Kasturbai's apprehension about their daughters-in-law?

[All India 2016 U]

(c) What solution did Gandhiji suggest for the problem posed by Kasturbai?

[All India 2016 U]

(d) How did Gandhiji serve the community?

[All India 2016 U]

19.2 Find meanings of the words given below from the options that follow :

(e) **incurable (Para 1)**   [All India 2016 U]

    (i) unreliable

    (ii) untreatable

    (iii) disagreeable

    (iv) unbeatable

(f) **motivated (Para 2)**   [All India 2016 U]

    (i) encouraged

    (ii) emboldened

    (iii) incited

    (iv) softened

(g) **upset (Para 4)**   [All India 2016 U]

    (i) puzzled

    (ii) furious

    (iii) confused

    (iv) distressed

(h) **renunciation (Para 5)**   [All India 2016 U]

    (i) giving up

    (ii) disagreement

    (iii) opposition

    (iv) termination

20. Read the passage given below:

Kausani is situated at a height of 6,075 feet in the Central Himalayas. It is an unusually attractive little town. It covers just about 5.2 sq. kms. It lies to the north of Almora in Uttarakhand's picturesque Kumaon region. Kausani provides the 300-km wide breathtaking view of the Himalayas. It is the most striking aspect of this place. Snow-capped peaks are spread in a stately row. They stare at you in silvery white majesty. The most famous peak on view is Nanda Devi, the second highest mountain in India. It is situated at a height of 25,645 feet and 36 miles away as the crow flies. The other famous peaks on view are Choukhamba (23,420 feet) and Trishul (23,360 feet). Then there are also Nilkanth, Nandaghunti, Nandaghat and Nandakot. On a clear day, the blue sky makes a splendid background to these peaks. At sunrise and at sunset, when the colour of the sky changes to a golden orange, the scene gets etched in your memory. When Gandhiji visited this place in 1929, its scenic beauty held him spellbound. He named it the 'Switzerland of

India'. He prolonged his two-day stay to fourteen days, making time to write a book, 'Anashakti Yoga'. The place where he was staying was originally a guest-house of the tea estate. It was renamed 'Anashakti Ashram' after the book.

Kausani is the birthplace of Sumitranandan Pant, India's poet laureate. Its natural surroundings inspired many of his poems. Its tea gardens mingle with dense pine forests and fruit orchards. The area is also host to many fairs and religious ceremonies. If Uttarakhand is the abode of gods, Kausani is God's own backyard. There is no traffic, no one is in a hurry. If serenity could be put on a canvas, the picture would resemble Kausani.

On the basis of your reading of the above passage, answer the following questions :

(a) Where is Kausani situated? **[All Indian 2015 U]**

(b) What is the most striking aspect of Kausani?

[All Indian 2015 U]

(c) Which is the most famous peak on view from Kausani? **[All Indian 2015 U]**

(d) How did Kausani influence Sumitranandan Pant?

[All Indian 2015 U]

(e) When does the view of peaks become so memorable?

[All Indian 2015 U]

(f) How can we say that Gandhiji was greatly charmed by the natural beauty of Kausani?

[All Indian 2015 U]

(g) What makes Kausani a calm and quiet place?

[All Indian 2015 U]

(h) Why do you think, is Kausani known as 'God's own backyard'? **[All Indian 2015 U]**

21. Read the passage given below:

1. I rested for a moment at the door of Anand Bhawan, on Market Road, where coffee-drinkers and tiffin-eaters sat still at their tables, uttering low moans on seeing me. I wanted to assure them, "Don't mind me, you hugging the cash box — you are a coward, afraid even to breathe. Go on, count the cash, if that is your pleasure. I just want to watch, that's all. If my tail trails down to the street, if I am blocking your threshold, it is because, I'm told, I'm eleven feet tip to tail. I can't help it. I'm not out to kill — I'm too full. I found a green pasture full of food on my way. I won't attack until I feel hungry again. Tigers attack only when they feel hungry, unlike human beings who slaughter one another without purpose or hunger."

2. To the great delight of children, schools were being hurriedly closed. Children of all ages and sizes were running helter-skelter, screaming joyously, "No school, no school. Tiger, tiger!" They were shouting and laughing and even enjoying being scared. They seemed to welcome me. I felt like joining them. So I bounded away from the restaurant door. I walked along with them, at which they cried, 'The tiger is coming to eat us; let us get back to school!"

3. I followed them through their school gate while they ran up and shut themselves in the school hall securely. I climbed up the steps of the school, saw an open door at the far end of a veranda, and walked in. It happened to be the headmaster's room. I noticed a very dignified man jumping on the table and heaving himself up into an attic. I walked in and flung myself on the cool floor, having a special liking for cool stone floors.

4. As I drowsed, I was aware of cautious steps and hushed voices all around. I was in no mood to bother about anything. All I wanted was a little moment of sleep; the daylight was very bright.

On the basis of your reading of the above passage, answer the following questions :

(a) How did the dinners at Anand Bhawan react on seeing the tiger?   **[All India 2015 Ⓤ]**

(b) When do tigers attack? In this context, how are human beings different from tigers?

[All India 2015 Ⓤ]

(c) Why were children happy and even enjoying being scared?   **[All India 2015 Ⓤ]**

(d) What did the headmaster do on seeing the tiger? What did the tiger like to do in the headmaster's office?

[All India 2015 Ⓤ]

(e) Identify the word which means the same as 'hugging'. (Para 1)   **[All India 2015 Ⓤ]**

   (i)   counting

   (ii) hiding

   (iii) rubbing

   (iv) holding tightly in the arms

(f) Identify the word which means the same as 'delight'. (Para 2)   **[All Indian 2015 Ⓤ]**

   (i)   pleasure

   (ii) fear

   (iii) sorrow

   (iv) nervousness

(g) Identify the word which means the same as 'dignified'. (Para 3)   **[All Indian 2015 Ⓤ]**

   (i)   tall

   (ii) honourable

   (iii) terrified

   (iv) tired

(h) Identify the meaning of the word, 'bounded'. (Para 2)   **[All Indian 2015 Ⓤ]**

   (i)   walked

   (ii) jumped forward

   (iii) walked with heavy steps

   (iv) ran lazily

22. **Read the passage given below and complete the statements that follow by choosing the most appropriate options.**

Cheraw is the most colourful Mizo dance. Bamboos are used in this dance. Hence the dancer moves by stepping alternately in and out from between and across a pair of horizontal bamboos, held against the ground by people sitting face to face at either side. They tap the bamboos open and close in rhythmic beats. Two bases support the bamboos, placed horizontally, one at each end. The bamboos, when clapped, produce a sharp sound, which forms the rhythm of the dance. It indicates the timing of the dance as well. The dancers step in and out to the beats of the bamboos with ease and grace. The patterns and stepping of the dance have many variations. Sometimes the steppings are made in imitation of the movements of birds, sometimes the swaying of trees and so on.

Little is known about the origin of Cheraw. It may be possible that the forefathers of the Mizos brought it with them when they left home in Far-East Asia. Cheraw is performed on any occasion these days. But, so goes the legend. It used to be performed in earlier times only to ensure a safe passage for a dead child to paradise. Cheraw is, therefore, a dance of sanctification and redemption performed with great care, precision and elegance.

(a) According to the passage, Cheraw is

______________ . **[All India 2014 U]**

(i)   a form of art

(ii) a festival of lights

(iii) a form of dance

(iv) a Mizo animal

(b) Cheraw is performed ______________ .

[All India 2014 U]

(i)   to show respect to the state

(ii) for sanctification and redemption

(iii) to please the goddess of dance

(iv) to earn money

(c) The dancers in Cheraw dance to ______________

. **[All India 2014 U]**

(i)   the beats of bamboos

(ii) the beats of drums

(iii) the clappings of the singers

(iv) the sound of a whistle

(d) The statement ______________ is correct.

[All India 2014 U]

(i)   Four bases support the bamboos

(ii) Cheraw is a solo dance

(iii) Cheraw is a dull stepping pattern

(iv) The sound of bamboos forms the rhythm of the dance

(e) The word 'redemption' in the passage means

_______________ .   **[All India 2014 U]**

    (i) performed with great care

    (ii) solution

    (iii) deliverance from evil ways

    (iv) compensation

23. Read the passage given below and complete the statements that follow by choosing the most appropriate options.

Himalayan valley is the geographical guard of the Indian territory against any foreign invasion keeping the enemy at bay from the western to the eastern subcontinent of the Asian sphere. The valley abounds with a classified variety of different glaciers, wildlife, peaks and thick vegetation liable to support the homo sapiens.

Pindari glacier is a range of four glaciers, namely Sunderdunga, Namik, Pindari and Kafni. To go to Pindari glacier it is a 54 km trek and the walking part is normally covered in four days. In this trek, we cross many mountains and forests and see a lot of wildlife. We were eight members in the team. The whole trip took us ten days in the mountains. Throughout the way, our guide and my father explained to us the various features of the Himalayas we were passing through. We had to face bad weather for two days. There was a steep climb at some places and as we climbed up we were affected by high altitude sickness and lack of oxygen and we felt very tired.

Pindari glacier is surrounded on all sides by snow-covered peaks such as Nanda Devi, Nanda Kot, Nanda Khat, Bailiuri and many more. This glacier is a frozen river of ice and settled in such a way that it looks like a huge staircase. There I saw all physical features such as gorges, moraines, hanging valleys, etc.

(a) Pindari glacier is _______________ .

     [All India 2014 U]

    (i) a glacier range of four mountains namely Sunderdunga, Namik, Pindari and Kafni

    (ii) a mountain peak surrounded by Sunderdunga, Namik and Kafni

    (iii) a forest in the Himalayan region

    (iv) a range of four glaciers, namely Sunderdunga, Namik, Pindari and Kafni

(b) A trip to Pindari glacier _____________ .

     [All India 2014 U]

    (i) is very informative

    (ii) helps in understanding the natural geography

    (iii) is an adventurous experience as one has to face bad weather and difficult treks

    (iv) is all of the above

(c) _____________ made the members suffer while trekking to their destination.   **[All India 2014 U]**

    (i) Steep climb and lack of oxygen

    (ii) High altitude sickness, lack of oxygen and steep climb

(iii) Lack of oxygen and tiredness

(iv) Lack of oxygen and snow-covered peaks

(d) The temperature in the area is ___________.

[All India 2014 U]

(i)   normal

(ii) below zero degree

(iii) very high

(iv) warm

(e) The word in the passage which means the same as

'characteristics' is ___________ .

[All India 2014 U]

(i)   features

(ii) altitude

(iii) treks

(iv) gorges

23. **Read the passage given below and complete the sentences that follow by choosing the most appropriate options.**

The tree is worshipped as the earth mother in tribal India. It provides food, air, occupation, materials for housing, fodder for animals and fuel. Without the trees there is neither soil nor water. There is nothing to prevent the soil from being washed away; there is nothing to prevent the water from evaporating. In the great tribal regions of India which are home to the Bhils, the Santhals, the Nagas, the Bishnois, whenever a child is born a tree is planted in the child's name. It forges a relationship between child and tree closer than the one between child and family. Naturally, so because that tree is specially the child's own. The trees are all slow growing. By the time the child reaches adolescence, his tree has just come into fruit. It starts its life as provider to the tribal and the tribal's life as guardian of the tree.

Nearly three hundred years ago, men and women of the Bishnoi tribe died in an attempt to stop the felling of trees. The Bishnoi faith prohibits the cutting of green trees. It demands absolute protection of the 'Khejri', the shade and fodder tree of the area. As a result, their lands are still fertile, while all around them fields have been reclaimed by the Thar Desert of Rajasthan.

(a) The tribals worship trees because trees provide them with ___________ .

[All Indian 2013 U]

(i)   food and occupation

(ii) materials for housing

(iii) fodder and fuel

(iv) all of the above

(b) The common practice adopted by the tribals at the time of a child's birth is ___________.

[All Indian 2013]

(i)   to plant a tree in the child's name

(ii) to name the child after a tree

(iii) to perform the rites under a tree

(iv) to arrange a feast in a forest

(c)   The advantage of the custom is that a mutual bond develops between ______________ when the child becomes an adult.   **[All Indian 2013 U]**

   (i)   the land and the tree

   (ii)   the adolescent and the tree

   (iii)   the soil and the water

   (iv)   all of these

(d)   The land of the Bishnois hasn't become a desert because ______________ .

[All Indian 2013 U]

   (i)   trees cannot grow in a desert

   (ii)   the Bishnois have planted trees on their land

   (iii)   they died in an attempt to stop the cutting down of trees

   (iv)   all of the above

(e)   The word in the passage which means the same as 'areas/regions' is ____________ .

[All Indian 2013 U]

   (i)   desert

   (ii)   fodder

   (iii)   soil

   (iv)   tracts

25.   Read the passage given below and complete the sentences that follow by choosing the most appropriate options.

In the year 1507 AD, the Portuguese sailors landing on the shores of the island of Mauritius discovered a strange looking bird. It was large and stubby, and could not fly. It had a hooked black beak, short yellow legs, grey-blue plumage, and a tuft of pale coloured feathers for its tail. Since this bird had never seen humans before, it was very friendly and trusting. In fact, the sailors mistook its gentle nature for stupidity, and called it 'Dodo,' which meant simpleton in Portuguese.

The dodo was an easy source of fresh meat for the Portuguese – and later, the Dutch who came to the island in 1598 – because it could be easily captured due to its friendliness. Dodos were killed in large numbers by the new inhabitants of the island. Those that survived men had to face new enemies like dogs and pigs that were introduced by these inhabitants. The dodo had no natural enemies on the island, but these new animals, together with man, hastened its extinction. By the year 1681, the last dodo had died, and today, the term 'as dead as dodo,' means something that has disappeared entirely from the face of the Earth.

(a)   In 1507 AD the Portuguese sailors discovered a bird which was ______________ .

[All Indian 2013 U]

   (i)   strange looking

   (ii)   large and stubby

   (iii)   could not fly

   (iv)   all of the above

(b) They mistook the bird for being foolish because it was _______________ .   **[All Indian 2013 U]**

(i)   unable to fly

(ii) friendly and trusting

(iii) had never seen humans before

(iv) was an easy source of fresh meat

(c) The new enemies referred to in the passage are _______________ .   **[All Indian 2013 U]**

(i)   dogs and pigs

(ii) the Dutch

(iii) the Portuguese

(iv) all of the above

(d) Dodos were wiped out from the face of the earth by _______________ .   **[All Indian 2013 U]**

(i)   their natural enemies

(ii) the sailors

(iii) both men and the new animals

(iv) all of the above

(e) The word in the passage which means the same as 'destruction' is _______________ .

[All Indian 2013 U]

(i)   strange

(ii) tuft

(iii) extinction

(iv) plumage

26. **Read the passage given below and answer the questions that follow :**

A 92-year-old lady who is fully dressed each morning by eight o'clock with perfect make-up, even though she is blind, moved to an old age home. Her husband recently passed away making the move necessary. After many hours of waiting patiently in the lobby she smiled sweetly when she was told her room was ready. She was provided a visual description of her tiny room.

"I love it," she stated with the enthusiasm of an eight-year-old having just been presented with a new puppy.

"But .... but Mrs. Jones, you haven't seen the room," said the attendant. "That doesn't have anything to do with it," she replied. "Happiness is something you decide. I have already decided to love it. It's a decision I make every morning when I wake up. I can spend the day in bed, recounting the difficulty I have with the parts of my body that don't work, or get out of bed and be thankful for the ones that do. Each day is a gift, and as long as I am alive I'll focus on the new day and all the happy memories I've stored away, just for this time in my life."

The attendant was greatly touched by the elderly woman's sense of cheer and boundless enthusiasm.

(a) Why did the old woman move to an old age home?

[All Indian 2013]

(b) How did she react when the attendant gave a description of the room she had to live in?

[**All Indian 2013**]

(c) What resolution was she used to making when she woke up every morning?   [**All Indian 2013**]

(d) What does the story tell about the old woman?

[**All Indian 2013**]

(e) Which word in the passage means the same as 'without limit'?   [**All Indian 2013**]

27. **Read the poem given below and answer the questions that follow:**

I Have a Dove

I had a dove, and the sweet dove died,

And I have thought it died of grieving;

O, what could it grieve for? Its feet were tied

With a silken thread of my own hand's weaving.

Sweet little red feet! Why should you die?

Why should you leave me, sweet bird, why?

You liv'd alone on the forest-tree,

Why, pretty thing, could you not live with me?

I kiss'd you oft, and gave you white peas;

Why not live sweetly as in the green trees?

(John Keats)

(a) How did the dove die?   [**All Indian 2013**]

(b) What were the dove's feet tied with?

[**All Indian 2013**]

(c) What does the expression, "Sweet little red feet" refer to?   [**All Indian 2013**]

(d) How did the poet take care of the dove?

[**All Indian 2013**]

(e) Which word in the poem means the same as 'intense sorrow'?   [**All Indian 2013**]

Topic-b: *Case-Based Factual Passages*

1. **Read the following text:**   [CBSE Sample 2023-24; **A**]

   1. Reduction in green areas has caused various environmental problems. People squeezed between concrete structures are looking for various ways to meet their longing for green. One of the ways to do so, is vertical gardens and green walls. Vertical gardening is a unique method of gardening where plants are grown in a vertical position or upward, rather than in the traditional method of planting them on the ground.

   2. The purpose of vertical gardens and green walls, which arises from the studies of different disciplines (landscape architects, architects, engineers, etc.), is to close the cold image of concrete and increase the visual value. In these systems, nature and structures are integrated, and thus, urban areas and the desired environment have become intertwined.

3. Vertical garden case studies often show that , though functionality should be in the foreground, when vertical gardens are planned, they are generally made as aesthetic elements in the city's underpasses and city squares, and decorative elements in residences, without seeking functionality.

4. Experts support that the visual quality and evaluation of landscape architecture is determined based on the satisfaction of the users. Hence, a survey questionnaire was prepared for residents of varied age groups from of a metropolitan city . The given Table 1, displays these responses:

Table 1 - Total number of participants : 400					
No.	**Survey statements**	**Strongly agree**	**Agree**	**Neutral**	**Disagree**	**Strongly disagree**
Vertical gardens-						
1	improve quality of life of people in urban areas	191	138	43	9	19
2	reduce noise pollution	128	164	77	25	6
3	increase air quality -indoors and outdoors	172	147	51	28	2
4	reduce energy and water consumption	58	47	125	68	2
5	positively impact global warming	114	144	106	30	6
6	have a relaxing and calming effect	161	177	44	7	11
7	cost too much	86	107	152	42	13
8	make plants look beautiful	195	139	44	6	16
9	add naturalness to the environs	135	173	55	25	12
10	are among the determining factor to visiting a place	59	133	141	54	13
11	are inconvenient indoors	9	84	123	126	48
12	can be applied in every place	71	132	97	77	23
13	have a functional feature	81	207	100	10	2
14	distract drivers	34	101	106	131	28
15	funds are best used for social issues	57	72	100	130	41

5. The study acknowledged that vertical gardening has the potential to transform urban spaces into green, sustainable areas, and further research should explore the impact of vertical gardening on the environment and human well-being.

Answer the following questions, based on the passage above.   **10 × 1 = 10**

(i) Complete the following analogy appropriately, based on your understanding of paragraphs 1 & 2.

We can say that the situation of people living in concrete structures is comparable with a fish living in a fishbowl, and the need for vertical gardens to the need for decorations in the fishbowl because

________________.

(ii) Fill the blanks with the appropriate option from those given in brackets, based on your understanding of paragraph 2.

The statement that , urban spaces have become more closely connected with the desired natural surroundings through the incorporation of nature and structures in vertical gardens and green walls, is a ___________ (fact/ opinion) because it is a _____________ (subjective judgement/ objective detail).

(iii) Justify the following, in about 40 words.

While the survey results suggest that vertical gardens may be effective in improving the quality of life in urban areas, further research and evaluation may be necessary to fully understand their effectiveness and potential drawbacks.

(iv) Based on the survey results, which two concerns should a city government, looking to install vertical gardens, address?

(v) In Table 1, the statement 3, "Vertical gardens increase air quality - indoors and outdoors," received the most neutral responses from participants, with 51 respondents indicating a neutral stance. State any one inference that can be drawn from this.

(vi) Select the option that correctly displays what 'intertwined' signifies. (Reference-Paragraph 2)

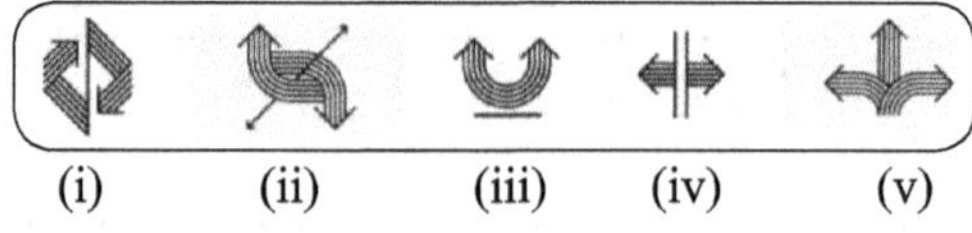

(a) (i) , (iv) and (v)

(b) Only (ii)

(c) Only (iii)

(d) (ii) and (v)

(vii) Infer one benefit and one drawback of vertical gardening, in comparison to other solutions, such as community gardens or parks. (Answer in about 40 words)

(viii) Which of the following is the main takeaway from the study mentioned in the passage?

(a) Vertical gardening has minimal impact on the environment or human well-being.

(b) Vertical gardening is a sustainable practice that can transform urban spaces into green areas.

(c) The impact of vertical gardening on the environment and human well-being has already been thoroughly explored.

(d) The study needs to include experts from horticultural firms to offer any recommendations for further research.

2. Read the following passage carefully:

[All India, 2023; A]

1. According to a new study, a vast blanket of pollution stretching across South Asia is cutting down sunlight by 10 per cent over India, damaging agriculture, modifying rainfall patterns and putting hundreds of thousands of people at risk.

2. It is said, "Acids in the haze may, by falling as acid rain, have the potential to damage crops and trees. Ash falling on leaves can aggravate the impact of reduced sunlight on the Earth's surface. The pollution that is forming the haze could be leading to several hundreds of thousands of premature deaths as a result of higher levels of respiratory diseases."

3. "The haze has cut down sunlight over India by 10 per cent (so far) – a huge amount! As a repercussion, the North-West of India is drying up," Prof. V, Ramanathan said when asked specifically about the impact of the haze over India. He said, "We are still in an early stage of understanding of the impact of the haze."

4. Prof. V. Ramanathan was asked whether the current droughts in most parts of India after over a decade of good monsoons was owing to the haze. He said, "It was too early to reach a conclusion. If the droughts persist for about four to five years, then we would start, suspecting that it may be because of the haze." India, China and Indonesia are the worst affected owing to their population density, economic growth and depleting forest cover.

Based on your understanding of the passage, answer the questions given below: **10 × 1 = 10**

(i) Infer one reason for the following based on the information in paragraph 1:

In India rainfall patterns are changing.

(ii) The pollution spreading across South Asia is affecting India by _______.

Choose the correct option from the ones given below:

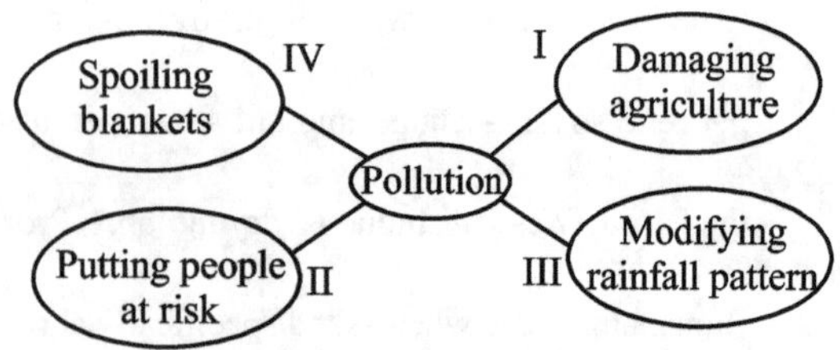

(a) I, II and III

(b) I, III and IV

(c) II, III and IV

(d) I, II and IV

(iii) Complete the following analogy correctly with a word/phrase from paragraph 2.

possibility : _______ : : suspecting : doubting

(iv) Select the correct option to complete the sentence.

_______ droughts were caused by the haze.

(a) Strong evidence suggested that

(b) Past surveys confirmed that

(c) There has not been enough time to determine that

(d) Superstitious people believe that

(v) From the following pie chart, identify one reason each which does and does not contribute to weather disruption:

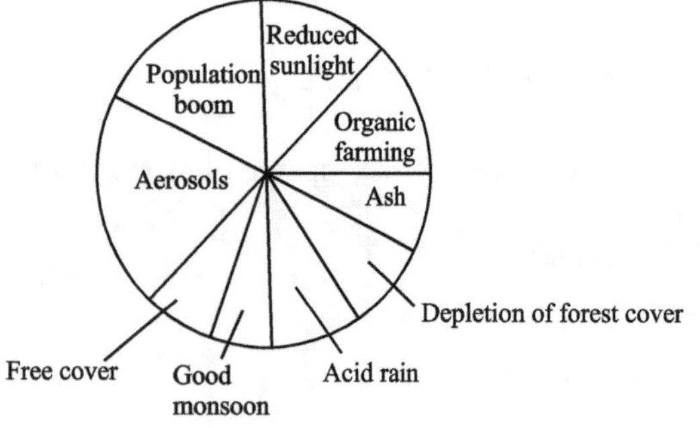

(v) (b) List two phenomena which lead to weather disruptions.

(vi) Fill in the blank by selecting the correct option.

Ash falling on leaves can _______ the impact of reduced sunlight on the Earth's surface.

(a) worsen

(b) encourage

(c) diminish

(d) support

(vii) Substitute the word 'repercussion' with one word similar in meaning in the following sentence from paragraph 3.

The haze has cut down sunlight over India ... As a repercussion, the North-West of India is drying up.

(viii) List any two countries which are affected due to depleting forest cover.

(ix) Which of the following mean the same as 'persist' in 'droughts persist' as used in para 4?

(a) destroying

(b) halting

(c) continue

(d) blocking

(x) Select the option that titles paragraphs 1-4 appropriately with reference to information in the text.

(a)   1.   Impact of Pollution in South Asia

     2.   Effects of Acid Rain

     3.   Understanding Consequences of Haze

     4.   Debate over Droughts

(b)   1.   Impact of Droughts

     2.   Understanding Acid Rain

     3.   Effect of Haze

     4.   Debate over Pollution

(c)   1.   Impact of Pollution in South Asia

     2.   Effects of Acid Rain

     3.   Debate over Droughts

     4.   Understanding Haze

(d)   1.   Impact of Haze

     2.   Understanding Acid Rain

     3.   Debate over Pollution

     4.   Effect of Haze

3.   Read the extract given below:

1.   Necessity is indeed the mother of invention. When areas in and around Leh began to experience water shortages, life didn't grind to a halt. Why? Because a retired civil engineer in the Jammu and Kashmir Government came up with the idea of artificial glaciers.

2.   Ladakh, a cold desert at an altitude of 3,000-3,500 meters above sea level, has a low average annual rainfall rate of 50 mm. Glaciers have always been the only source of water. Agriculture is completely dependent on glacier melt, unlike the rest of river/ monsoon-fed India. But over the years, with increasing effects of climate change, rainfall and snowfall patterns have been changing, resulting in severe shortage and drought situations. Given the extreme winter conditions, the window for farming is usually limited to one harvest season.

3.   It is located between the natural glacier above and the village below. The one closer to the village and lowest in altitude melts first, providing water during April-May, the crucial sowing season. Further, layers of ice above melt with the increasing temperature, thus ensuring continuous supply to the fields. Therefore, farmers have been able to manage two crops instead of one. It costs about 1,50,000 and above to create a glacier.

4.   Fondly called the glacier man, he has designed over 15 artificial glaciers in and around Leh since 1987. In recognition of his pioneering effort, he was conferred the Padma Shri by The President of India.

5. There are a few basic steps followed while creating an artificial glacier. River or stream water at high altitude is diverted to a shaded area of the hill, facing north, where the winter sun is blocked by a ridge or a mountain range. At the start of winter i,e., in November, the diverted water is made to flow on sloping hills facing distribution channels. Stone embankments are built at regular intervals which impede the flow of water, making shallow pools which freeze, forming a cascade of ice along the slope. Ice formation continues for 3-4 months resulting in a large accumulation of ice which is referred to as an 'artificial glacier'.

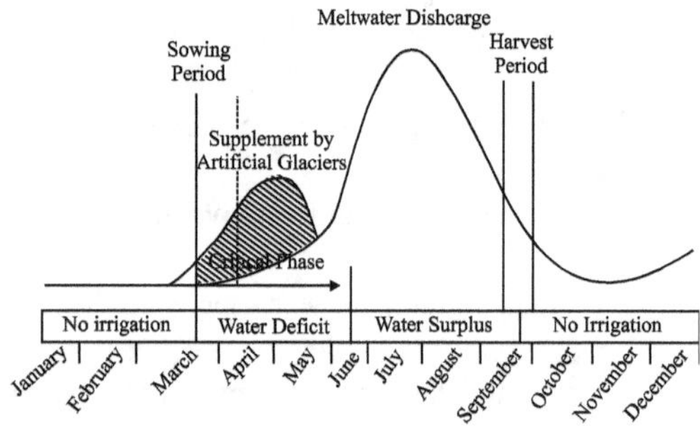

Based on your understanding of the extract, answer the questions below: 10×1=10

(i) Infer one reason for the following, based on information in paragraph1.

Areas in and around Leh began to experience water shortage but life didn't grind to a halt.

[Delhi, 2023; A]

(ii) Select from the passage the appropriate option to fill in the blanks: **[Delhi, 2023; A]**

Agriculture is completely dependent on.................unlike the rest of river/monsoon-fed India.

(a) rainfall pattern

(b) climate change

(c) glaciers melt

(d) extreme winter conditions

(iii) Complete the following analogy correctly with a word/phrase from paragraph 3:

[Delhi, 2023; A]

icing: cake:: layers:......................

(iv) Select the correct option to complete the following sentence: At the start of winter the diverted water is made to flow...................... **[Delhi, 2023; A]**

(a) on sloping hills facing distribution channels.

(b) on high altitude.

(c) on ice-cold water level.

(d) on mountain range.

(v) From the chart select the months of water surplus. **[Delhi, 2023; A]**

(a) January, February.

(b) November, December.

(c) July, August, September.

(d) March, April

(v) (b) Describe the number of months which result in large accumulation of ice. **[Delhi, 2023, , A]**

(vi) Fill in the blank by selecting from the passage the correct option: **[Delhi, 2023, A]**

The.................have been the only source of water in areas in and around Ladakh.

(vii) The word 'located' in paragraph 3 means:

[Delhi, 2023, A]

(viii) Write any two steps followed while creating the glaciers. **[Delhi, 2023, A]**

(ix) List one reason why artificial glaciers seem the best option. **[Delhi, 2023, A]**

(x) Select the most suitable title from the following for the passage: **[Delhi, 2023, A]**

4. Read the passage given below.

[CBSE Sample 2022-23 A]

1   The North-East of India is a melting pot of variegated cultural mosaic of people and races, an ethnic tapestry of many hues and shades. Yet, these states are lesser explored as compared to the rest of the country. The new generations of travellers who are 'money rich and time poor' are increasingly looking for unique experiences --a phenomenon being called the emergence of the 'experience economy'. For this new and growing breed of tourists, the North-East with its variety and uniqueness holds immense attraction.

2. A study conducted in 2020 by Dr. Sherap Bhutia, revealed that the foreign tourist arrival in the North-East increased from 37,380 persons in 2005 to 118,552 in 2014. The overall growth rate of tourist (both domestic and foreign) in the North-East was as high as 26.44% during 2005-06. A high and positive growth of 12.53% was registered in foreign tourist visits to North-East States of India during 2012 from 2011, which further rose to register a growth of 27.93% during 2013 from 2012. Foreign tourist arrivals in the North-East witnessed a growth of 39.77% during 2014 from 2013, according to data provided from the Ministry of Tourism, Government of India.

3   The study recommendations for tourism planners included the need to concentrate on some key areas like enhancement of tourist facilities, tourism financing, focus on community involvement and others for the formulation of a sustainable tourism strategy in the North-East States of India. (234 words)

1. Infer one reason for the following, based on information in paragraph 1.

The rate of tourism in the North-East of India puzzles tourism officials.

2. Select the appropriate option to fill in the blanks.

   From paragraph 1, we can infer that the _____________

   and _____________ of the North-Eastern states aid attracting the 'money rich and time poor' tourists.

   1. distinctiveness

   2. conventionality

   3. diversity

   4. uniformity

   5. modernity

   (a) 1 & 3   (b) 2 & 4

   (c) 2 & 5   (d) 1 & 4

3. Complete the following analogy correctly with a word/ phrase from paragraph 1:

   aroma: cooking:: _____________ : painting

   (**Clue:** Just like aroma is integral to cooking, similarly _____________ is/ are integral to painting)

4. Select the correct option to complete the following sentence:

   Travellers advocating the 'experience economy' seek a holiday package with _____________ (Paragraph 1)

   (a) grand facilities, expensive hotels and excellent services to pamper them.

   (b) a wholesome experience within the budget they have planned for.

   (c) places and cities to buy things from and opportunities spend money.

   (d) cost-effective services, affordable accommodation and many days of touring.

5. Select the chart that appropriately represents the trend of foreign tourist travels in the North-East, from 2011-2014, as per paragraph 2.

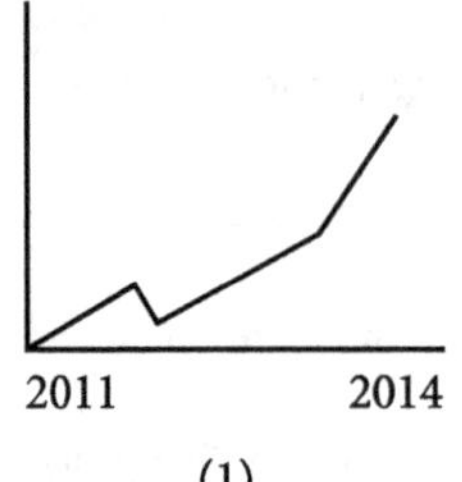

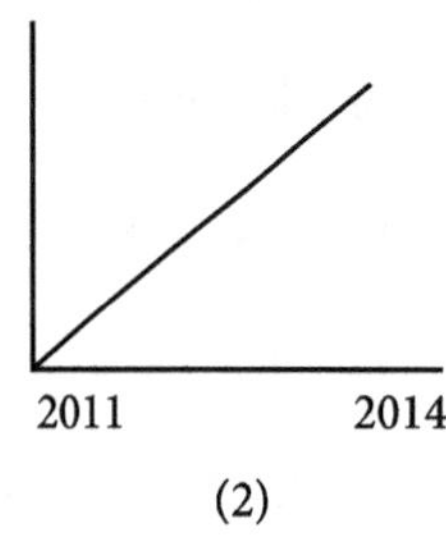

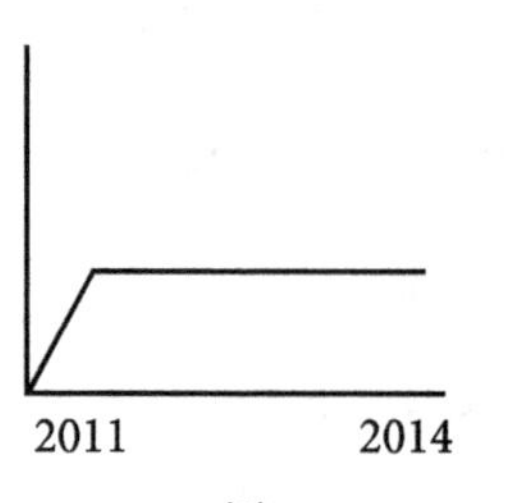

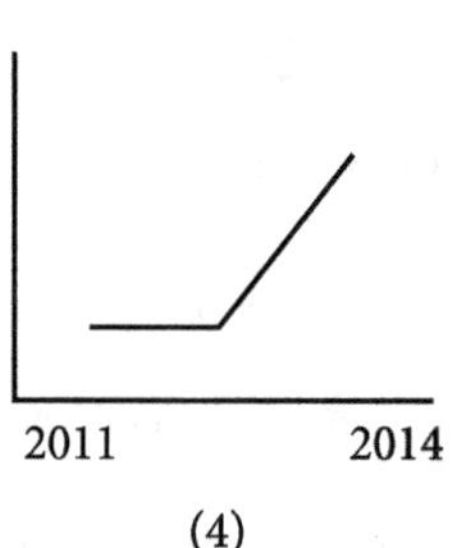

   (a) Option 1   (b) Option 2   (c) Option 3   (d) Option 4

(v) (b) Describe the trend of foreign tourist travels in the North-East, from 2011-2014 in ONE word, as per paragraph 2.

6. Fill in the blank by selecting the correct option.

The study of tourist travel statistics in the North-East, from 2005 to 2014 showed ________________ results.

(a) expected

(b) encouraging

(c) inconsistent

(d) questionable

7. Substitute the word 'witnessed' with ONE WORD similar in meaning, in the following, sentence from paragraph 2:

Foreign tourist arrivals in the North-East witnessed a growth of...

8. List any 2 examples of 'tourist facilities' as referred to, in Paragraph 3.

9. List one reason why the researchers recommend that the formulation of a tourism strategy in the North-Eastern States of India be sustainable.

10. Select the option that titles paragraphs 1-3 appropriately, with reference to information in the text.

(a) 1. Full Speed Ahead!

2. Ups and Downs

3. Cause for Concern

(b) 1. Winds of Change

2. Numbers Don't Lie

3. Time for Action

(c) 1. Inspecting Trends

2. Statistically Speaking

3. Let's Investigate

(d) 1. Cause & Effects

2. Dynamic Data

3. Dependable Facts

5. **Read the following excerpt from a case Study. J.K. Rowling – A Journey**

The story of Joanne Kathleen Rowling's near magical rise to fame is almost as well known as the characters she creates.

Rowling was constantly writing and telling stories to her younger sister Dianne. "The first story I ever wrote down was about a rabbit called Rabbit." Rowling said in an interview. "He got the measles and was visited by his friends including a giant bee called Miss Bee. And ever since Rabbit and Miss Bee. I have always wanted to be a writer, though I rarely told anyone so.

However, my parents, both of whom come from impoverished backgrounds and neither of whom had been to college, took the view that my overactive imagination was an amusing personal quirk the would never pay a mortgage or secure a pension.

A writer from the age of six, with two unpublished novels in the drawer, she was stuck on a train when Harry walked into her mind fully formed. She spent the next five years constructing the plots of seven books, one for every year of his secondary school life.

Rowling says she started writing the first book, Harry Potter and the Sorcerer's Stone, in Portugal, where she was teaching English.

At first nobody wanted to publish Harry Potter. She was told that plot was too complex. Refusing to compromise, she found a publisher.

In 1997 Rowling received her first royalty cheque. By book three, she had sky rocketed to the top of the publishing world. A row or zeroes appeared on the author's bank balance and her life was turned upside down. Day and night she had journalists knocking on the unanswered door of her flat.

Rowling's quality control has become legendary, as her obsession with accuracy. She's thrilled with Stepher Fry's taped version of the books and outraged that an Italina dust jacket showed Harry minus his glasses. "Don't they understand that the glasses are the clue to his vulnerability."

Annual earning of J.K. Rowling from 2010 to 2019.

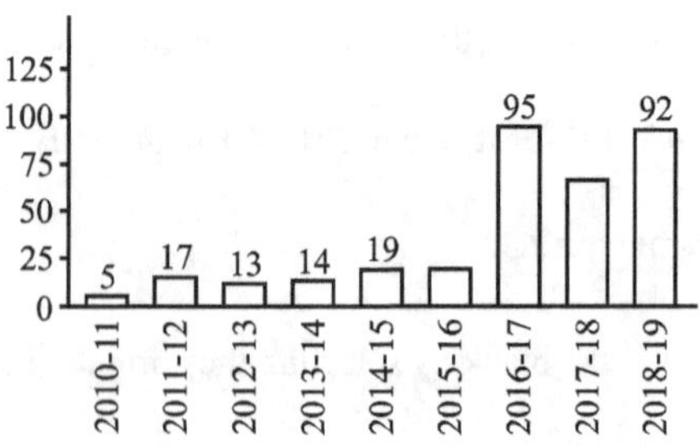

On the basis of your understanding of the passage answer any five of the six questions given below.

(1 × 5 = 5 Marks)

(i)   Explain J.K. Rowling's 'near magical rise to fame'.

[All Indian 2022, T-II, A]

(ii) What reason did the publishers give for rejecting Rowling's book ?   **[All Indian 2022, T-II, A]**

(iii) What was the drawback of achieving fame ?

[All Indian 2022, T-II, A]

(iv) Why was Rowling outraged with the Italian dust jacket?   **[All Indian 2022, T-II, A]**

(v)   Find a word in the last par that means the same as "insecure/helpless".   **[All Indian 2022, T-II; A]**

(vi) According to the graph, how many years did it take Rowling to become very successful ?

[All Indian 2022, T-II; A]

(vi) (b)   What has become legendary about Rowling ?   **[All Indian 2022, T-II; A]**

6. Read the passage given below and answer the questions / complete the statements that follow by choosing the most appropriate options out of the given ones :

[All Indian 2022, T-I; A]

Around 194 millions birds and 29 million mammals are thought to be killed each year on European roads, according to a new study that has ranked the most vulnerable species. The research has found that the species killed most often were not necessarily the endangered species. This means action to preserve wildlife when new roads are built risks being targeted at the wrong species based on current methods. Road densities in Europe are among the world's highest, with 50% of the continent within 1.5 km of a paved road or railway. Roads are therefore a significant thread to wildlife, and evidence shows deaths on them could even cause some species to disappear completely.

Despite this, the long - term protection of species is not currently considered when assessing the impact of new roads on wildlife, meaning we risk giving support to only the endangered species, doing nothing to help those most at risk. A better understanding of which species are most vulnerable to roads is therefore important if we are to take a more effective action of protection.

A research team based in Lisbon calculated road-kill rates for 423 bird species and 212 mammal species. They found that small animals with high population densities and which mature at an early age were most likely to be killed on roads. Nocturnal mammals and birds with a diet of plants and seeds were also shown to have higher death rates.

The study also used the road-kill surveys to rank the bird and mammal species whose long-term survival was most threatened by road-kill. The hazel grouse and ground squirrel were found to be the most at risk of local extinction. Both are common in Europe but are classified as species of Least concern Red list of Threatened Species.

The most vulnerable animals classified as threatened by IUCN were the red-knobbed coot, Balcan mole and Podolian mole, The study revealed that road-kill hotspots were not the areas with the highest population of endangered species. For example. house sparrows had a high road-kill rate (2.7 per km/year) but were ranked 420th of 423 bird species for vulnerability. Conversely, the hazel grouse had a low predicted road kill - rate (0.2 per km/yr) but was most vulnerable of all birds studied.

11. Study the following statements :

[All Indian 2022, T-I; A]

(A) Roads are killers for animals.

(B) Both birds and mammals are killed on roads.

(C) Species most killed are necessarily the endangered ones.

(a) (A) is correct and (B) is false

(b) (B) is correct and (C) is false

(c) (A) and (B) both are correct

(d) (C) is correct and (A) is false

12. Study the following statements :

[All Indian 2022, T-I; **A**]

(A) Roads have covered 50% of land in Europe.

(B) Road traffic causes a great risk to wild life.

(C) Some species can survive all kinds of traffic on roads.

(a) (A) is correct and (B) is false

(b) (B) is correct and (C) is false

(c) (C) is correct and (A) is false

(d) (A) and (B) both are false

13. Choose the correct statement

[All Indian 2022, T-I; **A**]

(a) While planning roads we should see which species to protect.

(b) We are doing a lot to protect those most at risk.

(c) 50% of Europe is covered only with roads.

(d) Small animals even with low population density are most at risk.

14. Choose the correct statement

[All Indian 2022, T-I; **A**]

(a) More mammals than birds are killed on the roads.

(b) Small animals generally keep away from roads.

(c) Number of road-kills depends upon the population density of small animals.

(d) Animals that come out only at night are saved.

15. (A) The surveys ranked the road-kill rate of birds and mammals. [All Indian 2022, T-I; **A**]

(B) the finding puts grouse and squirrel at great risk.

(a) (A) is an assertion and (B) is the response.

(b) (B) is an assertion and (A) is the response.

(c) Both (A) and (B) are false.

(d) Both (A) and (B) are unrelated to each other.

16. Hazel grouse and ground squirrel are classified as species of least concern. [All Indian 2022, T-I; **A**]

The statement is :

(a) a logical conclusion

(b) a piece of good news

(c) ironical

(d) a pleasant surprise

17. The title of the study should be

[All Indian 2022, T-I; **A**]

(a) A Birds and Mammals survey

(b) Road-kills

(c) Road density in Europe

(d) Need for conservation

18. The purpose of the study is   [All Indian 2022, T-I]

   (a) how to prevent road - kills

   (b) to see who is more at risk on the roads

   (c) how to plan better roads

   (d) to estimate the number of road accident victims

7. **Read the following excerpt from a case study titled Impacts of Festivities on Ecology.**

[CBSE Sample 2021-22 A]

5 Festivals are synonymous with celebration, ceremony and joy. However, festivals bring to fore the flip side of celebrations – pollution – air, water, soil and noise. This led to the need of assessing the awareness level among people about ecological pollution during festivals. So, a study was conducted by scholars of an esteemed university in India. This study was titled Awareness Towards Impact of Festivals on Ecology.

10 There were two main objectives of the study. The first one was to assess the awareness level among people about ecological protection during festivities. Exploring solutions to bring awareness about celebrating festivals without harming ecology was the second objective. The method used to collect data was a simple questionnaire containing 6 questions, shared with 50 respondents across four selected districts of a state in the southern region of India.

15 The research began by understanding the socio-economic conditions of the respondents before sharing the questionnaire. Once the responses were received, the data collected was tabulated (Table 1), for analysis.

Table-1: Awareness level among respondents

QUESTIONS	Yes%	NO %	CAN'T SAY%
1. Do you feel that bursting crackers is a must during festivities?	46	54	0
2. Do you think most people abuse environmental resources during celebration of festivals?	72	28	0
3. Do you think that celebrations & festivities result in uniting people?	64	32	4
4. Do you enjoy bursting crackers for amusement?	68	32	0
5. Do you feel pressured to burst crackers during festivals as an expectation of your social status?	82	12	6
6. Are you aware of waste segregation & disposal guidelines for better ecology?	56	40	4

20   The study recommended the imposition of strict rules and regulations as opposed to a total ban on all festive activities which have a drastic impact on our environment. The researchers believed that such measures would help in harnessing some ill-effects that add to the growing pollution and suggested further studies be taken up across the country to assess awareness about ecological degradation.

25   The observations made in the study pointed to the environmental groups and eco-clubs fighting a losing battle due to city traffic issues, disposal of plastics, garbage dumping and all sorts of ecological degradation. The researchers stressed that the need of the hour is increasing awareness among people to reduce ecological pollution which can be facilitated by celebrating all festivals in an eco-friendly manner.

On the basis of your understanding of the passage, answer ANY FIVE questions from the six given below.

1*5

(i)   Why do the researchers call pollution the 'flip side' of festivals?

(ii)   Comment on the significance of the second objective of the study with reference to lines 7-12.

(iii)   Justify the researchers' recommendation for limiting the drastic impact of festival pollution on the environment with reference to lines 16-21.

(iv)   Why do the researchers feel that environmental groups and eco-clubs are fighting a losing battle in the given scenario?

(v)   Even though a larger number of people say 'no' to bursting crackers than those who say 'yes', festival pollution persists. How does evidence from table 1 support this statement?

(vi)   What purpose does the 'Can't Say' column serve in the questionnaire (table 1)?

Solutions

Topic-a: *Discursive Passages*

1. (i) (c) Recognizes the challenges of studying poetry but also acknowledges the rewards it offers.

(ii) The tone is critical. The writer seems to be expressing their scepticism and dissatisfaction with poems that are overly obscure and difficult to understand. He suggests that such poems may not be worth the effort and compares them unfavourably to solving a riddle.

Or

The tone is sarcastic. The statement "if solving a riddle is what was intended, then playing Sudoku is a better option" suggests that the writer is not impressed with the level of complexity in some poetry. Additionally, the phrase "led to ponder if obscurity was the goal" implies that the writer believes some poets may intentionally make their work difficult to understand, which can be frustrating for readers.

(iii) The author's use of vivid imagery in the paragraph (3), such as "curl up in a ball and cry" and "jump up and down with joy", greatly affects the reader because it creates a powerful emotional impact and enhances the reader's understanding of the intensity of emotion that can be conveyed through poetry.

(iv) The two sets of antonyms are-

(a) intriguing and off-putting

(d) simple and challenging

[They represent opposite concepts, with "simple" meaning easy, uncomplicated, or straightforward, while "challenging" means difficult, demanding, or requiring effort. In the given passage, the author uses both terms to describe different types of poetry that a reader may encounter.]

(v) We can say that the author's tone becomes more neutral and objective when discussing weird poems, compared to other types of poetry **because the author acknowledges that weird poems can be off-putting, but also appreciates their uniqueness and the challenge they present to readers [hence,** the author is being neutral and objective with no bias]

(vi) Just as exploring a new city requires an open mind and a willingness to embrace the unexpected, studying poetry requires an openness to different styles and approaches, and a willingness to be challenged and surprised by what you find.

(vii). (b) Persistence makes studying poetry a rewarding pursuit.

(viii) Simple [This verse is simple in terms of its language, structure, and content. It describes a natural scene, which is easy to comprehend and has a peaceful effect on the reader.] **(10 × 1 = 10 Marks)**

2. (i) (d) it does not contain agricultural chemical.

(ii) (a) Denial

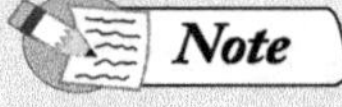

> **Note**
>
> With reference to the given lines, both denial and caution are close choices. Denial is a person's choice to deny the reality while caution is the suggestion for precaution.

(iii) demand overtook supply, big food companies that had been selling non-organic products for many years also began selling organic products.

(iv) organic food doesn't use chemicals for the growth whereas non organic food does.

(v) Reduces the chances of developing heart diseases.

(vi) The writer states that the germs get transferred from hands to the food so, washing hands can prevent contamination of food.

(vii) (a) the price decides the popularity.

(viii) Organic farms do not use agricultural chemicals such as pesticides that stop insects from damaging crops.

(ix) By Washing hands before touching it.

(x) foods that claim to be organic must have special labels that guarantee they're grown organically.

3. (i) (b) to hike **(10 × 1 = 10 Marks)**

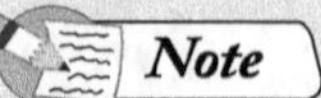

> **Note**
>
> To saunter means to walk in a slow and relaxed way, generally in not a particular direction. Rambles are usually aimless, walking for pleasure. Rambles are slower walks than hikes.

(ii) (d) because the depressing daily routine is forgotten.

(iii) a new meaning and significance to us.

(iv) One reason for feeling a connection with nature is that hiking takes us into the midst of natural surroundings, where we can appreciate and observe the beauty of natural elements such as waterfalls, flowers, streams, trees, and bushes. The various sounds of nature, like the murmur of a brook or the song of a bird, also contribute to establishing a connection with nature.

(v) flower.

(vi) (b) because of the excitement of climbing up and adventure of coming down.

(vii) (d) It is an escape from our busy schedule.

(viii) Two examples of minute observations that can be made while on a hike are a snake casting its slough and a mouse peeping out of its hole.

(ix) One point to justify the statement that hiking gives us a feeling of unlimited joy is that it provides an escape from the usual routine of daily life, allowing us to experience a sense of freedom and adventure in the open air. Additionally, the beautiful scenery, fresh air, and physical activity of hiking can produce endorphins and other positive feelings, contributing to a sense of joy and well-being.

(x) Merry.

here Leap with joy-to be very happy about something.

4. (i) (b) They evoke the wish in us to master them.

(ii) (d) The heavier the luggage- the higher the penalty

(iii) (c) conviction

(iv) hard to put in words

(v) very difficult/ requires perseverance

(vi) The writer says so because mountaineering includes difficulties like having to walk on icy sheets that cannot be accomplished without proper preparation of equipment. Moreover, one has to deal with several health hazards that cannot be managed without preparation.

(vii) If the weather is unpredictable, it makes it difficult to decide when to set up camp, as mountaineers would prefer to climb when it's sunny and camp when it's snowing.

(viii) (a) survival

(ix) Survival is key in mountain climbing, and it can be done with meticulous planning and careful decision-making.

(x) (d) Opportunity to use sophisticated mountaineering equipment

5. (i) Milkha singh is known as the flying sikh. When he was on the track during the Melbououne Olympics, he realized that his competitors were superbly fit and stronger than him and he needed to prepare more to succeed. **(1 Mark)**

(ii) Two achivements of Milkha singh

(a) He is the only Athlete to win gold in 400 meters at the Asian games as well as common wealth games.

(b) He won gold medals in the 1958 and 1963 Asian gaems. **(1 Mark)**

(iii) Milkha singh practised hard for becoming the best athelete in the world. He used to run two or three miles a day in the morning. **(1 Mark)**

(iv) Milkha singh's hard and strenuous practices drained out his energy leading him to vomit blood and some times dropping him down unconscious. **(1 Mark)**

(v) The view of packed stadium filled with cheering spectators, who applauded Milkha Singh as he would cross the finishing line motivated him to become the best athelete in the world. **(1 Mark)**

(vi) "I would start again" in the last sentence means doing and making a new beginning and Milkha singh started practising hard and much harder to become the athelete the best athelete in the world.   **(1 Mark)**

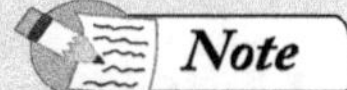
Note

In the passage first discuss the judiciary system of Romans then Saxons and after that Normans.

6.(i) (ci) Romans: Saxons: Normans

(ii) (a) The development of the system of justice in England. Article describes the development of judiciary system of justice in England.

(iii) (c) A and B are right.

Roman had 'highly-sophisticated' professionals. Normans and modern system do not have much difference. They both hired others to fight for their survival.

(iv) (b) A–(iii); B–(i); C–(ii); D–(iv)

The passage clearly shown that Roman had well educated legal professional members. A–(iii)

Roman: Educated judges and lawyers

Saxons: Authorities or a priest could be persuaded to swear an oath. Its clear from the passage. Saxons A priest to swear for the accused.

Modern times, a wealthy person hires a costly and brilliant barrister to defend him.

Modern: Highly paid lawyers can win a case. In 11th century Norman introduced trial by battle and hired champions who would fight on their behalf.

Roman: The winner in a battle declared innocent.

(v) (c) As clear from the passage, both the statements are directly stated. Money played a crucial role.

(vii) (d) (b) and (d) are right.

According to the passage Saxons had Noble and Rough aspects and if the accused could not produce enough oath helpers, he was found guilty and punished. So (B) and (D) are correct.

(viii) (a) (A) is an assertion and (B) is the response.

According to the passage, Early England comprised small villages with small population and crimes were rare.

Early middle age England grew as town then crime, cheating and fraud soared.

So (A) is assertion and (B) is the response.

(ix) (b) (B) and (C)

According to the passage in the 11th century both parties were allowed to hire champions, whoever could pay the more stood a good chance of winning and today a wealthy person hires a costly and brilliant barrister. So (B) and (C) are right.

(x) (b) (B) and (C)

According to the passage about the sixth century AD to the eleventh the majority of the trials were in the form of cruel physical torture and in the saxons authorities, a noble / a land lord or a priest counted for up to half a dozen ordinary peasants.

7. (b) a great hope

According to the passage Glimmering means a great hope.

1. (i) The writer calls handicrafts a 'valued tradition' because they showcase talents that are associated with artisans' lifestyles and history. They represent our rich culture and heritage.

(ii) If it continues, the worcation (work + vacation) trend will be a powerful boost to domestic tourism operators languishing in the economic slump caused due to the pandemic.

(iii) Artisans choose to work via machines rather than handcrafted tools because machines save labor and reduce drudgery. It also increases production and finesse.

(iv) Artisans need to be 'lured with incentives' because if they impart training to mass/bulk producers, they run the risk of losing their traditional livelihood to them. Therefore, they need to be tempted with benefits or rewards.

(v) One of the ways in which the government and private sectors support the culture of making handicrafts is by creating awareness and public support for artisans and their work.

(vi) The writer justifies an artist's act of abandoning her/his traditional craft for a more lucrative option by stating that they cannot be expected to continue their profession if it is not profitable, even though the loss of traditional crafts is perturbing.

8. (a) (i) Mohenjo-daro   **(1×8=8 Marks)**

(b) (iii) terracota animals

(c) (iv) she can not be rediscovered as she's bronze

(d) (i) it appeals to us despite a passage of time

(e) (i) consists of bangles of shell or ivory or thin metal only

(f) (ii) why museums in our country are exciting

(g) amid

(h) true

2.   **(2×4=8 Marks)**

9.1. (a) **Advantage:** It promotes a sense of togetherness and bounding.

Disadvantage: by the time a decision in reached at; tempers have risen, feelings injured and at least one person grumbling.

(b) Parents ask their kids:

(i) the cuisine they prefer

(ii) the movie they want to see

   (iii) the holiday they wish to go on

   (iv) the subjects they wish to study

(c) Two pieces of advice given by the writer are :

   (i) Listen to your children and their silences.

   (ii) Step into their world.

     Both the objectives can be achieved by spending at least half an hour quality time with your kids.

(d) The author appears to be supporting the parents but he actually presents both sides of the coin. He sympathises with parents but also suggests that they should listen to their children and understand their silences as well. So, I agree with him.

9.2. (1×4=4 Marks)

(a) injured   (b) cuisine

(c) conflicting   (d) complicated

Topper's Answer

2.1. (a) The advantage of allowing every family member to be part of the decision making process is that it promotes a sense of togetherness and bonding.

On the other hand, the disadvantage is that it can lead to arguments, opposition, injured feelings and frequent flaring out of tempers.

(b) In today's world, parents are asking their kids the cuisine they prefer and the movie they want to watch. They are also asking their kids about the holiday they wish to go on and the subjects they prefer to study.

(c) The writer advises the parents to listen to their children, their silences and ensure that they spend time with them. The writer also tells the parents to step into their children's world for about half an hour everyday and insist that their children share their stories with them.

(d) I completely agree with the author's views as I feel that in today's world where there is a continuous rat race, it is very essential for parents to understand their children, their views and opinions. Spending time. Parents spending some time with their children every day can help children to express and open up to their parents better.

2.2. (a) The synonym of 'hurt' is 'injured'
(b) (i) Cuisine
(c) The antonym of 'agreeable' is 'conflicting'
(d) (ii) complicated

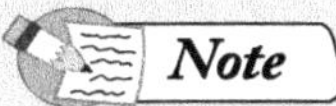 *Note*

a.   *You can answer these vocabulary questions correctly with an easy technique.*

b.   *Thoroughly read the paragraph mentioned in the question keeping in mind the meaning provided for the word you have to locate. You will see that the meaning fits appropriately in a particular context at a particular place. You will find the word you are looking for right there.*

c.   *To locate an antonym, first get a familiar antonym of the meaning word(s) provided; then, follow the same search method to get the required word in the passage.*

(1×8=8 Marks)

10.   (a)   Eleanor Roosevelt was a quiet, parentless girl growing up in the New York city. She grew up to become the First Lady of the United States.

(b)   Apart from being the first lady, Eleanor Roosevelt visited prisons and hospitals, travelled all over the country and helped people without food and jobs.

(c)   Eleanor Roosevelt suffered several personal tragedies. Her parents died when she was young; her second son died when he was a baby. Moreover, her husband was stricken with polio, which left him physically disabled for life.

(d)   She nursed her husband back to good health and encouraged him to remain in politics. She then helped him to become Governor of New York, and in 1933, President of the United States.

(e)   'She became her husband's legs and eyes' means that Eleanor Roosevelt shared her husband's responsibilities. While her husband was President, she took a great interest in all the affairs of the country. She visited prisons and hospitals; she went down into mines, up scaffoldings and into factories.

(f)   During the depression, she travelled all over the country bringing goodwill, reassurance and help to people without food and jobs.

(g)   She motivated the American soldiers during World War II by visiting them in camps all over the world.

(h)   Eleanor/Roosevelt kept in touch with the American people through a daily newspaper column called 'My Day'. She even broadcast on the radio and delivered lectures for the first time by a First Lady.

(i)   Eleanor Roosevelt was a remarkable woman who had great intelligence and tremendous strength of character.

11.1.   **(2×4=8 Marks)**

(a)   Russell's viper injects poison, whereas rat snakes opt for an alternative non-chemical method and catch and push their prey against the ground.

(b) Sand Boa produces secretions, particularly poisonous to birds. As an extra step, it crushes and injects poison to kill its prey.

(c) The hunting animals always compete with their prey. While hunting animals try their worst to kill most efficiently, their prey use any trick to avoid becoming a meal, such as developing immunity to poison.

(d) Mongooses are highly resistant to cobra poison, and with their speed and agility, kill snakes fearlessly.

(e) In the remote parts of India, local hospitality often involves leather tough meat which the writer finds difficult to chew. He cannot spit or refuse it as the hosts might get offended. So, he has to swallow it like a python stuffing a deer down its throat and hope he doesn't choke.

> ### 📝 *Note*
>
> *(a) These 2-mark questions are generally framed with 'why', 'what' and 'how' queries. You must consciously focus on the specific query and avoid diverting off track while writing out your answer. A 'why' requires reason(s), 'what' requires factual information, while 'how' requires the manner or process pertaining to the issue mentioned in the question.*
>
> *(b) In part (b) of the question above, for instance, the query is 'how' with regard to different methods a Russel viper employs to kill its prey. So, you should describe two different methods for the same.*

11.2 (i) (d) prey   **(1×2=2 Marks)**

     (ii) (c) softens

     (iii) (c) resistant to

11.3 (a) alternative   **(1×2=2 Marks)**

     (b) secretions

     (c) specific   **(1×8=8 Marks)**

12. (a) Some people believe that if they move up the time on their watch, it will help them be earlier.

     (b) Many others know that the time on their watch is wrong and they disregard it altogether.

     (c) Keep a clock, phone, computer or anything that displays time in each room.

     (d) One of the things that can be done is addition of five or ten minutes.

     (e) Many a time we do not realise that things usually take longer that what we expect.

     (f) Instead of pressing the snooze button, try to set your clock 10 minutes earlier than what you need.

     (g) If you have difficulty in getting up, move your clock to somewhere away from your bed.

     (h) It is a good habit to move your clock to somewhere away from your bed.

     (i) It is good to commit yourself to being 15 minutes earlier.

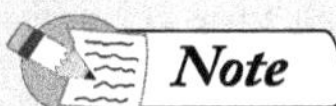

Note

(a)   *These 1-mark questions look simple but you risk getting them wrong if you are not mindful of how the complete sentence reads after you have filled your words.*

(b)   *It is imperative to double-check that you have used the correct tense, particularly in case of conditional sentences (with 'if' clause) and other complex sentences (with conjunction 'that'). For instance, in sentence (a) above, 'believe' and 'will' hint that the part you provide should also be in present tense, i.e., 'move'. In case, the given verbs were 'believed' and 'would'(past tense), you should have used 'believed' instead.*

13.1   **(2×4=8 Marks)**

(a)   It requires systematic, prolonged and strict training to become a professional singer. Since it is difficult and time consuming, the training part is conveniently ignored.

(b)   Music has the power to bring out the deepest emotions. It can make one cry or smile when depressed or obsessed. So music is called a magic medicine.

(c)   Hurried shortcuts and half-hearted attempts to gain some knowledge and training of music or singing are best described as 'Crash courses'.

(d)   The mindset of a student of music should be to make mistakes and be corrected by the teacher as this subsequently makes one flawless and educated.

(e)   Singing is a refined and intricate art because it requires systematic, prolonged and strict training to become acceptable.

13. 2   (a)   (i)   two thirds

(b)   (iii) fine arts

(c)   (ii) rise above

(d)   (iii) shelter from unhappiness.

(e)   (ii) incomplete   **(1×8=8 Marks)**

14.   (a)   A tourist attraction in Jammu and Kashmir is the Floating Post Office that is built on an intricately carved maroon houseboat, fastened on the western edge of the Dal Lake in Srinagar.

(b)   The seal used on everything posted from Floating Post Office is very unique along with the date and address as it bears the design of a boatman rowing a shikara on the Dal Lake.

(c)   The letters posted from here carry a special design which has the picturesque scenery of Dal Lake and Srinagar city. These pictures reach wherever these letters are posted, therefore promoting Kashmir as a tourist destination across the world.

(d) The chief postmaster John Samuel renamed the post office as 'Floating Post Office'.

(e) The post office's houseboat has two small rooms – one serves as the office and the other a small museum that traces the philatelic history of the state postal department.

(f) For the locals, the lake has several islets that are home to more than 50,000 people.

(g) The greatest fear is the recurrence of 2014 like floods in which the houseboat had gone for a toss uncontrollably pushed by the flood.

(h) The biggest boon to the people is that at no time of the year there is a need of a fan in this post-office.

(i) Fascination.

2.   **(2×4=8 Marks)**

15.1 (a) Smartphones make our communication very effective and instant. As a result, people are able to convey their message, all around the globe to their loved ones, without spending hefty sums of money.

(b) The internet facilities available on mobile phones, help the young generation broaden their minds and improve their skills by doing research.

(c) In the case of an emergency, smartphones can play a significant role. If any crime occurs in society, one can immediately inform the security forces with the help of smartphones and can prevent it from occurring.

(d) The youth waste too much time on mobile phones. They sometimes misuse them. They are prone to getting involved in undesirable activities on the internet. Besides, mobile phones adversely affect their academic performance.

(e) A prepaid card allows subscribers to load text credits to their handsets by the use of their credit cards, debit cards or by buying a prepaid card from the network they subscribe to.

15.2 (a) (iii) invention   **(1×4=4 Marks)**

(b) (ii) emails

(c) (iii) monitor

(d) (ii) negative

(e) (iii) monthly

Note

(a) These short-answer questions to test reading comprehension contain 2 marks each. The marking scheme is often hinted within the question. being mindful of the same will help you score high.

(b) You can clearly notice that each question requires you to make two clear points, i.e., 'helpful' in 2 ways, 2 benefits, 'lifesavers' in 2 ways, 2 demerits, and 'useful' in 2 ways, respectively.

(c) The MCQs appear direct and easy but need caution on your part. For example, no clear statement is there in the passage for 2.2 (b); you can answer it only if you comprehend the passage well.

(1×8=8 Marks)

16. (a) Nobody went into Miss Hilton's house because her front <u>gates were always locked and she seldom left the house.</u>

(b) Her house had only two colours, (i) <u>Grey,</u> and (ii) <u>Green</u>

(c) The high iron fence did not let the boys get <u>mangoes.</u>

(d) They never got it back if their <u>cricket ball</u> fell into her courtyard.

(e) The boys were ready to dislike the <u>new owners.</u>

(f) One resident of the street always <u>complained that the boys playing cricket on the pavement or made too much noise.</u>

(g) The new owners of Miss Hilton's house were (i) <u>a pretty woman, and</u> (ii) <u>an ugly man.</u>

(h) The man was shouting, the dog was barking, only <u>the woman was inaudible.</u>

17.1   **(2×4=8 Marks)**

(a) In our childhood and growing years, we were taught to pray and worship the pictures and idols of the Gods of our own religions. A few years later, we were taught to read books like Bhagwad Gita, Bible and Quran, as there were lots of valuable lessons to be learnt from them.

(b) We should respect our parents because they made our life comfortable with all their efforts. We should respect our teachers because they help and guide us to become good students and responsible citizens.

(c) The message that we get from nature is to save the environment and maintain ecological balance. We are taught to live in harmony with nature and recognise God's presence in our natural surroundings.

(d) When an obstacle, such as a heavy boulder or fallen trees blocks the flow of a river, the latterdoes not stop flowing. It either fights to remove the obstacle or takes a different path and moves on. Thus, it teaches us to be progressive and brave while facing obstacles in our life. It helps in keeping our fighting spirit alive.

17.2 (e) (ii)   advised   **(1×4=4 Marks)**

(f) (i)   search

(g) (iv)   useful

(h) (ii)   friendship

> *Note*
>
> (a) In questions starting with 'why or what for', it is necessary to give the reason(s). If they are more than one or two, write them all but if they are 6 or more, give only the main ones as suited to the length of your answer.
>
> (b) In questions starting with 'what', be cautious not to add any new information from your own side, keep your answer to the point and wholesome.
>
> (c) While answering the questions starting with 'when or where', the exact point of time or the exact location is a must to be mentioned.
>
> (d) While answering questions starting with 'How', it is expected that the students mention the way the action has taken place.
>
> (e) Identification of words with that of the similar ones given as choices calls for a rich vocabulary, you should learn more and more number of words – not only their meanings but also their proper uses.

(1×8=8 Marks)

18. (a) The doctors warn you to quit the habit if you are addicted to coffee.

(b) Caffeinated and de-caffeinated versions of coffee are drunk in America.

(c) The two potential health benefits of antioxidants are that they protect against heart diseases and cancer.

(d) Vinson, a dietitian says that the benefits of antioxidants ultimately depends on how they are absorbed and utilised in the body.

(e) Tea and milk are other popular sources of antioxidants.

(f) Coffee outranks dates as a source of antioxidants because dates are not consumed as much as coffee is.

(g) Coffee is beneficial because it has been linked to a number of potential health benefits including protection against liver diseases and colon cancer

(h) Researchers advise moderation in coffee consumption as excessive use can make one jittery and also cause stomach pain.

> **Note**
>
> (a) These are 1 mark questions.
>   Questions with 'What', 'Mention', 'State' and 'Name' should be answered with the exact fact asked. Do not add extra information.
> (b) The 'How' question will need a concise answer in a sentence or two. Do not write more.
> (c) Long answers will cause deduction in marks.

2.   **(2×4=8 Marks)**

19.2. (a) Gandhiji told Ranibala that her bangles were too heavy for her delicate little wrists.

(b) Kasturba's apprehension was that her daughters-in-law may want to wear jewellery

(c) Gandhiji said, "our children are young and when they grow up they will not surely choose wives who are fond of wearing jewellery."

(d) Gandhiji used the jewels to raise the community funds. He also donated every penny he earned in South Africa to the trustees for the service of South African Indians.

> **Note**
>
> a. These are 2-mark questions. You should answer these in 2-3 sentences, not more.
> b. Be very precise and exact.

19. 2 (e) (iv) unbeatable   **(1×8=8 Marks)**

(f) (i) encouraged

(g) (iv) distressed

(h) (ii) disagreement

> **Note**
>
> (a) To be able to answer vocabulary questions, you need to have a good vocabulary. So, you should make it a regular practice to read more to enrich your vocabulary.
> (b) However, in case you see unfamiliar words in this question, you can use an easy technique to get the correct answer. Read the paragraph mentioned replacing the given word with one option at a time. The one fitting the context will be your answer.
> (c) Another method is eliminating the obvious incorrect options so that the correct word is left as the answer.

20. (a) Kausani is situated at a height of 6,075 feet in the Central Himalayas.

(b) Kausani provides the 300-km wide breathtaking view of the Himalayas. It is the most striking aspect of this place.

(c) The most famous peak on view is Nanda Devi, the second highest mountain in India.

(d) Kausani is the birthplace of Sumitranandan Pant, India's poet laureate. Its natural surroundings inspired many of his poems.

(e) At sunrise and at sunset, when the colour changes to a golden orange, the scene gets etched in your memory.

(f) The scenic beauty of Kausani held him spellbound. He named it the 'Switzerland of India'.

(g) Kausani is a calm and quiet place because there is no traffic and the absence of busy people, unlike city.

(h) There is no traffic, no one is in a hurry. If serenity could be put on a canvas, the picture would resemble Kausani.

> *Note*
>
> a. *Before beginning to write the answers of questions based on an unseen passage, go through the questions first and while going through the passage, note and underline the relevant points given therein.*
>
> b. *Since all the questions carry only 1 mark, your answer must be very concise, sometimes merely a single word and sometimes, a simple sentence.*
>
> c. *Addition of any new information to the answers should be strictly avoided; only pin pointed answer should be given.*

21.   **(2×4=8 Marks)**

(a) The diners at Ananda Bhavan uttered low moans on seeing the tiger. Besides, the schools were hurriedly closed down and children of all ages were running helter -skelter, screaming joyously, "No school, no school, tiger, tiger!"

(b) Tigers don't attack until they feel hungry as it said, "I won't attack until I feel hungry again. In this respect, humans slaughter anyone and everyone whenever they want to as the tiger said, "Tigers attack only when they feel hungry, unlike human beings who slaughter one another without purpose or hunger."

(c) The children were ecstatic to find their schools being closed. But they were terrified by the appearance of the tiger and ran about helter-skelter, screaming joyously, "No school, no school. Tiger, tiger." They shouted, laughed and even enjoyed being scared.

(d) The headmaster jumped on the table and heaved himself up into an attic on seeing the tiger. The tiger flung itself on the cool floor as it had a special liking for cool stone floors and all it wished for was a little moment of sleep in the bright sunlight of the day.

(1×4=4 Marks)

(e) (iv) holding tightly in the arms

(f) (i) pleasure

(g) (ii) honourable

(h) (iii) walked with heavy steps

22. (a) (iii) A form of dance **(1×5=5 Marks)**

(b) (ii) for sanctification and redemption

(c) (i) beats of the bamboos

(d) (iv) the sound of the bamboos forms the rhythm of the dance

(e) (iii) deliverance from evil ways

23. **(1×5=5 Marks)**

(a) (iv) a range of 4 glaciers namely Sunder dunga, Namik Pandari and Kafni

(b) (iv) all of the above

(c) (ii) high altitude sickness, lack of oxygen and steep climb

(d) (ii) below zero degrees

(e) (i) features

 *Note*

a. To answer a question based on a poem and carrying 1 mark each, you should be as brief as possible. Exactly to the point and wholesome answer is required.

b. Understanding of the poem may require you to read and re read the poem. Read the poem twice or thrice.

c. Question on vocabulary is generally difficult to answer but you can make it out by reading the preceding and following lines of the concerned word(s).

24. (a) (iv) All of the above **(1×5=5 Marks)**

(b) (i) to plant a tree in the child's name

(c) (ii) The adolescent and the tree

(d) (iii) they died in an attempt to stop the cutting down of trees

(e) (i) desert

Note

a. To answer of MCQ's, you must take care to choose the option which is the closest answer. if the exact answer is not available in the passage.

b. In case the answer is not obvious, eliminate the wrong options so that you are left with the right choice.

25. (a) (iv) all of the above **(1×5=5 Marks)**

(b) (ii) Friendly and trusting

(c) (iv) All of the above

(d) (iii) Both men and new animals

(e) (iii) Extinction

26. **(1×5=5 Marks)**

(a) The 92-year-old lady moved to an old age home because she had lost her husband recently.

(b) She reacted with the enthusiasm of an 8-year-old who had been presented with a new puppy and said, "I love it."

(c) The resolution she makes every morning when she gets out of bed is that, "happiness is something you decide. I have decided to love it." Instead of recounting her problems she chose to believe that, "each day is a gift."

(d) It tells us that the woman has an extraordinary sense of cheer and boundless enthusiasm.

(e) boundless

Note

a. *In questions starting with 'why or what for', it is necessary to give the reason(s). If they are more than one or two, write them all but if they are 6 or more, give only the main ones as suited to the length of your answer.*

b. *In questions starting with 'what', be cautious not to add any new information from your own side, keep your answer to the point and wholesome.*

c. *While answering the questions starting with 'when or where', the exact point of time or the exact location is a must to be mentioned.*

d. *While answering questions starting with 'How', it is expected that the students mention the way the action has taken place.*

e. *Questions beginning with 'which' need to be answered in exact word(s) from the passage.*

27. (a) The dove died of grieving   **(1×5=5 Marks)**

(b) Its legs were tied with a silken thread weaved by the poet

(c) "Sweet little red feet," refers to the dove

(d) By kissing it often and feeding it peas

(e) grieving

Note

One way to attempt the reading section successfully questions first and then go to the passage. It saves time and makes you alert.

Topic-b: ***Case-Based Factual Passages***

1. (i) We can say that the situation of people living in concrete structures is comparable with a fish living in a fishbowl, and the need for vertical gardens to the need for decorations in the fishbowl **because a fish needs decorations such as plants or rocks to simulate a natural environment and improve its quality of life just like people living in urban areas need green spaces such as vertical gardens to improve their physical and mental wellbeing.**

(ii) The statement that, urban spaces have become more closely connected with the desired natural surroundings through the incorporation of nature and structures in vertical gardens and green walls, is an **opinion** because it is a **subjective judgement.**

[This statement expresses a viewpoint or belief about the benefits of incorporating nature and structures through vertical gardens and green walls in urban spaces. While there may be evidence to support this opinion, such as research on the positive effects of greenery on well-being or the visual appeal of vertical gardens, it is still ultimately a subjective judgment rather than an objective fact that can be proven or disproven.]

(iii) True, because the majority of participants strongly agreed that vertical gardens can improve the quality of life, increase air quality, and have a relaxing and calming effect. However, the survey does not provide information on the long-term effectiveness of vertical gardens or their potential impact on other aspects of urban life, such as traffic or community engagement.

(iv) A city government looking to install vertical gardens should consider addressing these concerns:

- cost of installation and maintenance [should be reasonable]

- areas of installation should be where driver distraction is less of an issue.

(v) Participants may not be fully informed or aware of the effects of vertical gardens on air quality, which could contribute to the neutral response.

(vi) (b) Only (ii)

(vii) Advantages of vertical gardens over other green spaces-

- They can be installed in small spaces, making them ideal for urban areas with limited space.

- They also offer aesthetic and design benefits, as they can be customized to fit specific architectural styles or preferences.

- Disadvantages of vertical gardens over other green spaces-

- May not provide as much space for outdoor recreation as community gardens or parks do.

- The cost of installation and maintenance may be higher than for other types of green spaces.

(viii) (b) Vertical gardening is a sustainable practice that can transform urban spaces into green areas.

2. (i) Because of a vast blanket of pollution.

(ii) (a) I, II and III

(iii) Potential

(iv) (c) There has not been enough time to determine that.

(v) Does- Depletion of forest cover.

Does not- organic farming.

(vi) (a) Worsen

(vii) Consequences

(viii) India and China

(ix) (c) Continue.

(x) (a) Impact of pollution in South Asia.

(b) Effects of Acid Rain.

(c) Understanding over Droughts

(d) Effect of Haze   **(10 × 1 = 10 Marks)**

3. (i) Because a retired civil engineer in the Jammu & Kashmir government came up with the idea of artificial glaciers.

(ii) Glaciers Melt

(iii) Glaciers

(iv) On sloping hills facing distribution channels.

(v) July, August, September.

4. (i) This is so because these states are lesser explored as compared to the rest of the country, despite having lots to offer.

(ii) (a) distinctiveness and diversity

(iii) hues and shades

(vi) (b) a wholesome experience within the budget they have planned for

(v) (b) Option 2

(vi) (b) encouraging

(vii) Any one of the following words can be used- observed/ recorded/showed/displayed

(viii) The 'tourist facilities' are as follows-

Accommodation – hotels, hostels, camps

Recreation- Parks, Gardens, Museums, Shopping areas

(ix) Researchers recommend that the formulation of a tourism strategy in the North-Eastern States of India be sustainable to create socio-economic benefits for the local community.

(x) Following are the options-

1. Winds of Change

2. Numbers Don't Lie

3. Time for Action

5. Case study

(i) JK Rowling's near "magical rise to fame" mentions her incredible journey of becoming a famous writer. **(1 Mark)**

(ii) Publishers told her that plot was too complex and the story being too long Rowling's book was rejected. **(1 Mark)**

(iii) The drawback of achieving fame was that she had journalists knocking on her door, day and night. **(1 Mark)**

(iv) Rowling was outraged with the Italian dust jacket because they showed Hary without her glasses. **(1 Mark)**

(v) Vulnerability **(1 Mark)**

(vi) According to the graph, Rowling took seven years to become very successful. **(1 Mark)**

For visually impaired candidates:

(vi) (b) JK Rowling is the first self made billionaire author in history, selling more than 400 million books. **(1 Mark)**

6. (i) (b) B is correct, C is false

(c) (A) and (B) both are correct.

According to the passage, it clearly shows that species must killed are not necessarily the endangered species.

Roads have become, killers for animals. Therefore, both (b) and (c) are correct.

(ii)　(b)　(B) is correct and C is false.

Passage states that Road traffic is dangerous for wild life and mammels so B is correct, and it is not possible that any one can survive on traffic on roads so C is false.

(iii)　(a)　While planning roads we should see which species to protect.

According to the passage, to preserve wildlife when new roads are built so option (a) is correct.

(iv)　(c)　Number of road-kills depends upon the population density of small animals.

According to the passage number of road kills depends upon the population density of small animals, so option c is correct.

(v)　(a)　(A) is an assertion and (B) is the response.

According to the passage in the research study the hazel grouse and ground squirrel were found to be the most at risk of local extinction, so option (a) (A) is assertion and (B) is response.

(vi)　(c)　ironical (a) logical solution.

Statement shows totally opposite sense from the passage detail, so the statement is ironic, according passage. The hazel grouse and ground squirrel were found to be the most at risk of local extinction.

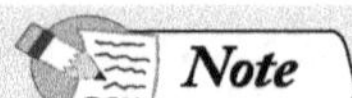
Note

It is also a logical conclusion as per the facts given in the passage. Hence, both (a) and (c) are correct.

(vii)　(b)　Road kills.

The summary of the passage in based on the road. Accidents and killing of mammals and birds in accidents. So the title should be road kills.

(viii)　(b)　To see who is more at risk on the roads.

The passage shows that the study is based on to see who is more at risk on the roads. Birds and Mammals are not safe on the roads.

7　(i)　Researchers call pollution the 'flip side' of festivals because the accepted norm is that festivals are synonymous with celebration, and people fail to see the other side, which is pollution.

(ii)　The significance of the second objective of the study is in knowing steps that need to be taken to address the problem investigated in the research and understanding what immediate actions need to be implemented to address the issue studied.

(iii)　Researchers recommend strict rules because they are better than a total ban. Banning does not serve the purpose of awareness. However, people do not generally conform to banning and tend to revolt. Nevertheless, strict rules pose some restrictions but still give the needed freedom.

(iv)　The researchers feel so because the festivals cause pollution along with other issues that add to it. Creating awareness is the only solution, and the lack of it accelerates the problem.

(v)　Festival pollution persists because still a large percentage of people (72%) abuse environmental resources to celebrate festivals. A high percentage of people (82%) continue to use crackers to celebrate festivals to live up to the expectation of their social status.

(vi)　The 'Can't say' column allows the respondents to choose not to express or answer. It allows an option for those who lack clarity and are unwilling to respond.

Writing Skills and Grammar

Topic-a: *Grammar*

Gap Filling

Fill in the blank by using the correct form of the word

1. Dear Sir   [CBSE Sample 2023-24 **Ap**]

This is with reference to committee's letter of recommendation that ________ (highlight) the nominations for 'Safe Residential Area' award for this current year.

2. A copy of the plan is enclosed and __________ (that/ then/ this) may be communicated to all Team Leaders for compliance.   [CBSE Sample 2023-24 **Ap**]

3. The experience of nursing an injured bird left me ____________ grateful for knowing the importance of being kind and compassionate to all creatures.

     [CBSE Sample 2023-24 **Ap**]

  (a)   feeling

  (b)   having felt

  (c)   felt

  (d)   feels

4. Congratulations Change Makers!

The regional competition awards have been announced and our school music club __________ the first prize.

     [CBSE Sample 2023-24 **Ap**]

  (a)   had been won

  (b)   will win

  (c)   was winning

  (d)   has won

5. The river runs through your veins

    The trees and mountains ______ your name

The moon and stars watch over

    You're guiding your way back home

To dream the night away.

     [CBSE Sample 2023-24 **Ap**]

  (a)   will call

  (b)   call

  (c)   had called

  (d)   calls

6. If I were attending the workshop. I _______ stay on till the end of the second session as well.

(a) would

(b) may

(c) can

(d) should

7. As a true patriot, I _______ lay down my life for my motherland. **[All India, 2023 Ap]**

(a) might

(b) could

(c) will

(d) should

8. When I was a very young girl, _______ grocery shopping was considered a major outing for me.

[All India, 2023 Ap]

(a) to be going

(b) going

(c) having gone

(d) went

9. The package _______ (arrive) at nine in the morning, the day after tomorrow. **[All India, 2023 Ap]**

(a) will arrive

(b) would arrive

(c) can arrive

(d) cannot arrive

10. Drivers _______ wear helmets for their safety.

[All India, 2023 Ap]

(a) must

(b) can't

(c) don't

(d) ought

11. Economics _______ difficult for the students of grade nine. **[All India, 2023 Ap]**

(a) is

(b) are

(c) has

(d) were

12. Parents must.................their children's leisure activities.

[Delhi, 2023 Ap]

(a) look at

(b) look into

(c) look away

(d) look up

13. Keep the environment clean. Do not litter.

You...................follow rules. **[Delhi, 2023 Ap]**

(a) should

(b) may

(c) must

(d) will

14. In times of trouble you can always.................your parents for help.   **[Delhi, 2023 Ap]**

   (a) turn in

   (b) turn to

   (c) turn on

   (d) turn away

15. The students with the help of their teacher.......................... (create) a beautiful poster.   **[Delhi, 2023 Ap]**

16. The doctor .... examined the patient when the family arrived.

   (a) was

   (b) had

   (c) has

   (d) have

17. The climate control comment by an activist __________________ on social media yesterday.

                                    [CBSE Sample 2022-23 Ap]

   (a) blow up

   (b) blew up

   (c) is blown

   (d) will be blown

18. The advertisement read, 'If you smoke, statistically your story _________________ end 15% before it should'.

                                    [CBSE Sample 2022-23 Ap]

   (a) must

   (b) should

   (c) will

   (d) ought to

19. As I was standing on the dock, looking out at the lake for the last time, a feeling of emptiness __________________ over me like darkness.

                                    [CBSE Sample 2022-23 Ap]

   (a) will wash

   (b) had washed

   (c) will have washed

   (d) washed

20. **Subject:** Request for Approval

   Dear Sir

   This is to respectfully submit that I __________________ (seek) approval for organising a tree plantation drive to be undertaken by the club.

                                    [CBSE Sample 2022-23 Ap]

21. _________________ WE AFFORD TO NEGLECT CHILDREN? THINK TWICE!!

                                    [CBSE Sample 2022-23 Ap]

   (a) WILL

   (b) MAY

   (c) NEED

   (d) CAN

22. Select the correct option to complete the narration of the dialogue between Latha and her father.

[CBSE Sample 2022-23 **Ap**]

Father: Why ask so many questions, Latha?

Latha: I believe that if you don't know the answer, keep asking till you do!

Father asked Latha the reason for the many questions she was asking. Latha exclaimed good-humouredly that in event of not knowing the answer one should ________________ .

(a) keep asking till one does.

(b) kept asking till one does.

(c) keep asking till one do.

(d) kept on to ask till one do.

23. I don't see why you ______ borrow his cycle. You have one of your own. [All India 2022, **Ap**]

(a) should

(b) could

(c) may

(d) might

24. My family___in Chennai for five years now.

[All India 2022, **Ap**]

(a) has lived

(b) has been living

(c) had lived

(d) lived

25. ____ the letter arrive in your absense, would you like me to forward it to you ? [All India 2022, **Ap**]

(a) If

(b) Could

(c) Should

(d) Might

26. If he came late he ______ be punished.

[All India 2022, **Ap**]

(a) will

(b) shall

(c) should

(d) would

27. By the time we reach the school the bell ____

[All India 2022, **Ap**]

(a) will be ringing

(b) will have rung

(c) would have been ringing

(d) would have rung

28. Three months ago I ____ a student of this school.

[All India 2022, **Ap**]

(a) was

(b) had been

(c) have been

(d) could be

29. A great advantage (a) _____________ early rising is the good start it gives us to our days' work. An early riser has done a large amount of hard work (b) _____________ other men have got out of their beds. In the early morning, the mind is fresh and there (c) _____________ few noises or other distractions, so that the work done (d) _____________ that time is generally well done.

[All India 2020 Ap]

(a) (i) and   (ii) of

    (iii) but   (iv) from

[All India 2020 Ap]

(b) (i) at   (ii) or

    (iii) upon   (iv) before

[All India 2020 Ap]

(c) (i) are   (ii) is

    (iii) will   (iv) was

[All India 2020 Ap]

(d) (i) at   (ii) for

    (iii) from   (iv) on

[All India 2020 Ap]

30. Reading books ____(a)____ a good hobby. Books open ____ (b)____ vast new world to us. They increase____ (c)____ knowledge and change our out-look____(d) ____ the world. **[All India 2020 Ap]**

(a) (i) has   (ii) was

    (iii) are   (iv) is

(b) (i) the   (ii) a

    (iii) an   (iv) some

(c) (i) his   (ii) one's

    (iii) our   (iv) your

(d) (i) towards   (ii) for

    (iii) by   (iv) from

31. Communication _(a)_ become very effective _(b)_ instant due to smart phones. People are able _(c)_ convey their messages all around the globe to _(d)_ loved ones _(e)_ spending hefty sums of money.   **[Delhi 2020 Ap]**

(a) (i)   is   (ii)   has

    (iii) have   (iv)   had

(b) (i)   but   (ii)   as

    (iii) or   (iv)   and

(c) (i)   for   (ii)   in

    (iii) to   (iv)   of

(d) (i)   his   (ii)   her

    (iii) their   (iv)   your

(e) (i)   with   (ii)   without

    (iii) and   (iv)   to

[All India 2019 Ap]

32. The caves of Ajanta and Ellora ___(a)___ magnificent works of sculpture. Whoever ___(b)___ there ___(c)___ spellbound. Thousands (d) ___ tourists visit these places every year. One can stay (e) ___ the guest houses.

[Delhi 2019 Ap]

(a) (i) is (ii) are (iii) was (iv) were

(b) (i) go (ii) going (iii) goes (iv) went

(c) (i) becomes (ii) became (iii) becoming (iv) has become

(d) (i) for (ii) of (iii) from (iv) at

(e) (i) on (ii) over (iii) upon (iv) in

33. The modern student __(a)__ the importance __(b)__ physical exercise. He spends one to two hours in open air __(c)__ he takes part in different sports. However, care should __(d)__ not to overstrain __(e)__ body.

[All India 2018 Ap]

(a) (i) understood

(ii) understand

(iii) have understand

(iv) understands

(b) (i) of (ii) by

(iii) from (iv) with

(c) (i) how (ii) which

(iii) where (iv) why

(d) (i) be taken (ii) took

(iii) takes (iv) has taken

(e) (i) a (ii) an

(iii) the (iv) some

34. Very few people (a) _______ loneliness. It seems to me that most people (b) _______ scared of (c) _______ left on their own.   **[All India 2017 Ap]**

(a) (i) enjoy (ii) enjoys

(iii) enjoyed (iv) enjoying

(b) (i) is (ii) am

(iii) are (iv) was

(c) (i) be (ii) being

(iii) been (iv) having

35. I met a smart young person (a) _____________ wanted a 'selfie' (b) _____________ me. So we (c) ___________ on top of a boundary wall.   **[Delhi 2017 Ap]**

(a) (i) which (ii) who

(iii) whose (iv) whom

(b) (i) with (ii) on

(iii) for (iv) to

(c) (i) sit (ii) sits

(iii) sat (iv) sitting

36. Kingfisher is (a) __________ beautiful bird with attractive colours. It (b) __________ found near lakes, river, canals (c) __________ ponds.

[All India 2016 Ap]

(a) (i) a (ii) an

(iii) the (iv) such a

(b) (i) are (ii) am

(iii) is (iv) has

(c) (i) and (ii) but

(iii) so (iv) or

37. He was (a) _______ at the news (b) ________ the success of a poor candidate (c) ________ got the highest number of votes in Bihar election. **[Delhi 2016 Ap]**

(a) (i) surprising (ii) surprise

(iii) surprised (iv) having surprised

(b) (i) of (ii) for

(iii) to (iv) by

(c) (i) which (ii) whose

(iii) whom (iv) who

38. There are ways and ways (a) _______ tackling a problem. But governments all over the world (b) ________ only one system (c) ____________ is : the carrot-and-stick one. **[All India 2015 Ap]**

(a) (i) in (ii) of

(iii) from (iv) on

(b) (i) prefer (ii) prefers

(iii) preferred (iv) preferring

(c) (i) who (ii) which

(iii) what (iv) whose

39. Today a good (a) ________ varieties of tea and tea brands are available in the market. Green tea is popular (b) ________ China and the Far East. In Japan, the tea ceremony is a traditional way of greeting guests, (c) ________ is a social occasion. **[Delhi 2015 Ap]**

(a) (i) very (ii) many

(iii) much (iv) more

(b) (i) on (ii) at

(iii) in (iv) for

(c) (i) and (ii) it

(iii) both (iv) this

40. A rich man from Punjab who (a) ____________ to Rohtak to purchase land, (b) ____________ of < 30 lakhs from his car on Monday. His son (c) ____________ inside the car when the robbery took place.

[All India 2014 Ap]

(a) (i) come   (ii) came

    (iii) was coming   (iv) coming

(b) (i) was robbed   (ii) is robbed

    (iii) robbed   (iv) has robbed

(c) (i) is sitting   (ii) sat

    (iii) was sitting   (iv) sits

41. Stranger : (a) ________________________________

      __________ here?

Policeman : They   (b) ________________ the

      shooting of a film.

Stranger :   Which film (c) ________________

      ________________?

[All India 2014 Ap]

(a) (i)   Why are the people gather

   (ii)   Why have the people gathered

   (iii)   Why did the people gather

   (iv)   Why have the people gather

(b) (i)   has come there to watch

   (ii)   had gone here to watching

   (iii)   have come here to watch

   (iv)   had come here to watch

(c) (i)   is being shot here

   (ii)   was being shot there

   (iii)   has been shooting here

   (iv)   has been shot there

42. I have been (a) ________________ to learn English for

the last three years. But, I haven't (b) ________________

yet. My teacher is very patient with me and he (c)

________________ me every time I fail.

[Delhi 2014 Ap]

(a) (i) tried   (ii) try

    (iii) tries   (iv) trying

(b) (i) succeeded   (ii) succeed

    (iii) succeeds   (iv) succeeding

(c) (i) encouraging   (ii) encourage

    (iii) encourages   (iv) encouraged

43. Shivani :   When did you arrive in Delhi, Mr. Shiv?

Shiv   :   I (a) __________ yesterday.

Shivani :   Did you (b) ________________ on the way?

Shiv   :   Nothing much, but someone (c) __________

      my bag while I was sleeping in the train.

Shivani :   It is very sad news.   **[Delhi 2014 Ap]**

(a) (i)   arrived

   (ii)   have arrived

   (iii)   was arrived

   (iv)   had arrived

(b) (i)   had any difficulty

   (ii)   have a difficulty

   (iii)   have any difficulty

   (iv)   had a difficulty

(c) (i)   ran away with

   (ii)   runs away with

   (iii)   has run away with

   (iv)   had run away

44. No matter how old you are, drink at least a glass of milk everyday (a) ______________ you want to sharpen (b) ______________ mental skills. A new study has claimed that drinking (c) ______________ glass of milk daily not only boost one's intake of much needed nutrients, but it also positively impacts one's brain power.

[All India 2013 **Ap**]

(a)   (i)   that   (ii)   if

        (iii) then   (iv)   how

(b)   (i)   her   (ii)   his

        (iii) my   (iv)   your

(c)   (i)   a   (ii)   and

        (iii) an   (iv)   the

45. Seema   :   (a) ______________________?

Nandish   :   My lucky charm is my 'Karha' (an iron ring).

Seema   :   (b) ______________________?

Nandish   :   I have been wearing it since childhood. It's my grandfather's 'Karha.' I believe when I am wearing it his blessing are with me.

Seema   :   (c) ______________________?

Nandish   :   No, I am not superstitious. I don't believe in fasting and going to a particular place of worship. I just believe in Karma.

[All India 2013 **Ap**]

(a)   (i)   What your lucky charm is

      (ii)   What was your luck charm

      (iii) What is your lucky charm

      (iv) What lucky charm is yours

(b)   (i)   Since when have you been wearing it

      (ii)   Since when are you wearing it

      (iii) Since when you have been wearing it

      (iv) Since when you are wearing it

(c)   (i)   You are not superstitious

      (ii)   You are superstitious

      (iii) You have been superstitious

      (iv) Are you not superstitious

Error Correction

1. Read the given sentence from a recipe review article. Identify the error and supply the correction in the sentence.

This delightful recipe must keep your hunger pangs at bay with its balanced spices and oriental flavour.

Use the given format for your response.

[CBSE Sample 2023-24; **Ap**]

error	correction

2. Identify the error and supply correction for the given sentence from a commercial company's current marketing strategy.

The company aimed at increasing authority in areas frequently visited by the clients.

Use the given format for your response.

[CBSE Sample 2023-24; **Ap**]

error	correction

3. Select the option that identifies the error and supplies the correction for the closing line, from an analytical report.

In conclusion, this study explores the association among short-sleep pattern and overweight youngsters.

[CBSE Sample 2023-24; **Ap**]

Option No.	error	correction
A	explores	explore
B	and	or
C	among	between
D	In	for

4. Identify the error and supply correction for the following note in a passengers' flight instruction manual:

Use the given format for your response.

[CBSE Sample 2023-24; **Ap**]

error	correction

5. Select the option that identifies the error and supplies the correction for the following line:

My sister lives at the ground floor of a two-storeyed apartment and hates living there.

[All India, 2023; **Ap**]

Option No.	Error	Correction
(a)	live	living
(b)	at	on
(c)	hates	hate
(d)	there	their

6. Identify the error in the given sentence and supply the correction:

Do you know that slouching should cause many problems?

Use the given format for your response.

[All India, 2023; **Ap**]

Error	Correction

7. Select the option that identifies the error and supplies the correction for the following line:

The sounds of laughter was echoing in the corridor.

[Delhi, 2023; **Ap**]

Option	Error	Correction
(a)	sounds	sound
(b)	laughter	laughing
(c)	was	were
(d)	in	of

8. Identify the error in the given sentence and supply the correction:

The children were exciting when they saw the leopard.

Use the given format for your response:

[Delhi, 2023; **Ap**]

Error	Correction

9. Identify the error in the statement given below and supply the correction. Use the given format for your response.

   Water was vital to human health and fitness.

   [Delhi, 2023; Ap]

Error	Correction

10. Select the option that identifies the error and supplies the correction for the following line, from a news report:

    Last week a child was not allowed to board the plane at Ranchi airport. **[CBSE Sample 2022-23; Ap]**

Option no.	error	correction
A.	child	children
B.	last	previous
C.	the	a
D.	at	in

11. Identify the error in the given sentence, from a school magazine report and supply the correction.

    In order to balancing the sentiments of the Eagles and the Hawks, the Student Council suggested a rematch between the teams.

    Use the given format for your response.

    [CBSE Sample 2022-23; Ap]

error	correction

12. Identify the error on a shop's hoarding and supply the correction, for the following sales offer:

    [CBSE Sample 2022-23; Ap]

Gumnaam & Daughters Pvt. Ltd.
Bindapur, Jharkhand
Massive discount for all senior citizen vaccinated with the precautionary dose.

Use the given format for your response.

error	correction

13. The following paragraph has an error in each line with a blank. Write the correct and the incorrect word in the blanks provided. The first one has been done for you.

    [All India 2022, Ap]

	Incorrect	**Correct**
A first Indian woman physician e.g.		
(1)	_____	_____
Anandibai Joshi graduated at 1886,		
(2)	_____	_____
About 125 years later, Indian women had start to		
(3)	_____	_____
outnumber men in admissions of medical		
(4)	_____	_____
colleges.		

14. The following paragraph has not been edited. There is an error in each line. Write the error along with its correction in the space provided.

[All India, 2020; **Ap**]

Error Correction

Spending time for their kids brings (a) _____ _____

immediate as well as long-last (b) _____ _____

gain for a parents. According to a (c) _____ _____

research, children with concerned (d) _____ _____

parents are more efficient.

15. The following paragraph has not been edited. There is one error in each line. Write the error and the correction in your answer book against the correct blank number.

[All India 2020; **Ap**]

	Error	Correction
The city police have decide		
(a)	_____	_____
to taking stern action against		
(b)	_____	_____
drivers which attempt to		
(c)	_____	_____
overtake in the left side		
(d)	_____	_____
on city roads.		

16. The following paragraph has not been edited. There is an error in each line. Write the error along with its correction in the spacc provided. [Delhi 2020; **Ap**]

	Error	Correction
Tallam is situated in an		
(a)	_____	_____
altitude of about 550 feet on a southern		
(b)	_____	_____
arm of a deep bay of the Western Ghats.		
(c)	_____	_____
Tallam boasts of delight forest scenery		
(d)	_____	_____

17. The following paragraph has not been edited. There is an error in each line. Write the error along with its correction in the space provided. Do **any four**.

[All India 2019; **Ap**]

	Error	Correction
e.g. Sachin Tendulkar is a best a the		
cricketer in India. He has play for		
(a)	_____	_____
more than 20 years on the country.		
(b)	_____	_____
He retired from the games		
(c)	_____	_____
last year. He is know for		
(d)	_____	_____
his skill in batting or fielding.		
(e)	_____	_____

18. The following paragraph has not been edited. There is an error in each line. Write the error as well as the correction as shown in the example. Do any four.

[All India 2018; **Ap**]

Error   Correction

In the prisoner's room a candle is

e.g.   is   was

burning dimly. A prisoner himself

(a) _______ _______

sat by the table. Only him back,

(b) _______ _______

the hair by his head, and his

(c) _______ _______

hands are visible from outside

(d) _______ _______

through any window.

(e) _______ _______

19. The following paragraph has not been edited. There is an error in each line. Write the error and its correction as shown in the example. [All India 2017; **Ap**]

Error   Correction

I met her by chance then I

e.g.   then   when

went to getting some medicine

(a) _______ _______

which Sister Amy use to give.

(b) _______ _______

It was amazing for meet M   other.

(c) _______ _______

I start loving just her presence.

(d) _______ _______

20. The following paragraph has not been edited. There is one error in each line. Write the error and its correction as shown in the example. [Delhi 2017; **Ap**]

Error   Correction

A saint walks the streets of Kolkata.

e.g.   walks   walked

It can happen only at India. It

(a) _______ _______

is time that us realised our

(b) _______ _______

strength. We are greater people. We

(c) _______ _______

have so much religious leaders.

(d) _______ _______

21. The following paragraph has not been edited. There is one error in each line against which a blank has been given. Write the error and the correction in your answer sheet against the correct blank number as given in the example. Remember to underline the word that you have supplied. [Delhi 2016; **Ap**]

Error   **Correction**

Research is an detailed study of a

e.g.   an   <u>a</u>

subject undertaking on a systematic

(a)   _______   ______

basis in order to increase a stock of

(b)   _______   ______

knowledge, including knowledge for man,

(c)   _______   ______

culture and society, that the use of this stock

(d)   _______   ______

of knowledge to devise new applications.

22. The following passage has not been edited. There is one error in each line against which a blank has been given. Write the incorrect word and the correction in your answer sheet against the correct blank number as given in the example. Remember to underline the word that you have supplied. **[All India 2015; Ap]**

Error   **Correction**

Summer camps develop a child confidence.

e.g.   child   <u>child's</u>

They also encourages children

(a)   _______   ________

to do things by their own.

(b)   _______   ________

The camps is beneficial to

(c)   _______   ________

aggressive children as we promote

(d)   _______   ________

mutual understanding.

23. The following passage has not been edited. There is an error in each line against which a blank has been given. Write the incorrect word and the correction in your answer-sheet against the correct blank number as given in the example. Remember to underline the word that you have supplied. **[Delhi 2015; Ap]**

Error   **Correction**

Most trees a single woody stem called

e.g.   has   <u>have</u>

a trunk who supports a mass of branches

(a)   _______   ________

carrying leaves. Trees clean an air

(b)   _______   ________

to removing tiny airborne particles. The

(c)   _______   ________

leaves of trees give in oxygen.

(d)   _______   ________

24. The following passage has not been edited. There is an error in each line against which a blank has been given. Write the incorrect word and the correction in your answer sheet against the correct blank number as given in the example. Remember to underline the word that you have supplied. **[2014; Ap]**

	Error	Correction

If your children is overweight,

e.g.   children   child

avoids fruit but vegetables,

(a)   ________   ________

and prefers computer games than real

(b)   ________   ________

ones, you should being concerned.

(c)   ________   ________

25. The following passage has not been edited. There is an error in each line against which a blank has been given. Write the incorrect word and the correction in your answer sheet against the correct blank number as given in the example. Remember to underline the word that you have supplied. **[Delhi 2014; Ap]**

Error   Correction

Boys who have never fight

e.g.   fight   fought

each other in the class is today

(a)   ______   ______

bitterly annoyed or fearful

(b)   ______   ______

Even during a Holi festival

(c)   ______   ______

the school has been peaceful.

26. The following passage has not been edited. There is an error in each line against which a blank is given. Write the incorrect word and the correction in your answer sheet against the correct blank number as given in the example. Remember to underline the word that you have supplied. **[All India 2013; Ap]**

Have you being criticized by

e.g.   being   been

teachers for shouted in the

(a)   ______   ______

class room? Here is something

to cheered you up. Now experts

(b)   ______   ______

have found as impulsive children.

(c)   ______   ______

that cannot resist shouting.

(d)   ______   ______

in the class score higher in

tests to those who appear to be.

(e)   ______   ______

better behave and quiet.

(f)   ______________

Sentence Transformation

Report the Following

1. Abhilash and Neha had a conversation about the inauguration of Neha's Dance Academy. Report Abhilash's question.

   Is your best friend helping you in this venture?

   [CBSE Sample 2023-24; **Ap**]

2. Read the dialogue between Shabnam and her mentor, Sara, regarding her summer internship programme.

   [CBSE Sample 2023-24; **Ap**]

   Sara: Why did you choose to participate in this internship programme?

   Shabnam: Ah! I am convinced this programme has the potential to enhance my abilities.

   Select the correct option to complete the reporting of the above dialogue.

   Sara asked Shabnam ______________ in that internship programme. Shabnam sighed and exclaimed that she was convinced that programme had the potential to enhance her abilities.

   (a) why to choose to participate

   (b) to choose participation

   (c) why he had chosen to participate

   (d) with her choice in participating

3. Vendor: It is nice to see you, Sir!

   Customer: Yes, indeed! Unlike last month, I have been away for quite some time this month.

   The vendor greeted his customer respectfully and mentioned that he was pleased to see him. The customer answered in the affirmative and explained that

   ____

   [CBSE Sample 2023-24; **Ap**]

4. Complete the sentence by reporting the reply correctly.

   [All India, 2023; **Ap**]

   The clerk at the ticket counter : Where do you want to go?

   Passenger: Please give me a ticket to Bhopal.

   The clerk at the ticket counter enquired where the passenger wanted to go. The passenger requested the clerk ______.

5. *Tony:* Why did you call me?

   Sarita : Will you go to the museum with me?

   Tony asked Sarita why she had called him. Sarita wanted to know whether Tony ________.

   [All India, 2023; **Ap**]

6 Roma asked Gopal to go by the metro. Report Gopal's question. Which way is the metro station?

   [All India, 2023; **Ap**]

7. The father said, "I bought a watch." (Change the speech)

[All India, 2023; Ap]

(a) The father said that I bought a watch.

(b) The father said that he bought a watch.

(c) The father said that he had bought a watch.

(d) The father said that he has bought a watch.

8. **Chief guest:** Who inspired you to learn classical dance.

Student : I was inspired by my grandfather who was a renowned dancer.

The Chief Guest asked the student who had inspired the student to learn classical dance. The student replied....................... [Delhi, 2023; Ap]

9. **Receptionist:** When would you like to check into the hotel.

Customer: I will send you an email and give the details.

In response to the question regarding when he would like to move in, the customer replied............

[Delhi, 2023; Ap]

10. Samiksha shared some information with Sameer regarding the annual blood donation camp. Report Sameer's question:

How did you feel when you were donating blood?

[Delhi, 2023; Ap]

11. Select the correct option to complete the narration of a dialogue between a passerby and a farmer.

Passerby: Can you tell me the way to Rampur.

Farmer: Drive for four kms and then turn right.

The passerby asked the farmer if he could tell him the way to Rampur. The farmer replied that...................

[Delhi, 2023; Ap]

(a) he may drive for four kms and then turn right.

(b) he should drive for four kms and then turn right.

(c) he might drive for four kms and then turn right.

(d) he had to drive for four kms and then turn right.

12. Doctor: Do you feel down from time-to-time Mr. Gopalan? Patient: Yes, I do not stay in a good mood.

The doctor, while trying to figure out his patient's ailment, asked about his well-being, to which, the patient affirmed ___________________.

[CBSE Sample 2022-23; Ap]

13. Sunil shared some information, with Tariq, about a holiday at sea. Report Tariq's question.

Did you enjoy travelling by sea?

[CBSE Sample 2022-23; Ap]

14. **Ritika :** Can I borrow your Math book for a couple of days?

Mohit : Yes certainly, I have already studied for the best tomorrow.

Ritika asked Mohit (1) _______ for a couple of days.

Mohit agreed and said that (2) _______.

[All India 2022, Ap]

15. **Biology Teacher:** I instructed you to draw the diagram of bacteria. Why did you submit a blank sheet?

Sameer: Sir, I had drawn the diagram of bacteria, but you can't see it because it is not visible to the naked eye.

The biology teacher had instructed Sameer to draw the diagram of a bacterial cell and asked him (a) ....a blank sheet. Sameer respectfully answered that he had drawn the diagram but (b) ....to the naked eye.

Topic-b: *Writing*

Letter Writing–Formal Letter

1. As Vaishali Nathani of 214, Indrayani Apartments, Vaishali Street, Daipur, you believe that forming Ecology clubs and appointing Eco-minders in your city can aid in the preservation and conservation of nature.

   Write a letter to the MLA of your city area, in about 120 words, suggesting the need to form such clubs. Share their importance and implications. Recommend the involvement of resident volunteers for implementation of eco-club activities that nurture and protect the local ecosystem.   **[CBSE Sample 2023-24; Ap]**

2. As Armaan Khan, the School Literary Captain of Ujjwal Academy, Old City, Kiladerabad, you believe that languages can help bridge regional divides and promote unity.   **[CBSE Sample 2023-24; Ap]**

   Write a letter to the Editor of a national daily, in about 120 words, suggesting the introduction of an online regional language learning programme managed and run by student councils and language clubs in the city. The programme aims to help residents who have recently relocated to a new region in picking up the local language organically. Share the importance and credibility of such a programme and suggest a feasible way to execute it along with possible activities.

3. You are Armaan/Anjali of C-63. Panvel. You recently read a magazine article which highlighted the condition of underage children working in hazardous conditions. Instead of going to school, they are working in dimly lit factories, tea stalls, in garages, etc. to supplement, family incomes. Write a letter to the editor of "The Times of India' is about 100 - 120 words, drawing attention to this national problem and suggesting solutions.

   [All India, 2023; Ap]

4. You are Rohit/Riya of Hauz Khas, New Delhi. You bought a pair of shoes from M/s. Shoe Factory, GK-II, New Delhi. On unpacking them, you found to your amazement that both the shoes are meant for your left foot. Write a letter of complaint to the Manager of M/s. Shoe Factory asking for replacement at their cost. (Word limit : 100 - 120 words)

5. Stakeholders associated with education of children are concerned about the poor reading habits of students today. There are multiple reasons for this disinterest in students. Academic pressure, technology and distraction, social media, parents don't read, children don't visit libraries, lack of leisure time are some of the reasons. As a concerned parent write a letter to the editor in about 100–120 words, expressing your concern. Suggest innovative ways in which children can be brought back to books. You are Sahil/Sushila. **[Delhi, 2023; Ap]**

6. You are Aruna/Arjun C.C.A. incharge of St. Joseph's High School. You have read an advertisement in a newspaper regarding admission into a foreign languages institute. **[Delhi, 2023; Ap]**

   Write a letter in about 100–120 words to the Director of the institute 'Lingua for All' making relevant inquires:

   (a) Eligibility

   (b) Duration of Course

   (c) Time Schedule

   (d) Fee Structure

   (e) Faculty

   (f) Placement

7. You are Sunidhi Prakash, the Vice Captain of Brilliant Vidyalaya, Barra, Kanpur. You have recently noticed several posters around your school premises conveying a hazardous message: **[CBSE Sample 2022-23; Ap]**

8. You are Zac Skaria, a resident of # 412, Magna Greens Apartments, Gandhi Marg, Jonpara, Mumbai. Three students of grade 10 from your residential complex have rescued and rehabilitated a few old beggars from the neighbourhood. You think that their work deserves appreciation and recognition. Write a letter to the President of the RWA, seeking recommendation for these youth, to be nominated for 'Serving Citizens' Award'. Suggest other ways such acts of kindness could be recognised and awarded in the future.

   [CBSE Sample 2022-23; Ap]

9. You are Niharika, Incharge of the Neighbourhood Library for children. Write a letter to Manautal Publishers placing an order for books 2 sets each of Panchatantra and Amar Chitra Katha in about 120 words. Mention mode of payment, library discount and date of delivery.

   [All India 2022, Ap]

10. You are Arun. Near the gate of your colony there is a motor mechanic's workshop. Many care are parked outside on the pavement and even beyond. Repair work goes on. The surroundings have become filthy; pedestrians are put to trouble. Arun decides to write a letter of complaint, of course, for wider audience / readership.

A. The letter will be addressed to :

[All India 2022, **Ap**]

(a) The Sanitary Inspector

(b) The Municipal Commissioner

(c) State Minister of Health

(d) Editor of a local newspaper

B. Subject of the letter should be

[All India 2022, **Ap**]

(a) Problems caused to pedestrians

(b) Inconvenience caused by the next door workshop

(c) Insanitary conditions at the colony gate

(d) A health hazard

C. Arun decides to write this letter as :

[All India 2022, **Ap**]

(a) he has a personal problem with the owner of the workshop

(b) a matter of social concern.

(c) he intends to contest the next municipal election.

(d) he is very health conscious.

D. He will arrange the contents of the letter in this way :

[All India 2022, **Ap**]

A. noisy surroundings

B. action requested

C. garbage littered

D. public inconvenience

E. the health hazard

F. location of the workshop

(a) B, A, C, E, D, F

(b) F , D, A, C, E, B

(c) A, C, E, B, D, F

(d) F , C, E, D, A, B

E. What kind of action would Arun suggest ?

[All India 2022, **Ap**]

(a) Fine to be imposed on the workshop

(b) Notice on lack of cleanliness to be issued

(c) Workshop to be shifted.

(d) Periodic visits of the Health Inspector

F. The correct closing of the letter should be :

[All India 2022, **Ap**]

(a) Your's faithfully

(b) Yours faithfully

(c) Yours truly

(d) Your's truly

11. You are Samina Zaveri, Class X, Vadodara, Gujarat. You come across the following information on a local library's notice board.

Create Your Own Board Game Competition! Create an educational board game, and send it to us at Teen-Toggle Games Pvt. Ltd, 307, Satija building, Colaba, Mumbai by July 2022. The top 10 winning board games will be featured on our international portal. Attractive scholarships for the winners!

You wish to participate but require more information. Write a letter to Teen-Toggle Games Pvt.Ltd in about 120 words, enquiring about rules, scholarship details and deadlines. Also enquire about specifications for solo or group entries.

12. You are Shammi/Sapna, resident of 12 Mall Road, Agra. You have noticed that majority of the water taps in your colony keep on leaking. Also water drips from various joints in the supply pipes. All these lead to a big wastage of potable water. Write a letter of complaint to the Municipal Commissioner, Agra Municipal Corporation requesting him to get the necessary repairs done.

[All India 2022; Ap]

13. You are Sonia/Sunil of M-3, Ashok Vihar, New Delhi. You placed an order with Messers Bright Publishers, Darya Ganj, Delhi for the supply of some books and stationery item. When you checked the received parcel, you found that it contained some damaged items. Write a letter to the publishers to replace the defective items at their cost **[100 – 150 words].**   **[All India 2020; Ap]**

14. You are Kapil/Komal, living at C-424, Sector-18, Green Park, New Delhi. You bought a washing machine from Balaji Electricals Private Limited, Lajpat Nagar, New Delhi. It started giving trouble within a few days. Write a complaint letter (100-150 words) to the Sales Manager seeking immediate repair or replacement. Invent the details of defects.   **[Delhi 2020; Ap]**

15. You are Tanvi/Shirish of Safdarjung Development Area, New Delhi. You are extremely disturbed about the attacks on old people living alone. Write a letter in 100-120 words to the Editor, 'The New Indian News' making people sensitive to the problem. Make suggestions to the people living alone and the authorities to ensure that such attacks do not take place.   **[All India 2019; Ap]**

16. As a health conscious person, you have noticed an advertisement in a newspaper on yoga classes in your neighbourhood. Write a letter in 120 words to the Organiser, Yoga for Public, R.K. Puram, New Delhi–100 requesting him/her to send you information about the duration of the course and other relevant details. You are Shweta/Srikar of 15, R.K. Puram, New Delhi .

[Delhi 2019; Ap]

17. You are Prabhu Kumar/Parvati of I7E, Ravi Dass Road, Kochi. Write a letter in 100-120 words to the editor of a newspaper about the nuisance caused by loudspeakers in the city during examination days drawing attention of the concerned authorities to the problem.

[All India 2018; Ap]

18. The road that leads to your market is broken and full of potholes. Mosquitoes and flies breed there. Write a letter in 100 – 120 words to the editor of a local newspaper drawing attention of the concerned authorities to get the road repaired. You are P.V. Prabhu/Prabha, 112, Aram Nagar, Delhi.   **[All India 2017; Ap]**

19. There is a busy road in front of your school. A large number of students have to cross the road while going back home. They run a great risk. Write a letter in 100-120 words to the Editor, Navjiwan Times, Agra drawing attention of the concerned authorities to the problem. Make a request to mark a zebra crossing and to put traffic lights in front of your school. You are Amit/Anita, Class X, New Age Public School, Ram Nagar, Agra.

[Delhi 2017; Ap]

20. Your locality has witnessed a number of cases of theft in recent weeks. The local law and order authorities were approached but you find no change in the situation. Write a letter in 100-120 words to the editor of a local newspaper drawing attention of the higher authorities to the problem. You are Ram/Rama 4, Gobind Road, Meerut.   **[All India 2016; Ap]**

21. Nowadays, we see the rise in prices of edible things like pulses, onions, oils and some other products. The layman is facing hardship on account of it. Write a letter in 120-150 words to the editor of a reputed daily requesting him to highlight the difficulties faced by common man due to rise in prices. Sign yourself as Pranjal/Praneeta living at 124, Vivek Vihar, Delhi.   **[Delhi 2016; Ap]**

22. Recently a serious quarrel took place in a colony in Delhi due to the use of loudspeakers at a public place and caused disharmony among the people. Write a letter in 100–120 words to the Editor of *The Hindustan Times* expressing your concern over the unpleasant incident, highlighting the fact that the loudspeakers cause noise pollution and discord, suggesting that the unauthorised use of loudspeakers at public places should be banned. You are Anjana/Arjun, F-112, Kailash Colony, Delhi.

[All India 2015; Ap]

23. The recent increase in crimes against people of the North-east, especially in the cities, has highlighted the growing problem faced by the community. Fear of violence continues to worry them. Write a letter in 100-120 words to the Editor of The Times of India expressing your concern over the recent death of a young student resulting from a racial comment against people from North-east. Suggest what steps the government should take to solve this problem. You are Aanchal/Aryan, resident of A-12, East of Kailash, N. Delhi.

Hints: racial comments, attacks – rude behaviour, hurt feelings of our own fellow citizens – disharmony – dents the image of our country – steps to solve this problem.

[Delhi 2015; Ap]

24. You are Rahul / Rohini, a resident of J-Block, Rajouri Garden, New Delhi. The water pipe that supplies drinking water to your area is damaged and there has not been any water supply for two days now. Write a letter, in about 120 words, to the editor of a local daily drawing the attention of the authorities towards the difficulties of the residents and asking for immediate repair of the pipe. Demand the supply of drinking water through tankers.

[All India 2014; Ap]

25. Floods in Uttarakhand in June 2012, wiped out hundreds of village; people have been left homeless; sources of liveliness gone, no roads. In this hour of their need, all the countrymen must come forward to help. An a responsible citizen, write a letter in about 120 words to the Editor, The Times, N. Delhi, expressing your concern about the miserable condition of those who have been uprooted. Make an appeal to the people to donate generously to the Uttarakhand Relief Fund.   **[Delhi 2014; Ap]**

26. Your hostel room-mate has recently gone to his home-town being urgently called by his parents. Write a letter in 120-150 words informing him about the postponement of periodical tests. Don't forget to mention that the course will remain the same. You are Atul, Room No 10, Kaveri Hostel, Delhi Senior Secondary School, Delhi.

[All India 2013; Ap]

Analytical Paragraph Writing

1. Tsering, of class X, is contesting for the post of the Junior School Captain, in the upcoming student council elections. Given below is her character traits' graphic, shared in the public domain, by the school counsellor, for the awareness of student voters, at school.

[CBSE Sample 2023-24; A]

All Tsering's peers have been asked to write a paragraph in about 120 words, analysing these traits, to either **support or oppose** her candidature. As one of her peers, write this analytical paragraph, by selecting some of the traits that support your analysis.

You may begin like this :

As a responsible student voter, I believe Tesring possesses / does not possess the necessary traits to be a School Captain.

You may end like this:

For these reasons, I believe she has / does not have the potential to be a good School Captain and I support / oppose her candidature.

2. As the Captain of the school's Cultural Club, you have been asked to study the given itinerary provided by a tour-organizing vendor.

[CBSE Sample 2023-24; A]

A 3N/2D Educational Tour for the Senior School Students: Jabalpur and Ranha National Park (Vandhya Pradesh)

- Tour Travel & sightseeing by bus.
- Accommodation on quad sharing basis.
- One staff complimentary for every 20 students.
- Bottled mineral water throughout the tour.
- Dance Party on 22 November.
- Insurance policy of ₹ 20,000/- per head.
- Provision of Tour Manager's assistance to all places.

Day	Estimated time of departure from	Estimated time of arrival	Sight-seeing Destination/ Activity	Time spent at the destination
22 Nov. 2023	8:49 am (Nagpur Junction)-8 hrs. 30 min	5:23 pm	Reporting at the hotel	
23 Nov. 2023	9:00am (hotel)	10:00am	Bhawartal Garden	1 hr.
	11:00am (garden)	11:40am	Bhedaghat Dhuandhar Falls	1hr.
	12:40pm (falls)	1:00pm	Lunch (nearby restaurant)	1 hr.
	2:00pm (restaurant)	2:15pm	Marble Rocks Cable car tour	1hr. 30 mins
	3:45pm (Marble Rocks)	4:45 pm	Rani Durgavati Museum	1 hr. 30 mins
	6:15pm (museum)	7:00pm	Back to the hotel	
24 Nov. 2023	5:30am (hotel)- 170 kms- 4 hrs. drive	9:30am	Ranha Tiger Reserve	7hrs.
	4:30pm (Tiger Reserve)	9:00pm	Back to the hotel	
25 Nov. 2023	7:54 am (Jabalpur Railway station)- 8 hrs. 45 min	4:21 pm	Nagpur Railway Junction	

Analyse this itinerary to either approve or reject the tour proposal, while focusing on the students' safety, interest, and physical wellness. Write this analytical paragraph in about 120 words, by selecting features that support your analysis.

You may begin like this :

A thorough analysis of the itinerary provided by the tour organizing vendor reveals that the tour proposal should be accepted / rejected.

You may end like this:

Therefore, the tour proposal for the educational trip should be approved / rejected.

3. Given below are the pollution figures for some major towns and cities in India: **[All India, 2023; A]**

	Suspended Particulate Matter	Sulphur Dioxide	Nitrogen Oxide
Permissible Limits	200	80	80
Ludhiana	453	20	64
Delhi	680	124	137
Mumbai	485	27	53
Chennai	262	45	34

Using the information given above along with your own ideas, write an analytical paragraph in 100-120 words.

4. The given pie chart represents the amount of money spent by a family on different items in a month. Write an analytical paragraph in 100 - 120 words using the information given in the pie chart.

[All India, 2023; A]

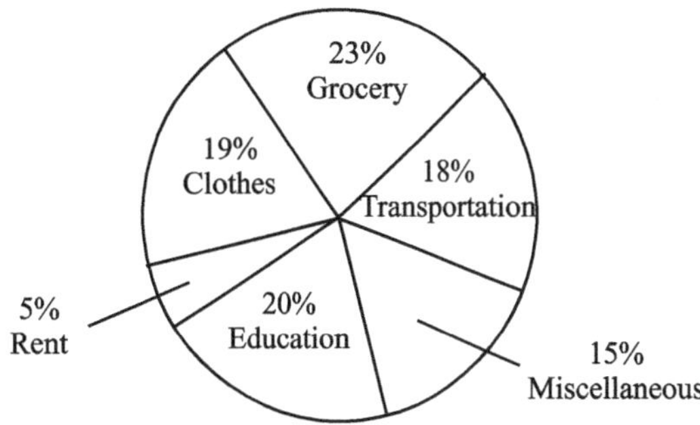

5. The given pie–chart shows how water is consumed in households in a metropolitan city in India. Study the information carefully and write a paragraph in about 100–120 words drawing a comparative analysis of water consumption. Emphasize on wasteful water consumption and suggest possible ways to save water.

[Delhi, 2023; A]

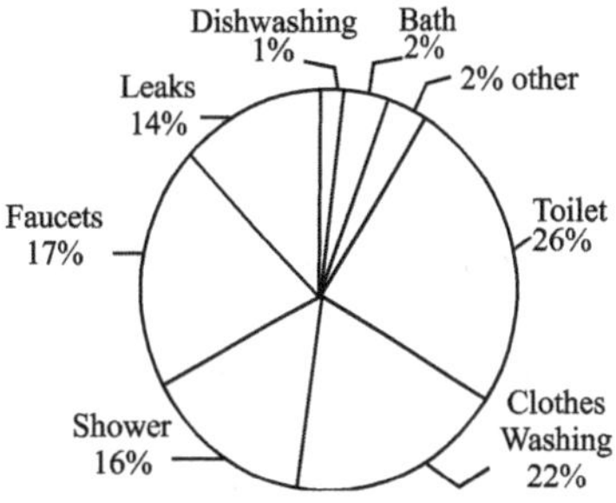

6. The chart below gives the percentage of social media users by age in India in 2020. Write a paragraph analysing the given information, drawing comparisons among different age groups in 100–120 words.   **[Delhi, 2023; A]**

Internet Activities by Age Group

Age Group							
Activity %	Teens	20s	30s	40s	50s	60s	70+
Get News	76	73	76	75	71	74	70
Online games	81	54	37	29	25	25	32
Downloads	52	46	27	15	13	8	6
Product research	0	79	80	83	79	74	70
Buying a product	43	68	69	68	67	65	41
Searching for people	5	31	23	23	24	29	27

7. Gurmeet Kaur is an aspiring candidate for a public-funded engineering college in the suburbs.

[CBSE Sample 2022-23; A]

She belongs to a nearby village, has minimal technological skills and exposure, has the required cut-off percentage and is looking for a complete or partial scholarship.

Write a paragraph in about 100-120 words, analysing her SWOT notes to support your stand on whether she should join/ not join the college.

STRENGTH	WEAKNESS
• Strong Curriculum • Quality faculty • Vibrant Activity Clubs • Green location • Close proximity to residential areas	• Lack of diversity • Students' behavioural problems • No hostel facility • Slow repair and maintenance work • Underutilization of IT Services • Lack of targeted advertisements to out-state students
OPPORTUNITIES	THREAT
• Practice based research • Partnership with professional organisations • Strong alumni • Acclaimed Student Exchange Programme with European countries	• Lack of publicity in areas of excellence • Public perception towards funded colleges • Declining students' interest towards technical subjects • Low employee morale due to budget cuts

8. Read the following excerpt from an online post of a website on educational practices.

[CBSE Sample 2022-23; **A**]

Kids who appreciate how much effort, time and care goes into growing food will understand how important farmers are, and why it's important to take care of our Earth. In the world of today, gardening needs to be given more importance than sports, music and dance in all schools because it creates environmental stewards and outdoor learning laboratories that help the child and community for years to come.

Write a paragraph in 100-120 words to analyse the given argument.

You could think about what alternative explanations might weaken the given conclusion and include rationale / evidence that would strengthen / counter the given argument.

9. A survey was conducted in the National Capital in over twenty schools about the different activities that interest the children in the age group of 13 years to 15 years. Write a paragraph in not more than 120 words, analyzing the following information.

[All India 2022, **A**]

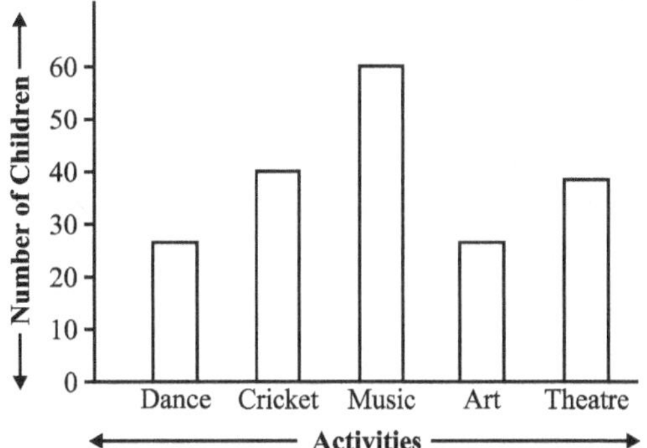

Solutions

Topic-a: *Grammar*

Gap Filling

1. highlights **(1 Mark)**

2. this **(1 Mark)**

3. **(a)** feeling **(1 Mark)**

4. **(d)** has won **(1 Mark)**

5. **(b)** call **(1 Mark)**

6. **(a)** would **(1 Mark)**

7. **(c)** will **(1 Mark)**

8. **(b)** going **(1 Mark)**

9. **(a)** will arrive **(1 Mark)**

10. **(a)** must **(1 Mark)**

11. **(a)** is **(1 Mark)**

12. **(a)** Look at **(1 Mark)**

13. **(a)** Should **(1 Mark)**

14. **(b)** turn to **(1 Mark)**

15. created **(1 Mark)**

16. **(b)** had **(1 Mark)**

17. **(b)** Blew up **(1 Mark)**

18. **(c)** will **(1 Mark)**

19. **(d)** washed **(1 Mark)**

20. seek **(1 Mark)**

21. **(d)** CAN **(1 Mark)**

22. **(a)** keep asking till one does **(1 Mark)**

23. **(a)** should **(1 Mark)**

   May, might and could are not suitable for sentences so option (a) should is correct.

24. **(b)** has been living **(1 Mark)**

   The sentence is following the rule of present perfect continuous so option (b) has been living is correct.

25. **(a)** If **(1 Mark)**

   First according to the sentence. If is suit with first part so option (A) if is correct.

26. **(d)** would **(1 Mark)**

   First part of sentence has 'if', then in the second part 'would' will come so option (d) would is correct.

27. **(b)** will have rung **(1 Mark)**

   The sentence is of future perfect tense. Option will have rung is correct.

> **Note**
>
> When we use this tense we are projecting ourselves forward into the future and looking back at an action that will be completed some time later than now.

28. **(a)** was   **(1 Mark)**

The sentence is of past tense so, the first option 'was' is correct.

29. **(a)** (ii) of   **(1×4=4 Marks)**

(b) (iv) before

(c) (i) are

(d) (i) at

30.

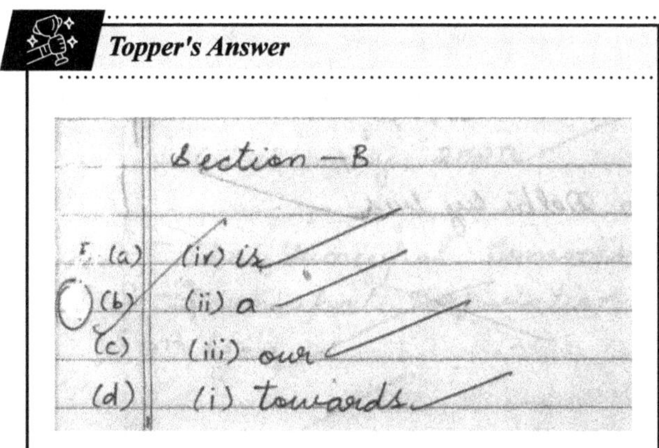

31. (a) – (ii)   **(1×4=4 Marks)**

(b) – (iv)

(c) – (iii)

(d) – (iii)

(e) – (ii)

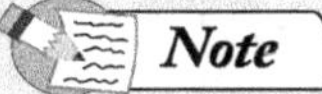 **Note**

a. To choose the correct words to fill in the blanks, you should first read the whole passage with blanks. This will give you an idea about the main theme or subject of the passage. This will help selecting the most suitable option.

32. **(a)** (ii) are   **(1×4=4 Marks)**

(b) (iii) goes

(c) (ii) becomes

(d) (ii) of

(e) (iv) in.

33. **(a)** (iv) Understands   **(1×4=4 Marks)**

(b) (i) of

(c) (iii) Where

(d) (i) be taken

(e) (iii) the

34. **(a)** (i)   enjoy   **(1×3=3 Marks)**

(b) (iii)   Are

(c) (ii)   Being

Note

(a) Such questions are designed to test your understanding of, and proficiency in, the rules of grammar. You should practice as much as possible to master the basic grammar topics and their usage to be able to answer such questions correctly.

(b) The above questions are based on subject-verb agreement. Unless you are proficient in this concept, you are likely to make mistakes in any sentence you form.

35. **(a)** (ii)   Who   **(1×3=3 Marks)**

(b) (i)   with

(c) (iii)   Sat

36. (a) (i) a   (1×3=3 Marks)

   (b) (iii) is

   (c) (i) and, (iv) Or

> **Note**
>
> *(a) This question is based on the prescribed grammar topics. You must possess a good understanding and practice of each of those to be able to choose the correct options.*
>
> *(b) The easiest method of solving this question is to read the given passage and keep filling in the blanks on the question paper itself in a flow. Next, check your answers among the options and select the correct ones for each.*

37. (a) (iii)   Surprised   (1×3=3 Marks)

   (b) (i)   of

   (c) (iv)   Who

38. (a) (ii) Of   (1×3=3 Marks)

   (b) (i) prefer

   (c) (ii) Which

39. (a) (ii)   many   (1×3=3 Marks)

   (b) (iii)   In

   (c) (i)   and

40. (a) (iii) was coming   (1×3=3 Marks)

   (b) (i) was robbed

   (c) (iii) was sitting

41. (a) (iii) why have the people gathered here?

                                    (1×3=3 Marks)

   (b) (iii) have come here to watch

   (c) (i) is being shot here?

42. (a) (iv) trying   (1×3=3 Marks)

   (b) (i) succeeded

   (c) (iii) encourages

43. (a) (i) arrived   (1×3=3 Marks)

   (b) (i) has any difficulty

   (c) (i) ran away with my bag

> **Note**
>
> *a. For dialogue completion, you can take your cues from the words and sentences provided. For example, in Q.7, 'have been' is already provided, so, verb+ing is the only form suited here.*
>
> *In Q.8, 'did you arrive' in Shivani's query is simple past tense in active voice. So, Shiv's reply will take its verb in the same tense and voice, i.e., 'arrived'. Options (ii) and (iv) are perfect tenses while option (iii) is simple past in passive voice; hence they get eliminated.*
>
> *b. You must be proficient in the concepts of 'Tense' and Voice' to complete the given dialogue correctly.*

44. (a) (ii) if   (1×3=3 Marks)

   (b) (iv) your

   (c) (i) a

45. **(a)** (iii) What is your lucky charm?   (1×3=3 Marks)

  (b) (i)   Since when have you been wearing it?

  (c) (iv) Are you not superstitious?

Error Correction

1. error-must; correction-will   **(1 Mark)**

2. error-aimed; correction-aims   **(1 Mark)**

3. c- among-between   **(1 Mark)**

4. error-will; correction- should   **(1 Mark)**

5. **(c)** at- in   **(1 Mark)**

6. should-can   **(1 Mark)**

7. **(a)** sound   sounds   **(1 Mark)**

8. Exciting   Excited   **(1 Mark)**

9. Was   is   **(1 Mark)**

10. the/a   **(1 Mark)**

11. error- balancing; correction- balance   **(1 Mark)**

12. error- all; correction- each   **(1 Mark)**

13.

Incorrect	Correct
1. A	The
2. At	in
3. Start	Started
4. of	to

(3 Marks)

14. **Error**   **Correction**   (1×4=4 Marks)

Topper's Answer

6.	Error	Correction
(a)	for	with
(b)	long-last	long-lasting
(c)	a	the
(d)	with	having

15. **Error**   **Correction**   (1×4=4 Marks)

  (a) decide   decided

  (b) taking   take

  (c) which   who

  (d) in   from

16.   **Error**   **Correction**   (1×4=4 Marks)

  (a) in   at

  (b) a   the

  (c) of   in

  (d) delight   delightful

17.   **Error**   **Correction**   (1×4=4 Marks)

  (a) play   played

  (b) on   for

  (c) games   game

  (d) know   known

  (e) or   and

18.   **Error**   **correction**   (1×4=4 Marks)

  (a) A   the

  (b) Him   his

  (c) By   on

  (d) Are   were

  (e) Any   the

> **Note**
>
> *(a) The question on error-correction is designed to test your knowledge and practice of the rules of grammar.*
>
> *(b) Part (a) test you on Article, (b) on Pronoun, (c) on Preposition, (d) on Verb and (e) on Determiners as well as Article.*
>
> *(c) Students cheat themselves by believing that they know the English language well while they commit blunders in such simple looking exercises as above in their ignorance of the rules of grammar and usage. So, you must gain proficiency in grammar to score in such simple questions as the above.*

19.   **Error   Correction**   (1×4=4 Marks)

  (a) Getting   get

  (b) Use   used

  (c) For   to

  (d) Start   started

20.   **Error   correction**   (1×4=4 Marks)

  (a) At   in

  (b) Us   we

  (c) Greater   great

  (d) Much   many

21. Error   Correction   (1×4=4 Marks)

  (a) Undertaking undertaken

  (b) A   the

  (c) For   of

  (d) That   and

22.   **Error   Correction**   (1×4=4 Marks)

  (a) encourages   encourage

  (b) By   on

  (c) Is   are

  (d) We   they

23.   **Error   Correction**   (1×4=4 Marks)

  (a) Who   which

  (b) An   the

  (c) To   by

  (d) In   us

24.   **Error Correction**   (1×3=3 Marks)

  (a) but   and

  (b) than   to

  (c) being be

25.   **Error   Correction**   (1×3=3 Marks)

  (a) is   are

  (b) bitterly   bitter

  (c) a   the

26.   **Error   Correction**   (1×6=6 Marks)

  (a) Shouted   shouting

  (b) Cheered   cheer

  (c) As   that

  (d) That   who

  (e) To   than

  (f) Behave   behaved

Sentence Transformation
---

1. Abhilash asked Neha whether/ if her best friend was helping her in that venture. **(1 Mark)**

2. **(c)** why he had chosen to participate **(1 Mark)**

3. unlike the previous month, he had been away for quite some time that month. **(1 Mark)**

4. To give him a ticket to Bhopal. **(1 Mark)**

5. Would go to the museum with her. **(1 Mark)**

6. Gopal asked Roma which way into the metro station. **(1 Mark)**

7. **(d)** The father said that he had bought a watch. **(1 Mark)**

8. That he had been inspired by his grandfather who had been a renowned dancer. **(1 Mark)**

9. he would send her an email and give the details **(1 Mark)**

10. How she had felt when she had been donating blood? **(1 Mark)**

11. **(b)** he should drive for four kms and then turn right **(1 Mark)**

12. that he does not stay in a good mood **(1 Mark)**

13. Tariq asked Sunil if/ whether he had enjoyed traveling by sea. **(1 Mark)**

14. Ritika asked Mohit if she borrowed his math book for a couple of days. **(1 Mark)**

    Mohit agreed and said that he had already studied for the test the next day. **(1 Mark)**

15. The biology teacher instructed Sameer to draw the diagram of bacteria and asked him **why he had submitted** a blank sheet. Sameer respectfully answered that he had drawn the diagram, but **the teacher couldn't see it because it was not visible** to the naked eye. **(1 Mark)**

Topic-b:

Writing

Letter Writing–Formal Letter
---

1. 124, Indrayani Apartments **(5 Marks)**

   Vaishali Street, Daipur

   21 August 2023

   The MLA

   Janta House

Rajajipura, Daipur

Subject: Suggestion Regarding the Need to Form Ecology Clubs

Madam

This letter is written to express my concern about the environmental degradation in our city and suggest a solution that I believe could help in preserving and conserving nature. I believe that forming Ecology clubs and appointing Eco-minders in our city can aid in this endeavour.

Ecology clubs can be run by resident volunteers who may undertake activities such as making bird-houses, planting native trees, water harvesting and creating compost piles to nurture and protect the local ecosystem. By involving the residents in these activities, we can raise awareness about the importance of preserving nature and instil a sense of responsibility towards it.

Some of the implications of forming Ecology clubs are reduction of pollution levels, increase in biodiversity and promotion of sustainable practices. This initiative will enhance the quality of life of the residents by providing them with a green and healthy environment.

Madam, you are requested to kindly consider this suggestion to ensure better preservation and conservation of nature.

Yours sincerely

Vaishali Nathani

2.   Ujjwal Academy   **(5 Marks)**

Old City, Kilandarabad

30 August 2023

The Editor

India Samachar

Jamnagar, Kilandarabad

Subject: Introduction of Online Regional Language Learning Programmes

Dear Sir

As someone who believes that languages can help bridge regional divides and promote unity, I am writing to suggest the introduction of an online regional language learning programme in our city to help the recently relocated residents (of all ages) establish a healthy rapport with the local residents and promote mutual understanding.

This online programme, organised and run by student councils and language clubs, can help these residents pick up the local language organically. This initiative may be conducted only on weekends for three months, making it feasible for participants to attend without hindering their work or studies. Activities such as language exchange programmes, cultural events, and group discussions on the virtual platform can be undertaken to make this programme more engaging.

I hope that publishing of this letter in the columns of your Daily shall urge the community to support this programme for its potential, to bring people together, promote language proficiency, and foster a sense of brotherhood.

Yours truly

Armaan Khan

(Captain, Literary Club)

3. Armaan/Anjali (**5 Marks**)

C- 63, Panvel

Delhi

Dated 20th march, 2023

The Editor

The Times of India

Subject- Critical issue of children

Dear Editor,

I am writing to bring your attention to a critical issue that is affecting the lives of countless children across our nation. The recent magazine article that I read highlighted the plight of underage children who are forced to work in hazardous conditions, instead of going to school. These children are toiling away in dimly lit factories, street stalls, garages, and other places to supplement their family incomes. This situation is not only illegal but also immoral and needs urgent attention.

It is a national problem that needs immediate attention from the government, civil society, and media. The government should enforce laws and regulations to ensure that every child gets access to education and a safe childhood. They should also provide financial assistance to families who are living in poverty to help them sustain themselves without sacrificing the education and future of their children.

Civil society can play a vital role in addressing this issue. By raising awareness, providing resources and support, and partnering with the government, they can work towards eradicating child labor from our society. The media can also play a crucial role in highlighting the plight of these children and creating a public discourse around the issue.

In conclusion, we must take collective responsibility to end child labour and provide every child with a safe, healthy, and happy childhood. We cannot afford to ignore this issue any longer.

Sincerely,

Armaan/Anjali,

C-63, Panvel

4. Hauz Khas, (**5 Marks**)

New Delhi

Dated- 20th march, 2023

Manager Department

M/s Shoe Factory

New Delhi

Subject- Complaint letter for replacement of shoes

Dear Sir/Madam,

I am writing to bring to your notice a problem I encountered with the pair of shoes that I recently purchased from your store. I am a resident of Hauz Khas, New Delhi, and I bought the shoes from your store located in GK-II, New Delhi.

To my surprise, upon unpacking the shoes, I discovered that both of them are meant for my left foot. This has caused me great inconvenience as the shoes are unwearable and I am unable to use them.

As a valued customer, I expect that the products I purchase from your store are of high quality and are free from any defects. However, this was not the case with the shoes that I received. I am therefore requesting a replacement pair of shoes at your cost as I am not willing to incur any further expenses due to the mistake that was made by your store.

I am hopeful that you will take immediate action to resolve this issue and provide me with a replacement pair of shoes. I look forward to your response and expect that this matter will be resolved as soon as possible.

Thank you for your attention to this matter.

Sincerely,

Rohit/Riya

5. The Editor   **(5 Marks)**

The Hindustan times

Bahadur shah zafar marg

Delhi

Dear sir

As a concerned parent . I am deeply worried about the declining interest of children in reading books. There are multiple factors responsible for this, including academic pressure, technological distractions, and the influence of social media. With the lack of leisure time, children are spending more time on their screens, which has led to a decline in their reading habits.

I would like to suggest some ways to bring children back to books. Firstly, parents should inculcate a reading habit at a young age by reading to their children and creating a comfortable reading space at home. Secondly, schools should encourage children to read by introducing book club and organizing literary events. Thirdly, libraries can be made more accessible by providing digital lending facilities and hosting interactive reading sessions.

By implementing these solutions, we can help children develop a love for reading, which will enhance their horizons . I would be highly obliged if you will publish my letter in your esteemed newspaper.

Yours sincerely

Sahil/ Susheela

6. A/32   **(5 Marks)**

Saint Joseph high school

Jaipur

27 Feb'23

Director

lingua for all

XYZ City

Dear Director

Sub: Inquiry for admission process

As the CCA in charge of Saint Joseph High School, I have come across your advertisement in the newspaper, and I believe that your institute can provide quality language education to our students. I am writing this letter to inquire about the admission process, course details and other relevant information regarding the foreign language courses offered at Lingua for All.

I would like to know about the eligibility criteria for admission, the duration of the course, the time schedule, and the fee structure. Moreover, it would be helpful to know about the faculty members who will be teaching the course and their qualifications and experience. Finally, I would like to inquire about the placement opportunities available for the students who complete the course successfully. It would be great if you could provide us with some information about the companies that have hired your students in the past and the average salary package.

Thank you for taking the time to read this letter. I look forward to hearing from you soon.

Yours sincerely

Aruna/Arjun.

7. Brilliant Vidyalaya, Barra **(5 Marks)**

Kanpur

29 August 2022

The Editor

The DWA

K-21, Anjana Pura

Kanpur

Subject: Need for Promoting Healthy Eating Routines

Dear Madam

This is with reference to posters bearing the message of 'crash diet' being posted around our school premises. Such posters impact youngsters negatively and can be hazardous to their self-esteem. I would like to propose the idea of implementing "Wholesome Lunch Month' for all school students to counter the implications of such misleading advertisements. This initiative is sure to encourage all students to bring nutritious and healthy lunch daily and develop healthy eating routines. To ensure that this project gains strength, schools may organize puppet shows, street plays, and Ted Talks (by Nutritionist/ Psychologist), encompassing the theme of fostering healthy eating routines and a positive body image.

I hope that the publishing of my letter in the columns of your renowned Daily helps spread awareness and promotes a healthy lifestyle among students.

Yours truly

Sunidhi Prakash

Vice-Captain

8.   421, Magna Greens Apartments   **(5 Marks)**

Gandhi Marg, Jonpara

Mumbai

19 July 2022

The President

RWA, Magna Greens Apartments

42, Gandhi Marg, Jonpara

Mumbai

Subject: Seeking Recommendation for 'Serving Citizens' Award' Nominations.

Dear Sir

This is with reference to the empathetic social service done by Miss Jiya, Mas Adwait, and Master Pranit (residents of our complex) in rescuing and rehabilitating a few old beggars from our neighborhood. These students ensured that the beggars were rehabilitated at 'Seva Sadan'- an NGO which takes care of the needy of our city.

This selfless initiative, carried out with dedication and responsibility, deserves due recognition. I, therefore, request you to issue a letter of recommendation for these students to be nominated for the 'Serving Citizens' Award' organized by the local Municipal Corporation.

I would also like to submit that the RWA set up a special committee that looks into such acts in the future. This would aid dedicated attention and appropriate screening of nominations. Arrangement of academic sponsorships for such children would also be an encouraging gesture.

I entreat you to address this at your earliest convenience and issue the recommendation letters.

Yours sincerely

Zac Skaria

9.   Dariyaganj

Delhi

Date.................

Manautal Publishers,

Nehru Place

New Delhi

Sub : To place an order for children books

Sir,

I am Niharika, Incharge of the Neighbourhood library for children.

I want to place an order for the library. Required books are 2 sets each of Panchtantra and Amar Chitra Katha. I would like the book to be delivered by 25th June 2022.

The half payment will be made once the order has been confirmed by the online payment I expect a resonable library discount would be adjusted in the invoice.

Waiting for your response.

Thanking you

Niharika (Incharge)

Children library   **(5 Marks)**

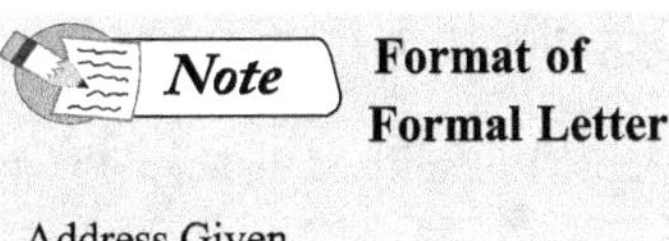

Format of Formal Letter

Address Given

Date

Name of the Company

Address

Sub.

Body of the letter

Yours faithfully/thanking you

Name

Designation

10. A. (d) Editor of a local news paper

The Arun decides to write, the letter for wider audience and readership so it will be addressed to editor of local Newspaper. **(1 Mark)**

B. (c) Insanitary conditions at the colony gate.

According to the letter near the gate there is motor mechanic's shop and many cars are parked outside on the pavement so the subject should be insanitary conditions at the colony gate. **(1 Mark)**

C. (b) a matter of social concern

This problem is not only Arun's problem, it is the problem of the whole colony. So the matter is of social concern. **(1 Mark)**

D. (b) F, D, A, C, E, B

First he will arrange (F) the location of the workshop, then public inconvenience from it after it surrounding become noisy and garbage littered here and there and so many health problems related pollution so at last the action requested so the option (b) F, D, A, C, E, B is correct. **(1 Mark)**

E. (c) Workshop to be shifted

Arun, suggests that workshop to be shifted to another place so option (c) is correct.

(1 Mark)

F. (c) Your truly

Closing of the letter should be from yours truly it should without apostrophe sign. **(1 Mark)**

11. Samina Zaveri

Vadodara, Gujarat

1st July 2023

Teen Toggle Games Pvt. Ltd.

307, Satija Building,

Colaba, Mumbai

Subject- Enquiry regarding scholarship details and deadlines

Dear Ma'am/Sir,

I am Samina Zaveri, a class X student from Vadodara, Gujarat. I had come across the information about creating one's own board game on my local library's notice board. I wish to know more about the same. The poster mentioned that contestants had to make an educational poster that, if selected, would be eligible for scholarships. I wanted to know about the rules and regulations to enter this contest and the deadline to participate. Furthermore, I'd like to know whether we need to participate individually or in a group.

Kindly assist me with the above details. I hope to hear from you soon so I may prepare for it at the earliest.

Regards,

Samina Zaveri

12.

colony. There is also leakage of water from various joints in the supply pipes.

All this leads to a huge waste of potable water notwithstanding the fact that there is an acute water shortage in various parts of India. Therefore it is saddening to see the lack of concern among people for the conservation of water. The constant dripping of water leads to a waste of water which can otherwise be used for domestic purposes like cooking, washing and bathing. We sometimes have a low supply of water in our houses owing to this problem. Even the animals in our locality sometimes face a shortage of water.

I hope that you will take appropriate measures to rectify this problem and get the necessary repairs done to avoid wastage of potable water

at the earliest.

Yours faithfully

Sapna

13. M-3, Ashok Vihar

New Delhi

Messers Bright Publishers **(8 Marks)**

Daryaganj,

New Delhi

15th Feb. 2020

Subject: Consignment received against my order is spoiled.

Sir,

This is to bring to your kind notice that the consignment received against my order no 153216 did 10th Jan. 2020 is of no use because almost every important page is either faulty or spoiled. The book 'The wheel of Fire' misses pages from 113 to 159. The pen and register supplied are faulty and do not serve the purpose.

I therefore, request you to replace the defective items at your cost and save me from the encumbrances that I am going through.

Thanking you

Yours faithfully

Sonia/Sunil

14.   **(8 Marks)**

C-424, Sector - 18,

Green Park

New Delhi

28th Feb. 2020

Messrs Balaji Electrical Private Ltd. Lajpat Nager, New Delhi

<u>Subject:</u> To seek redressal or replacement of the faulty washing machine.

Sir,

With reference to receipt no. 4107 dated 17th Jan. 2020. I am to bring to your notice that the IFB washing machine that I bought from your store last month does not run smoothly: causes jerks and unpleasant shrill sound. It sometimes stops in the middle without completing its task. Since this is still in warranty period, you either repair it to our satisfaction or replace altogether with a new one.

Anticipating an early response

Yours truly,

Kapil/Komal

15.   15, Block D   **(8 Marks)**

Safdarjung Development Area

New Delhi

16th September, 2019

The Editor

The New Indian News

Delhi-110025

Subject: Attacks on old people living alone

Sir/Ma'am

Through the columns of your renowned newspaper, I would like to put forward my views to draw the attention of concerned authorities to the danger that senior citizens living alone in the city are facing.

Most of the senior citizens in the city live alone with their domestic helps, some of which take advantage of their helplessness. The old and infirm are often burgled, poisoned or beaten to death. It is indeed a sad plight for our senior citizens and a shame for the society.

It is my humble request to the authorities concerned to make it mandatory to get the verification of the domestic helps done before they are hired by our senior citizens and also to set up a neighbourhood watch where everyone can contribute to ensure the safety of the elderly.

I hope my plea will reach the ears of the authorities concerned through your newspaper and an immediate action would be taken.

Yours truly,

Tanvi

(A concerned citizen)

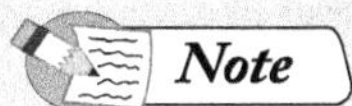

Note

(a) *There are different types of letters and there is a specific format to be followed for each. You will therefore be marked on the format you present your letter in.*

(b) *It is important for you to remember the marking scheme for this question so that you consciously pay attention to each aspect of your letter.*

(c) *The format you should follow for formal letters, including a letter to the Editor of a newspaper as in the question above, is as follows:*

16. 15, R.K. Puram

New Delhi

1st July, 2023

The Organiser

Yoga for Public,

R. K. Puram,

New Delhi,

Sub: To seek information about yoga classes.

Sir,

It has been learnt through the advertisement in the Hindustan Times that you have started to run yoga classes for public in R. K. Puram, New Delhi. Since I am a resident of this place and am very much interested to learn it, I seek relevant informations about it like the duration of the course, fees, timing, venue etc.

I request you to be kind enough to send me these informations on the address given below.

Thanks and regards.

Yours faithfully,

Shweta/Srikar,

15, R.K. Puram,

New Delhi.

17. 17E,   **(8 Marks)**

Ravi Das Road

Kochi

Date

The Editor

The Times of India

Kochi

Sub: Nuisance caused by loudspeakers

Dear Sir/Ma'am

I want to draw your kind attention towards the nuisance caused by the loudspeakers in our locality. The noise pollution has been affecting every single resident. I request to publish our anxieties in your newspaper so as to us help in resolving this issue.

The students are preparing for their final examinations' day and night. But unfortunately, the loud speakers being used for the election campaign is creating a very difficult situation for our children. The students are facing anxiety and stress issues, which is indeed not good for their health.

On behalf of all the students of our society, I request you to publish our concern in your esteemed newspaper, and seek a redressal.

Thanking you,

Yours sincerely,

Parvati Nair

18. 112, Aram Nagar **(5 Marks)**

Delhi

08 Sept., 20XX

The Editor,

The Times of India

Delhi

Subject: Pathetic condition of public roads.

Dear Sir,

I am writing today to draw attention to the necessity in repairing the broken roads in my locality.

The residents who commute regularly to the market for daily needs, face many problems while traveling on foot or in a vehicle on the road leading to the market because it is broken and full of potholes. The holes also fill up with water on rainy days and have become breeding grounds for mosquitos and flies. This is affecting public health. There is no maintenance by the concerned authorities as they choose to neglect the struggles of the residents and take no initiative to repair the road.

I request you to publish an article in your newspaper so that the concerned authorities get informed and act.

Thanking you

Yours sincerely

P.V. Prabha

19. New Age Public School **(5 Marks)**

Ram Nagar

Agra

20 July,20XX

The Editor,

Navjiwan Times

Agra

Subject: Students at risk

Sir,

This is to draw the attention of the concerned authorities to the problem of heavy traffic in front of NewAge Public school. Indiscipline of the drivers, traffic snags, and the apathy of the traffic police is putting the life of the students at risk.

A large number of students have to cross the road in front of the school every day amidst heavy traffic. Small children, even though accompanied by an elder, barely escape from what could be a horrifying accident. There are no traffic lights or zebra crossing on the road and this is making the problem worse.

I hope your esteemed daily will reach our concern to the concerned authorities and spur them on to restore safety for the students of my school as well as the people around the area at large.

Yours sincerely

Amit Sen

20. Gobind Road (5 Marks)

Meerut

xx/xx/20xx

The Editor

The Times of India

Meerut

Subject: Repeated theft in Gobind Road.

Sir/Madam,

Through the columns of your esteemed newspaper I'd like to express my concerns on the recent cases of theft in Gobind Road. In the past few weeks we have witnessed more than one hundred theft cases here. There is a group of unidentified people who are carrying this process unhindered.

The local authorities have been informed but in vain. Yesterday, the situation was bad as a lady whose chain was snatched, suffered serious injuries and is admitted in the hospital. Her condition continues to remain critical.

I request your help, as there is an urgent need for the higher authorities to look into the matter and secure our lives.

Regards

Yours faithfully

Ram Madhav

21. 124, Vivek Vihar (5 Marks)

Delhi

xx/xx/20xx

The Editor,

Times of India

Delhi

Subject: Indiscriminate rise in prices of essential products

Sir,

I write this letter to your esteemed daily, with a hope that you will be able to initiate a process, towards the redressal of the woes of the common man of our country. I have approached all concerned, to solve the problem of rising prices of essential commodities. But all my efforts have been in vain.

The prices of what one calls 'staple diet', has been increasing by leaps and bounds. Pulses, onions, oil, vegetables, rice, wheat, milk and dairy products are beyond the reach of the common man. What will the common man feed his family? Can he afford to keep them hungry till his pockets jingle with the adequate number of coins?

The situation is becoming alarming. Kindly help bring a solution to this very dangerous situation. It is only the media that can now open the eyes of those who are in authority.

Thanking you

Yours faithfully

Pranjal Shah

22. F-112   **(5 Marks)**

Kailash Colony

Delhi

Xx/xx/xxxx

The Editor,

The Times of India

Delhi

Sub: Unauthorized use of loudspeakers at public places

Sir,

I, a resident of F-112, Kailash Colony, wish to hereby, appeal through the columns of your esteemed newspaper, the need to cease the unauthorized use of loudspeakers in the public spaces. People fail to understand the havoc this noise pollution causes on the lives of people. I want you to spread awareness, against this menace. Enjoyment can be experienced without such awfully loud sounds that make one disbalanced and fatigued. Thus, I believe playing of music above the permissible decibels should be banned, at least in the public domain.

Kindly look into this issue and publish this in your national daily, so as to reach the concerns of a vast majority of people, to the concerned authorities. .

Thanking you

Yours sincerely,

Anjana Mitra

23. A-12   **(5 Marks)**

East of Kailash

New Delhi

Xx/xx/xxxx

The Editor,

The Times of India

New Delhi

Sub: Racial Discrimination

Sir,

It is with immense grief that I write this letter to you.

I am completely taken aback by what the indiscriminate racial comments, attacks and rude behaviour being extended by the Delhiites, towards our brethren from the North-east. This is creating so much of disharmony, thereby, presenting a very dismal picture of our country to the world.

It is a very distressing situation. I therefore request you, to take the initiative to dispel the fear and agony that is prevailing. People must be made aware, that every Indian is free in the country, covered by the tenets of the constitution, no matter which part of the country he or she is a native of.

I look forward to your efforts in this regard.

Yours faithfully

Anchal D'Souza

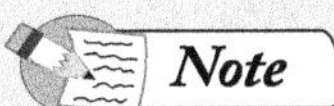

Note

a. *Different types of letters follow their own standard formats and you will be marked for format as well as content of your letter. So, read the question carefully and write in the correct format required.*

b. *Avoid the common mistake of signing your own name in the end. Remember to sign as the person named in the question. Always divide the body of your letter in at least three paragraphs including the introductory and the closing ones.*

24. J Block

Rajouri Garden

New Delhi

28th March 2014

The Editor

Times of India

New Delhi

Subj: Need for drinking water

Sir

I am an aggrieved resident of Rajouri Garden. The residents in this area are facing an acute shortage of drinking water. The pipe supplying drinking water to our area has been damaged. We have not been getting any supply for the past more than 48 hours.

I am appealing to you and your esteemed newspaper to help us get a redressal, as all the pleas to the concerned authorities in the PWD department have fallen on deaf ears. Infants, school going children, office goers, house-wives, and the aged are all suffering due to the apathy of people who matter. We request to be supplied with water through tankers till the problem is resolved.

I hope you would address our problem and reach our woes to the department.

Thanking your

Yours faithfully

Rahul

25. ABC Apartments

M G Road

Uttarakhand

28th June 2012

The Editor

The Times of India

New Delhi

Sub: Uttarakhand relief fund

Dear Sir,

The floods that have lashed the state of Uttarakhand has resulted in the loss of thousands of lives and rendered several survivors homeless and jobless. The crops, businesses, roads and all means of communication has been destroyed, leaving the state in a state of utter despair.

Through the columns of your esteemed newspaper, I wish to appeal to all my beloved countrymen to help Uttarakhand in her hour of need. As a responsible citizen of India, I request each and every one to donate according to their might to the Chief Minister's relief fund and help our brethren.

I sincerely hope you would adhere to my humble request and do the needful to help restore the state.

Thanking you

Yours faithfully

Adarsh Singh.

26. Room No. 10

Kavery Hostel

Delhi Senior Secondary School

Delhi

26th March, 2013

Dear Vikram

Hope you have reached your home town safely. I know that you were called urgently because of the failing health of your grandfather. Hope he is better now. Convey my best wishes to everyone at home.

I write this letter to inform you, that our periodic tests have been postponed by a week. However, there is no change in the portions. I am aware that you were extremely worried about missing out on the exams. God has been kind. Therefore, you need not come back immediately. Take time to be with your grandpa. He would really like that you are there with him. If you need any support from me do let me know. Read through your books if you get some time. I will keep in touch.

Warm regards and godspeed to your grandpa.

Yours affectionately

Atul Sharma.

Analytical Paragraph Writing

1. Supporting Tsering's candidature: **(5 Marks)**

As a responsible student voter, I believe Tsering possesses the necessary traits to be an excellent School Captain. Her disciplined study routine and hard work ethic indicates her ability to prioritize and manage her time effectively. Tsering is less impulsive but sensitive and focuses on the excellent outcome of tasks assigned to her demonstrating good decision-making skills. Additionally, her willingness to help peers in academic and personal difficulties highlights her empathetic and caring nature. Furthermore, Tsering believes in the "One for all and all for one" policy, which is pivotal in fostering a sense of community and promoting inclusivity in the school. While she may be an average academic performer, her positive attitude and desire for appreciation will motivate her in her pursuit of excellence. For these reasons, I believe she has the potential to be a good School Captain and I support her candidature.

Opposing Tsering's candidature:

As a responsible student voter, I have reservations about Tsering's candidature for the School Captain's position. While she maintains a disciplined study routine, her average academic performance suggests a lack of academic discipline. Additionally, her quest for appreciation may cause her to prioritize recognition over the well-being of the school community. Moreover, Tsering's sensitivity, while admirable, may hinder her ability to make tough decisions and exercise effective leadership skills. While her willingness to help peers is commendable, it may also distract her from her responsibilities as the School Captain. Finally, Tsering's focus on the excellent outcome of tasks assigned to her may cause her to overlook the process and teamwork required to achieve those outcomes which are crucial for the school's smooth functioning. For these reasons, I believe she does not have the potential to be a good School Captain and I oppose her candidature.

2. Accepting the proposal: (5 Marks)

A thorough analysis of the itinerary provided by the tour organizing vendor reveals that the tour proposal should be accepted. It is well-planned and includes an array of educational activities for the students. The inclusion of visit to Bhawartal Garden, Bhedaghat Dhuandhar Falls, Marble Rocks Cable car tour, and Rani Durgavati Museum offers an opportunity for the students to learn about nature, history, and art. The tour to Kanha Tiger Reserve adds an element of adventure and allows students to connect with wildlife. The provision of bottled mineral water, insurance policy, and tour manager's assistance ensures the safety and well-being of the students. Inclusion of a DJ party adds to the entertainment, enjoyment and enthusiasm quotient of the tour. The complimentary staff provided for every twenty students further adds to the security of the students. Therefore, the tour proposal for the educational trip should be approved.

Rejecting analytical paragraph:

A thorough analysis of the itinerary provided by the tour organizing vendor reveals that the tour proposal should be rejected. While the tour includes 7 of 14 various educational activities, we have concerns about the safety and wellbeing of the students. The tour includes a long journey of nearly nine hours from Nagpur Junction to Jabalpur and vice versa. Also, it mentions an early morning departure at 5:30 am to the Kanha Tiger reserve and late evening arrival back to the hotel, on the last day. Long hours of travel and the hectic schedule may lead to physical exhaustion and hamper the learning experience of the students. Additionally, the inclusion of a DJ party may not be suitable for an educational tour. The tour organizing vendor has not provided details on the quality of the hotel and the quad-sharing basis may not be comfortable for all students. Hence, considering the well-being of the students, the tour proposal for the educational trip, should be rejected.

3.   The given paragraph is showing the data of four cities' pollution.   **(5 Marks)**

Out of all the cities, Ludhiana is not a metropolitan city as Delhi, Mumbai or Chennai but it has a huge cloth industry. That is the reason that it has 453 Suspended Particulate Matter which is higher than even Chennai. If we talk about Sulphur Dioxide and Nitrogen Oxide then Delhi has it maximum because of pollution done by vehicles. Delhi is at the top in pollution as all the pollutants are maximum in comparison to other cities. Ludhiana has minimum Sulphur Dioxide but Nitrogen is near to the level of Mumbai.

Mumbai is also having very less Sulphur Dioxide may be because of the use of CNG. We must say that Delhi is at the peak of pollution and it must be curbed otherwise this will harm the health of the people living there. The high rate of Suspended Particulate Matter in Ludhiana and Mumbai must be taken care.

4.   The given pie chart has given the expenditures on different things in a family. The expense percentage on Grocery is 23% which is maximum in comparison to clothes, transportation, education, rent and miscellaneous expenses. In the chart we see clothes with 19% expenses, education with 20%, and transportation with 18% expenses are almost similar.   **(5 Marks)**

It is surprising to see that 15% expenses are miscellaneous which are apart from core essential amenities like food, shelter and clothes.

If we want to cut the expenses then the amount spent on clothes and miscellaneous can be reduced as other things are extremely important, so these can't be compromised with.

5.   The pie chart shows that 26% of People waste a lot of water while using the toilet and 16% of people waste to use the shower. Almost 14% of the water is wasted because of pipeline leaks.   **(5 Marks)**

However, 22 % of water is wasted in cloth washing which is a huge amount.

Possible ways to save water:

- Use a toilet flush which consumes less water.

- Put a plastic bottle in your toilet bank.

- Install water shaving shower heads or flow restrictors.

- When watering plants, apply water only as fast as the soil can absorb it.

- Use size cycles while washing clothes, skip the extra rinse.

- Use watering-can instead of a running hose.

- Take a quick shower.

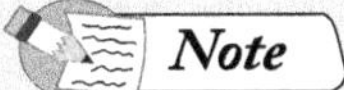

For analysis writing one should able to understand the wastefull and usefull water consumption from the pie chart. As we can see dishwashing and bathing are the usefull. Water consumption from the pie chart.

6. We notice from the chart given that there are groups of individuals that grouped together according to their age. The table shows the internet activities of each age group. In the 20s column, we see that the internet activities are very high as that is the prime age when children are most free and active on social media, online games, online shopping etc. In the 30s, we see that the online games and downloads decreases among individual who are in their 30s and their product research, product purchase increases. Before 20s also mention: that the Teens are the most active on the internet activities as it is that adolescent time where everyone is eager to learn more. Individuals in their 40s, hardly download anything using internet resources or barely play online games as most of them might be busy in their corporate life and personal life. But however the product research is a bit more that individuals in their 30s. Those who are in their 50s, a similar pattern is seen in their consumption of internet activities. Those who are in their 60s are heading retirement or already have hit retirement and use the internet to get more news. Their gaming and download consumption for the internet are low.

And lastly those who are in their 70s watch a lot of news but they hardly use internet activities like downloading, online games and buying products online.   **(5 Marks)**

7. **In support of the decision:** The given information illustrates the options Gurmeet would weigh to make the right decision about her admission to a public-funded engineering college. With the availability of a strong curriculum, quality faculty, and vibrant Activity Clubs, she will be assured of an enriching educational journey. Though a hostel facility is unavailable, she may take up accommodation in the suburbs or choose to travel daily from her village. Good opportunities for practice-based research, partnership with professional companies, and an international student exchange program will enhance her professional and interpersonal skills. Hard work, responsible behavior, and prudent decision-making could help Gurmeet thrive in the college, even though it has a rigid and conventional culture. The strengths and opportunities work in favor of Gurmeet. Taking this opportunity will allow her to mend the incorrect public perception of public-funded colleges and students' outlook toward technical subjects.

Against the decision: The given information indicates Gurmeet's dilemma about seeking admission to a public-funded college. Though equipped with a strong curriculum, engaging activity clubs, and an able faculty, the college lacks diversity and good conduct among the students, giving rise to concerns about a safe environment for a novice like Gurmeet. Underutilization of IT services will be further detrimental to the progress of Gurmeet's educational journey and add to extra costs related to research work. If she does not qualify for a complete or partial scholarship, the arrangement of her accommodation and additional expense of the students' exchange program will increase her expenditure, too. Such a college environment may dampen her endeavoring spirit. The weakness and threats outweigh the strengths in the case of Gurmeet. So, it is recommended that Gurmeet does not apply for admission to the said college.

(5 Marks)

8. **Argument FOR the subject of the statement:** In the world of today, gardening needs to be given more importance than sports, music, and dance in all schools. While sports, music, and dance contribute towards personal growth, the current times mandate attention towards a global issue ---nature and natural processes. With growing food wastage in many homes today and the urban young believing that vegetables are grown and harvested at the supermarkets, the efforts of the farmers are discredited. Gardening at school will open a world of first-hand learning experiences of sowing, watering, and harvesting processes. Waiting for the saplings to grow will inculcate sensitivity, patience, empathy, gratitude, and value for one's hard work. They will feel accountable for their piece of Mother Earth, resulting in making them efficient and enterprising environmental stewards. Unlike sports, music, or dance, gardening goes beyond just enjoyment to create aware and responsible citizens of the future. **(5 Marks)**

Argument AGAINST the subject of the statement: Gardening certainly, should not be given precedence over sports, music, and dance in all schools. Gardening at school requires good planning with hands-on guidance and continued supervision by the teachers. Students tend to lose interest due to the slow and natural growth progress of plants as well as the investment of continuous hard work. Small targets or goals would be missing, whereas the danger of destruction of their work due to rains, intrusion of grazing animals, or a pest attack is like set in a feeling of defeat. It may be noted that sports, music, and dance are uplifting activities that display faster results, are enjoyable, and inculcate team spirit, collaboration, and confidence. Unlike gardening, setbacks in these activities can be addressed with some sense of personal control. These activities help students express and de-stress successfully. So, maintaining their due importance in the school's co-curriculum is imperative.

9. The survey shows the data collected from National Capital. Over 20 schools recorded entries of over 200 students. The age group varied from 13 to 15 years. Every student has shown interest in at least one activity among art, music, dance, theatre, and cricket. Students are primarily interested in music. With a count of 60 students, music is the most liked activity. Cricket and Theatre are the next most populous activities of interest. Total of forty students like cricket and theatre each. Art and dance are the least liked activities among all the options. Only 20-30 students like them. **(5 Marks)**

It shows that every child has his/her own area of interest. Every child is different from others. Therefore, the interest of every child varies from one another.

CBSE Competency Focused Practice Questions

TENSES

1. Choose an appropriate answer to complete the conversation given below. **[CFPQ, CBSE 2022]**

Kartika : How old are you?

Ron : I am turning twenty in the coming week.

Kartika : For how many years have you been playing the guitar?

Ron : _______________

(a) Next week, when I turn twenty, I have played the guitar for twelve years.

(b) Next week, when I turn twenty, I am going to play the guitar for twelve years.

(c) Next week, when I turn twenty, I will have been playing the guitar for twelve years.

(d) Next week, when I turn twenty, I was going to be playing the guitar for twelve years.

2. In which of these sentences is the action expected to happen before a particular time in the future?

[CFPQ, CBSE 2022]

(a) I will visit Aunt Rose and Cousin Sebastian in Paris this weekend.

(b) My parents as well as my brother will have arrived at the venue by 7 pm.

(c) We suggest that you take the shorter route to the hospital to reach earlier.

(d) They would have to take the train if they do not reach the airport by 10 pm.

3. Choose the option that completes the sentences below correctly. **[CFPQ, CBSE 2022]**

I just heard the journalist report that several highway in Uttarakhand _______________ bloocked due to landslides as incessant rain batters the hill state.

(a) had been

(b) have been

(c) were being

(d) will have been

4. Choose the correct option to complete the given dialogue.

[CFPQ, CBSE 2022]

Pintu :

Why do you look so stressed? Is everything alright?

Mithu:

No! I just got some bad news __________________.

(a) Aditya is in a car accident.

(b) Aditya has been in a car accident.

(c) Aditya had been in a car accident.

(d) Aditya will have been in a car accident.

5. Complete the following sentences with the appropriate verbs. **[CFPQ, CBSE 2022]**

The crew _____________ work at the crack of dawn.

Each of its members __________ for three hours before taking a break.

(a) begin, work

(b) begins, work

(c) begin, works

(d) begins, works

6. Which underlined phrase indicates that the subject will complete the action in the very near future?

[CFPQ, CBSE 2022]

(a) Arvind <u>will train</u> for his tournament today.

(b) Jay will be playing the piano at my wedding today.

(c) Rehana <u>will have reached</u> the office by the time you get here.

(d) 1Carol <u>will be completing</u> her exam preparations sometime this week.

7. Choose the option that best completes the given conversation correctly. **[CFPQ, CBSE 2022]**

Ann : *You are panting heavily. You _______ be exhausted!*

Sofia : *When I was in college, I _______ run everyday.*

Ann : *You __________ resume exercise. It will make you more fit.*

(a) could, would, might

(b) must, would, should

(c) must, ought to, would

(d) might, ought to, should

8. Choose the option that correctly completes the sentence below. **[CFPQ, CBSE 2022]**

She is highly creative and likes to work at her own pace. I doubt whether she _______ cope with the stress of a corporate job.

(a) could have to

(b) will be ablve to

(c) may not have to

(d) must not be able to

9. Choose the correct option below to meaningfully complete the conversation. **[CFPQ, CBSE 2022]**

Sanith : *I _______________ get tickets for the football match last week.*

Sanil : *You _______________ tole me. I had extra*

tickets since my sisters backed out at the last minute.

(a) did not, need to have

(b) might not, could have

(c) could not, should have

(d) would not, ought to have

10. **Raju makes the following statement :**

[CFPQ, CBSE 2022]

If you are very hungry, you will eat a lot of food.

If Raju is not completely sure about his statment, he will

change it to : _______________

(a) If you are very hungry, you had better eat a lot of

    food.

(b) If you are very hungry, you should eat a lot of food.

(c) If you are very hungry, you will not eat a lot of food.

(d) If you are very hungry, you might eat a lot of food.

11. Which sentence shows that Edward is <u>able</u> to finish a

painting in two days?   **[CFPQ, CBSE 2022]**

(a) Edward can finish a painting in two days.

(b) Edward may finish a painting in two days.

(c) Edward has to finish a painting in two days.

(d) Edward ought to finish a painting in two days.

12. The sentence below has been divided into three parts.

The President of Italy, accompanied by his cabinet

members, is expected to arrive at the embassy by 5 pm.

A. The President of Italy,

B. Accompanied by his cabinet members,

C. is expected to arrive at the embassy by 5 pm.

Which of these options, when replaced with part B, will

change the verb form in part C?   **[CFPQ, CBSE 2022]**

(a) in addition to his cabinet members

(b) together with his cabinet members

(c) as well as his cabinet members

(d) and his cabinet members

13. How many shops in this lane are open during the night?

Choose the option that BEST serves as a reply to the

question above.   **[CFPQ, CBSE 2022]**

(a) Only one of the shops are open during the night.

(b) Only one of the shops is open during the night.

(c) Neither of the shopes are open during the night.

(d) A number of shops is open during the night.

14. Which of these sentences is grammatically

INCORRECT?   **[CFPQ, CBSE 2022]**

(a) Shawn, as well as his friends, are studying for the

    test.

(b) Neither the employees nor the manager was at the

    meeting.

(c) The captain or the club members note down special

    requests every week.

(d) Each of the employees, who attended the talk, was

    fine with the session being recorded.

15. Choose the correct option to complete the passage given below.

With a government always wanting more financial help, in season and out of season, with the reduced value of the currency and with enemies on _________ side, the position of the directors of the bank was no enviable one. It was only by great energy, united effort, and perseverance that they _________ able to keep their heads above water and struggle on until at last, they found themselves on safer and firmer ground. **[CFPQ, CBSE 2022]**

(a) all; was

(b) some; is

(c) each; are

(d) every; were

16. The sentence below has been divided into five sections. Which of these sections contain errorts?

[CFPQ, CBSE 2022]

(1) *Although the sting of certain scorpions* **(2)** *are rarely dangerous,* **(3)** *they cause swelling* **(4)** *and pose health risks to infants,* **(5)** *who are vulnerable to its venom.*

(a) only sections (2) and (3)

(b) only sections (3) and (5)

(c) only sections (2), (3) and (4)

(d) only sections (2), (4) and (5)

17. Read the following instruction for a Language exam. Identify the number of errors in the instruction below.

[CFPQ, CBSE 2022]

The sentences given below lists rules of grammar incorrectly. One out of every four sentences are designed to test basic grammatical rules while the other three sentences are created to test higher concepts.

(a) one

(b) two

(c) three

(d) four

18. Option 1, 2, 3 and 4 below together from a paragraph. There is a grammatical MISTAKE in one part of the paragraph. **[CFPQ, CBSE 2022]**

Identify the option with the **MISTAKE**.

(a) Neither Jeff nor Martin were paying attention when the outer lock swung open and a

(b) grey, space-suited figure raced for protection under the shed. It was a dash of no more

(c) than five seconds duration, but to Jeff and Martin it seemed like their father took an

(d) Eternity to reach safety. Engulfed by fear and excitement, they ran to him.

REPORTED SPEECH

19. Read the conversation below and choose the option that best presents the designer's words to Rachel. **[CFPQ, CBSE 2022]**

Ross : *Hey, Rachel! What did the interior designer say about the new design?*

Rachel : *The designer informed me that he would have the design ready by the following week.*

(a) The designer said, "I will have the design ready by next week."

(b) The designer said, "I would have had the design ready by next week."

(c) The designer said, "I would have the design ready by the following week."

(d) The designer said, "I will be having the design ready by next week."

DETERMINERS

20. The cash prize will be awarded to _______________ student who scores the highest in English across all sections. **[CFPQ, CBSE 2022]**

(a) a

(b) X

(c) the

(d) this

PREPOSITIONS

21. Wilson was reading the document very carefully this time yesterday. **[CFPQ, CBSE 2022]**

Rewrite the given sentence to indicate that the action described will occur in the future and continue for an expected length of time.

22. The conversation given has two errors. Identify the INCORRECT phrases and rewrite them correctly. You need not rewrite the entire dialogue.

Taylor : *Why is everybody worried?*

Selena: *The news are pretty upsetting. Some wild animal has attacked Mrs. Packletide's cattle that was grazing in the field.* **[CFPQ, CBSE 2022]**

23. Fill in the blanks to complete the sentences given below. Do not rewrite entire sentences. The police _______________ prepared a list of suspects for the robbery case. Each of the suspects _______________ not allowed to leave the town until further notice.

[CFPQ, CBSE 2022]

24. Combine the phrases given below to form a passive sentence in the present continuous tense.

investigate / for fraud / this organisation / the government

[CFPQ, CBSE 2022]

25. Rewrite the given sentences by identifying and correcting the error. Underline the changed word in the sentence.

    [CFPQ, CBSE 2022]

    (a) Meera bought earrings for her mother, a ball for her brother and a new pair of shoes for her.

    (b) By showing us how to make baskets from bamboo, she has not only revived an old tradition but also showed us how to fend for herself.

26. Identify the type of phrase used in the underlined part below and make a sentence using the same type of phrase. **[CFPQ, CBSE 2022]**

    Ray was determined to paint *using the ancient fresco technique with natural dyes.*

27. Given below is an except from a newspaper article. There are two errors in the excerpt. Identify the phrases that need to be corrected and rewrite them correctly. Do not rewrite the entire sentnece.

    [CFPQ, CBSE 2022]

    To enable a greater number of COVID-19 tests and reduce the burden against laboratories, the Indian Council of Medical Research (ICMR) has recently approved a COVID-19 home testing kit that can be used by all adults at home. Thetest kit is called CoviSelf and is designed to give results over 15 minutes of taking the test.

28. Given below is an edited extract from Love and Friendship by Jane Austen. Complete the extract with appropriate prepositions. **[CFPQ, CBSE 2022]**

29. Complete the sentences given below with appropriate determiners. **[CFPQ, CBSE 2022]**

    Raju said, "___1___ book is mine, I don't know where yours is, Check if its there on ___2___ table by the window."

30. Rewrite these sentences into indirect or reported speech without changing their meaning.

    [CFPQ, CBSE 2022]

    (a) *"I want to be a motor mechanic," he repeats.*

    (b) *"Can a god-given lineage ever be broken?" she asks.*

31. Identify the tense in the underlined part of the given sentences. **[CFPQ, CBSE 2022]**

    (a) *We were shocked to find our house engulfed by the fire.*

    (b) *She had thought about the problem for a long time before attempting it.*

32. Rewrite the folowing sentences by changing their tense to the form given in brackets. **[CFPQ, CBSE 2022]**

    (a) *She has been feeling terrible and wants to apologise for her behavour. (Simple Past Tense)*

    (b) *They were working together on this project back in 2008. (Past Perfect Tense)*

33. Rewrite these sentences using the tense that is appropriate for the given context. **[CFPQ, CBSE 2022]**

(a) *I did the exercise hundreds of times before.*

(b) *If he had shown some patience, I answered his question.*

34. The sentences given below describe two different events/ actions/situations. Write them down in the order of their occurrence in the box given below. One sample has been done for you. **[CFPQ, CBSE 2022]**

(a) *Benson was surprised that someone had sent him a postcard.*

(b) *The heavy rains destroyed the crops that we had planted.*

(c) *Dany could not buy cupcakes because he had forgotten his wallet.*

(d) *Abigail and Sarah hadn't spoken before attending the summer camp.*

Occured First	Occured Later
1. Some sending a postcard	Benson being surprised
2.	
3.	
4.	
5.	

35. Fill in the blanks with the appropriate form of the verbs given in the brackets. **[CFPQ, CBSE 2022]**

When we found out that the Prussians __________ (ask) M. Hamel to leave the school, we were shattered. Despite his strict demeanour and harsh words, M. Hamel __________ (take) great efforts with our French. Nothing would be the same now. I wished we __________ (defeat) the Prussians in the war – the wretches!

36. Rewrite each sentence using the tense given in brackets. **[CFPQ, CBSE 2022]**

(a) Have you thought about the matter? (Present Continuous Tense)

(b) The doctor encourages his patients to exercise on a regular basis. (Past Continuous Tense)

(c) Does your leg hurt too much? (Present Continuous Tense)

37. Each of the given sentences has an error. Rewrite the sentences by correcting the error and underlining the change. Sentence 0 has been done for you as an example. **[CFPQ, CBSE 2022]**

Question: I does my homework in the evening.

Answer : I <u>do</u> my homework in the evening.

(a) A big group of people have arrived at the hotel today.

(b) Why are everyone late for the most important event?

(c) The unique features of a starfish makes it different from other sea creatures.

38. Read the given comic strip. In the pragraphs below, there are numbered blanks. In your paper, write the serial number of each blank and the appropriate phrase to complete the text in INDIRECT SPEECH without any change in meaning. Do NOT copy the comic strip.   **[CFPQ, CBSE 2022]**

Source (edited) : 'Dishrack' –

https://commons.wikimedia.org/wiki/File:Hots_Dishrack.png

The wife called her husband from her hotel room. She _____(i)_____.

The wife was _____(ii)_____ there was something wrong with the dish rack. Her husband continued to say that it had been four days and it hadn't gone down. She _____(iii)_____. He added that it was also causing the sink to back up.

ANALYTICAL PARAGRAPH

1. The chart below displays data about the production (in metric tonnes) of three crops– wheat, pulses and cotton — in India for five specific years between 1950-51 and2010-2011. write a paragraph in 100-120 words analysing the given data.

[CFPQ, CBSE 2022]

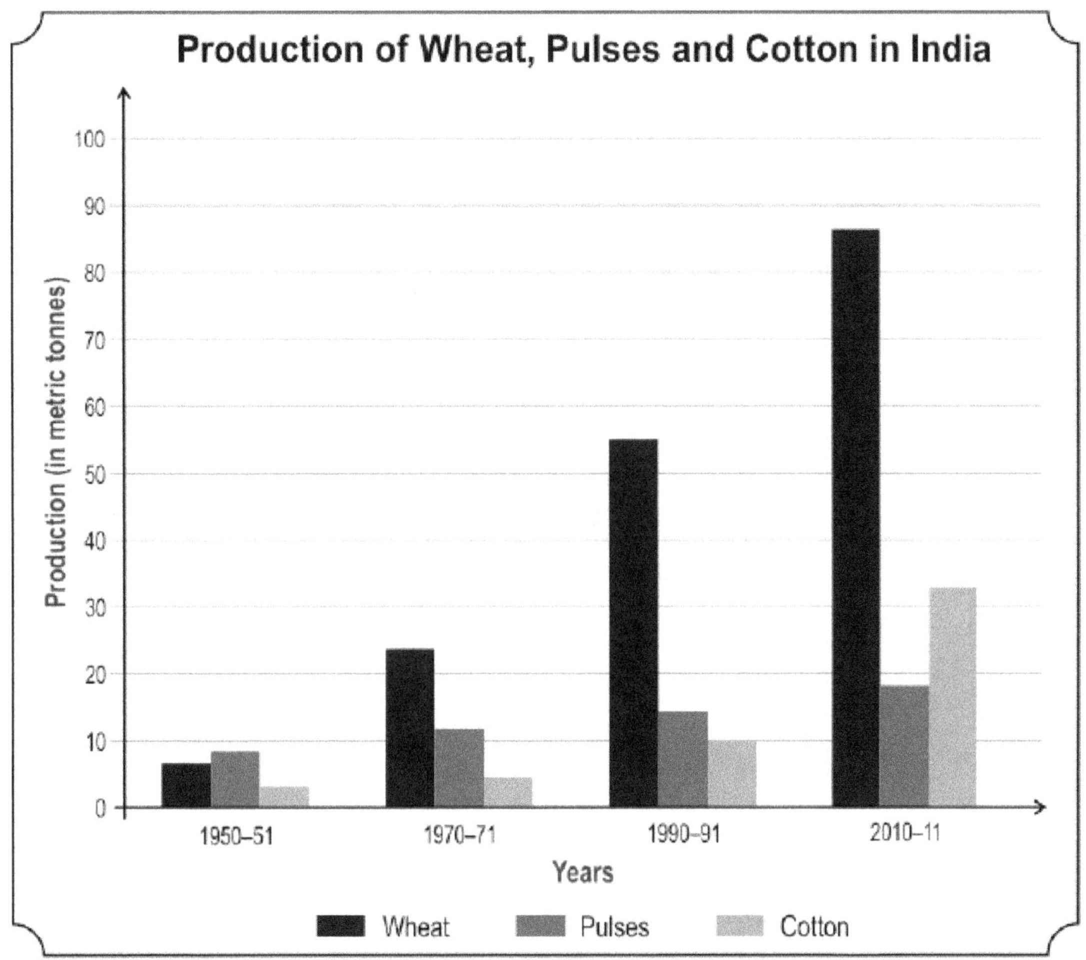

Source (Edited): 'Levels of Agricultural Development and Environmental Issues in

India: A Geographical Perspective' - IJRAR, Volume 7, Issue 2, April-June 2020

2. Read the statement given below. Social media is a useful platform for many teenagers as it exposes them to news and helps

    them interact with people across the globe. It also gives them a platform to be creative. Write a paragraph in about 120

    words analysing the given argument. You can think about what alternative explanations might weaken the given conclusion

    and include rationale/evidence that would strengthen/counter the given argument.   **[CFPQ, CBSE 2022]**

3. Read the statement given below. Newspapers should go online completely and we should do away with printed copies.

    Printing newspapers wastes ink and paper in a digital age where most people get information from the internet. Write a

    paragraph in about 120 words analysing the given argument. You can think about what alternative explanations might

    weaken the given conclusion and include rationale/evidence that would strengthen/counter the given argument.

                                                                                              [CFPQ, CBSE 2022]

FORMAL LETTER

4. You are Shoaib/Saiqua, a resident of 80A11 B Tops a Road, Kolkata. You noticed that the elderly in your community are reluctant to get vaccinated against COVID-19. write a letter in 120 -150 words to the Editor of a newspaper expressing your concern about this reluctance and mentioning the need to create awareness about the vaccination programme.

[CFPQ, CBSE 2022]

5. During one of your visits to a bank in your city, you noticed that the bank is not easily accessible to people with disabilities. The absence of ramps makes it highly difficult for people in wheelchairs to avail the services of the bank. write a letter in 100-120 words to your District Magistrate highlighting the issue and requesting him/her to take necessary action. You are Sneha/Shahid from Madhuban Apartments, Kanpur.

[CFPQ, CBSE 2022]

Solutions

---

1. (c)	2. (b)	3. (b)	4. (b)
5. (d)	6. (c)	7. (b)	8. (b)
9. (c)	10. (d)	11. (a)	12. (d)
13. (b)	14. (a)	15. (d)	16. (c)
17. (b)	18. (a)	19. (a)	20. (c)

21. Wilson will be reading the document very carefully this time tomorrow. **(1 Mark)**

22. Identifies the incorrect phrases and rewrites them correctly (the news is pretty/news is pretty; cattle that were/Mrs Packletide's cattle that were) Accept any other valid answer. **(1 Mark)**

23. Fills in the blanks with the correct answers
(Blank 1: have Blank 2 : is) **(1 Mark)**

24. This organisation is being investigated for fraud./This organisation is being investigated by the government for fraud./The government is being investigated by this organisation for fraud. **(1 Mark)**

25. **(a)** Meera bought earrings for her mother, a ball for her cousin and a new pair of shoes for <u>herself</u>. **(½ Mark)**

    (b) By showing us how to make baskets from bamboo, she has not only revived an old tradition but also showed us how to fend for <u>ourselves</u>. **(½ Mark)**

26. Type of phrase : adverbial phrase **(½ Mark)**

    Sample sentence: I will go to the market tomorrow/s the sang with her heart and soul/any other valid answer.

    (½ Mark)

27. Identifies the incorrect prepositional phrases (against laboratories, over 15 minutes) **(½ Mark)**

    Accept any other preposition that fits the phrase correctly.

28. (a) on **(2 Marks)**

    (b) with

    (c) in

    (d) of

29. (a) This/any other valid answer **(1 Mark)**

    (b) that/the/any other valid answer **(1 Mark)**

30. (a) He repeated that he wants to be a motor mechanic. **(1 Mark)**

    (b) She asked if a good-given lineage could ever be broken. **(1 Mark)**

31. (a) Simple past tense **(1 Mark)**

    (b) Past perfect tense **(1 Mark)**

32. (a) She felt terrible and wanted to apologise for her behaviour. **(1 Mark)**

    (b) They had worked together on this project back in 2008. **(1 Mark)**

33. (a) I had done the exercise hundreds of times before./I have done the exercise hundreds of times before. (past perfect tense/present perfect tense) **(1 Mark)**

(b) If he had show some patience, I would have answered his question. (past perfect tense for if clause)

34. 2. planting of crops; heavy rains destroying the crops

3. Dany forgetting his wallet; Dany not able to buy cupcakes

4. Selin leaving; Sam placing order

5. Abigail and Sarah attending the summer camp; Abigail and Sarah speaking to each other.

(2 Marks)

35. (a) had asked (perfect past tense) **(1 Mark)**

(b) had taken (perfect past tense) **(1 Mark)**

(c) had defeated (perfect past tense) **(1 Mark)**

36. (a) Are you thinking about the matter? **(1 Mark)**

(b) The doctor was encouraging his patients to exercise on a regular basis. **(1 Mark)**

(c) Is your leg hurting too much? **(1 Mark)**

37. (a) A big group of people has arrived at the hotel today. **(1 Mark)**

(b) Why <u>is</u> everyone late for the most Important event? **(1 Mark)**

(c) The unique features of a starfish make it different from other sea creatures. **(1 Mark)**

38. (i) wanted to know if everything was alright at home without her/wanted to know whether everything was alright at home without her/enquired if everything was alright at home without her/enquired whether everything was alright at home without her/asked him if everything was alright at home without her/asked him whether everything was alright at home without her/any other valid answer. **(1 Mark)**

(ii) confused when she heard her husband tell her that/confused to hear her husband tell her that/surprised when she heard her husband tell her that/surprised to hear her husband tell her that/taken aback when she heard her husband tell her that/taken aback to hear her husband tell her that/bewildered when she heard her husband tell her that/bewildered to hear her husband tell her that/surprised to hear that/taken aback to hear that/confused to hear that/bewildered to hear that/any other valid answer **(1 Mark)**

(iii) suggested that he should call someone/advised that he should call someone/proposed that he should call someone/any other valid answer **(1 Mark)**

1. India's agrarian economy is the leading producer of wheat pulses and cotton. Between 1950-1952, wheat production was recorded at 7 metric tonnes, pulses were produced at 9 metric tonnes and cotton was produced in lesser quantity than the two. Between 1970-71, crop production increased a little as compared to the previous years. Wheat was produced at 25 metric tonnes, pulses at 10, and cotton at 5 metric tonnes. Compared to the previous years, the period between 1990-1991 witnessed a significant increase in both wheat, pulses, and crop production. The period between 2010-2011 did not show much progress in the production of the pulse but cotton and wheat production exacerbated amounting to 32 and 87 metric tonnes respectively. **(5 Marks)**

2. Social media has become the widely used networking platform among teenagers nowadays. People, especially teenagers, do not have to depend on newspapers for updates on recent happenings. They can easily know about all current events and news from around the globe through social media. Besides, social media makes interaction with people all across the globe possible. Teenagers get exposed to newness and difference. Moreover, they get multiple options to enhance their creativity through social media. It is a great platform that they can use to showcase their work or talent to a global audience and get feedback in return. They can find motivation and inspiration and feel more encouraged to follow their passion which in turn can increase their dedication toward work. So, if used properly, social media opens many ways of growth and productivity for youngsters. **(5 Marks)**

3. The printed newspaper is the conventional source of news existing since the time of the printing press. In recent times, however, people are more dependent on technology and the internet. They prefer reading news bulletins on their smartphones and laptops. It saves their time and effort as phones are easier and more handy. Besides, ink and paper are used to print newspapers, which can be saved to protect our environment. However, in printed newspapers, one can find many ways to broaden knowledge with the help of word puzzles, stories, cooking recipes, etc. So, even though the online newspaper is more convenient for our busy lifestyles, we should not completely discard the use of printed newspapers. **(5 Marks)**

4. 80 A/1B Topsia Road

Kolkata

5th July 20XX

The Editor

The Hindu

Kolkata

Subject- Reluctance to get vaccinated

Sir/Madam

Through the column of your esteemed daily, I wish to express my concern regarding the elderly who are reluctant to get vaccinated against Covid-19.

Vaccines save 2 to 3 million lives each year and are amongst the greatest advancements of modern medicine. The development of safe and effective covid-19 vaccines is a huge step forward in our global effort to combat the virus. But there are still some people who are sceptical about the vaccines. People should understand that vaccinating themselves can help their loved ones while being careful not to overstate the vaccine's power to reduce or eliminate transmission.

I hope that after the publication of this letter, the message would reach the masses and the youth would motivate the elderly to get vaccinated. Also, the elderly themselves would bust this myth and create a healthy society for themselves and others too.

Thanking you

Yours truly

Saiqua   **(5 Marks)**

5.   Madhuban Apartments

Kanpur

5th July 20XX

District Manager

Kanpur

Uttar Pradesh

   Subject- Absence of ramps in the bank

Sir/Madam,

With due respect I want to state that the local branch of xyz Bank is not easily accessible to people with disabilities. They cannot avail the services all by themselves for there are no ramps for them to grant them access to the bank. A wheelchair is provided to them but it becomes inconvenient and at times risky for them to use without proper infrastructure in place. I've myself observed differently abled individuals feeling uncomfortable in seeking help for the tasks that they otherwise manage on their own.

Therefore, I request you to review this issue seriously and take immediate actions for solving it. It will be a big help and relief for many needy people.

Thanking you

Yours sincerely

Sneha

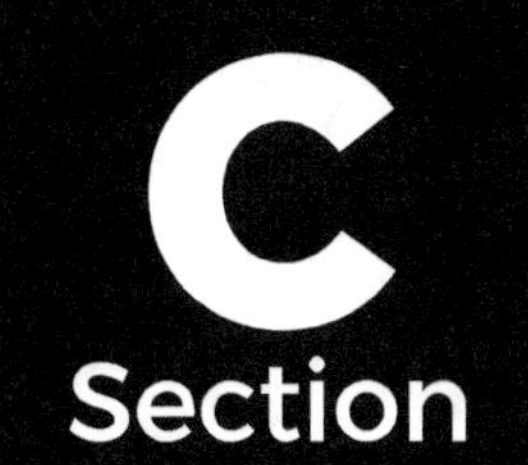

Literature Textbook & Supplementary Reading Text

Topic-a: *First Flight: Prose*

---

1. A Letter to God

1   *Extract Based Questions*

The moment the letter fell into the mailbox the postmaster went to open it. It said : " God : of the money that I asked for, only seventy pesos reached me. Send me the rest, since I need it very much. But don't send it to me through the mail because the post office employees are a bunch of crooks. Lencho."

(i) Lencho wrote the second letter as he was :

[All India 2022, T-I; U]

(A) unhappy

(B) curious

(C) hopeful

(D) thoughtful

(E) confident

(a) (A), (C) and (E)

(b) (A), (B) and (C)

(c) (B), (E) and (A)

(d) (C), (D) and (E)

(ii) The postmaster opened the letter expecting it to:

[All India 2022, T-I; U]

(A) be full of thanks to God

(B) show his happiness

(C) be full of anguish for getting less money

(D) be accusing God of being miserly

(a) (C) and (D)

(b) (A) and (B)

(b) (A) and (D)

(d) (D) and (B)

(iii) On reading the letter the postmaster was

[All India 2022, T-I; U]

(a) surprised

(b) dismayed

(c) pleased

(d) puzzled

(iv) 'the post office employees are a bunch of crooks'

The statement is :   **[All India 2022, T-I; U]**

(a) thoughtful

(b) sad

(c) dismissive

(d) ironic

(v) Find the suitable word from the extract to complete the following :

sanctioned : approved : : demanded : _________

[All India 2022, T-I; U]

(a) fell

(b) reached

(c) went

(d) asked

2   *Short Answer Type Questions*

1. Explain how the description of the devastation caused by the hailstorm reflects the sadness within Lencho, in A Letter to God   **[CBSE Sample 2023-24; U]**

Refer to the given lines, from the text -

"Not a leaf remained on the trees. The corn was totally destroyed. The flowers were gone from the plants. Lencho's soul was filled with sadness."

2. In what way would writing a letter to God help Lencho tide over his crisis?   **[All India, 2023; U]**

3. Why did the night after the rains turn sorrowful for Lencho?   **[Delhi, 2023; U]**

4. What did Lencho's happy happy mood change into concern?   **[All India 2020; U]**

5. (a) Why did Lencho write a letter to God ?

[Delhi 2019; U]

---

2. Nelson Mandela - Long Walk to Freedom

---

1. 'In life, every man has <u>twin obligations</u>',

[All India 2022, T-I; U]

The 'twin obligations' are

(a) first to his <u>community</u> and the second to his <u>country.</u>

(b) first to his <u>family</u> and the second to his <u>country.</u>

(c) first to his <u>country</u> and the second to his <u>parents.</u>

(d) first to his <u>community</u> and the second to his <u>family.</u>

2   *Short Answer Type Questions*

1. What did Nelson Mandela remember on the day of the inaugural ceremony?   **[All India 2020; U]**

3 *Long Answer Type Questions*

3. Two Stories About Flying

1. You have been chosen to address a student gathering from the neighbourhood schools, to speak on the resilience of human spirit required to transcend discrimination. Prepare the speech draft in not more than 120 words, with reference to the commonality of themes in Nelson Mandela: Long Walk to Freedom and The Trees by Adrienne Rich. **[CBSE Sample 2023-24; ]**

You may begin this way:

Good morning, everyone. Today, I'd like to discuss two pieces of literature that offer a powerful insight into the resilience of the human spirit required to transcend discrimination.

You may end this way.

To conclude, I'd like to say that ...

Thank you

2. Mandela said, "People must learn to hate, and if they can learn to hate, they can be taught to love." Discuss.

[All India, 2023; U]

3. 'No one is born hating another person because of the colour of his skin, or his background or his religion'. Do you agree? Elaborate on the basis of the chapter "Nelson Mandela – Long walk to freedom".   **[Delhi, 2023; U]**

4. Why was Nelson Mandela overwhelmed with a sense of history? How did he succeed in ending the apartheid regime in South Africa?   **[Delhi 2020; U]**

1. 'He had in fact seen his older brother catch his first herring and devour it.' (His First Flight)

How did 'he' feel ?   **[All India 2022, T-I; U]**

A. Angry

B. Greedy

C. Jealous

D. Hungry

(a) A and B

(b) B and C

(c) C and D

(d) D and A

1 *Extract Based Questions*

1. Inside the clouds, everything was suddenly black. It was impossible to see anything outside the aeroplane. The old aeroplane jumped and twisted in the air. I looked at the compass. I couldn't believe my eyes the compass was turning round and round and round. It was dead. It would not work. The other instruments were suddenly dead, too. I tried the radio. "Paris Control? Paris Control? Can you hear me?" There was no answer. The radio was dead too. I had no radio, no compass, and I could not see where I was. I was lost in the storm.

(i) As soon as the pilot was inside the cloud ....

[**Delhi, 2023; U**]

    (a) his ears got blocked.

    (b) he choked with fear.

    (c) his vision was obstructed.

    (d) he was jumping up and down.

(ii) The devices in the aeroplane were ....

[**Delhi, 2023; U**]

    (a) malfunctioning.

    (b) broken completely.

    (c) giving wrong readings.

    (d) stopped responding completely.

(iii) The Paris air control did not reply to the pilot's call because ....   [**Delhi, 2023; U**]

(iv) Select the option that correctly captures the application of the word 'twisted' as used in the extract.   [**Delhi, 2023; U**]

    (a) Ragini **twisted** Raghav's wrist.

    (b) Ragini **twisted** the story to suit the occasion.

    (c) Ragini did not appreciate Raghav's **twisted** bent of mind.

    (d) Ragini matched the swimmer as he **twisted** twice in the air before diving into the water.

(v) Fill in the blank with ONE WORD only:

[**Delhi, 2023; U**]

The narrator's .... comes through clearly when he sees the compass turning round and round.

2 *Short Answer Type Questions*

1. "I'll take the risk." What is the risk? Why does the narrator take it? (The Black Aeroplane)

[**All India, 2023; U**]

2. Describe the young seagull's first flight.

(Two stories about flying)   [**Delhi, 2023; U**]

3. Validate the given statement with reference to baby seagull's fear. 'Fear doesn't exist anywhere else other than one's mind.' (His First Flight- Two Stories about Flying)   [**CBSE Sample 2022-23; U**]

4. "The sight of the food maddened him." What does this suggest? (His First Flight)   [**Delhi 2020; U**]

3 *Long Answer Type Questions*

1. You have been asked to present an evaluation of the approaches of the mothers of both, the baby seagull and Amanda, towards helping their children. Write this presentation draft including your insights, in about 120 words, comparing the approaches of both parents.

You may begin this way:

One acknowledges that both parents, Amanda's mother and the baby seagull's mother both....however, ...

(Reference -Amanda! & His First Flight)

> ### 4. From the Diary of Anne Frank

1. Mr Keesing was annoyed with Anne as :

[All India 2022, T-I; U]

(a) she was week is maths.

(b) she had not done her home work.

(c) she was a naughty girl.

(d) she was very talkative.

2. 'Paper has more patience than people' (Anne Frank)

[All India 2022, T-I; U]

Which of the following is not true ?

(a) One can write anything on paper

(b) People have good ears for listening

(c) One can write one's diary even at night

(d) One may express one's anger on paper

1   *Extract Based Questions*

1. Read the following extract and answer the questions that

follow: **[All India, 2023; U]**

I wrote the three pages Mr. Keesing had assigned me and

was satisfied. I argued that talking is a student's trait and

that I would do my best to keep it under control, but that

I would never be able to cure myself of the habit since

my mother talked as much as I did, if not more, and that

there's not much one can do about inherited traits.

(i) Who was Mr. Keesing?   **[All India, 2023; U]**

(a) English teacher

(b) Social Science teacher

(c) Warden

(d) Principal

(ii) According to the extract, the incorrigible habit possessed by the speaker was. **[All India, 2023; U]**

A making noise in class

B talking too much

C procrastinating

D coming late to class

E asking irritating questions

Select the correct option:

(a) A and C

(b) Only B

(c) A, D and E

(d) Only C

(iii) Complete the analogy by selecting the suitable word from the extract.   **[All India, 2023; U]**

routine: habit : : characteristic: ____

(iv) Select the reason why the narrator is unable to control her trait.   **[All India, 2023; U]**

(a) She had deliberately practised it.

(b) She wanted to be different from her brother.

(c) Her teacher had encouraged her to continue as she was.

(d) She had inherited it.

(v) Which of the following most nearly means the opposite of the phrase 'under control'?

[All India, 2023; U]

(a) to spend less

(b) unable to take on the challenge

(c) find it difficult to manage

(d) being very stubborn

2   *Short Answer Type Questions*

1. Kitty was a trusted friend to Anne. Elaborate.

(From the Diary of Anne Frank)

[CBSE Sample 2023-24; U]

3   *Long Answer Type Questions*

1. How did Kitty help Anne overcome her loneliness?

[All India 2019; U]

2. What is the main theme of 'The Diary of a Young Girl'?

[All India 2019; U]

3. Justify the title, 'The Diary of A Young Girl'.

[Delhi 2019; U]

4. Write a character sketch of Anne Frank.

[Delhi 2019; U]

5. Anne's diary is as important for Anne as any other character in the annexe. What is your opinion?

[All India 2017; U]

5. Glimpses of India

1   *Extract Based Questions*

1. [CBSE Sample 2022-23; U]

"Hey, a tea garden!" Rajvir cried excitedly. Pranjol, who had been born and brought up on a plantation, didn't share Rajvir's excitement. "Oh, this is tea country now," he said. "Assam has the largest concentration of plantations in the world. You will see enough gardens to last you a lifetime!"

"I have been reading as much as I could about tea," Rajvir said. "No one really knows who discovered tea but there are many legends."

(i) Why was Pranjol not as excited as Rajvir about the tea gardens? [CBSE Sample 2022-23; U]

(a) He disliked looking at tea gardens.

(b) He had worked in tea gardens himself.

(c) He had grown up in and around tea gardens.

(d) He was bored with tea gardens.

(ii) What does Pranjol mean by saying that Assam has the largest concentration of plantations in the world? [CBSE Sample 2022-23; U]

(iii) Fill in the blank with ONE WORD only.

[CBSE Sample 2022-23; U]

Pranjol's _________________ comes through clearly when he exclaims, "You will see enough gardens to last you a lifetime!"

(iv) How according to Rajvir does the world know about the discovery of tea? **[CBSE Sample 2022-23; U]**

(a) Historical places

(b) Traditional tales

(c) Authentic anecdotes

(d) Popular publications

(v) Select the option that correctly captures the application of the word 'cried' as used in line 1 of the extract. **[CBSE Sample 2022-23; U]**

(a) Jaspreet cried a lot in spite of winning second place in a competition.

(b) Jaspreet cried out loud when she saw a white tiger in the sanctuary.

(c) Jaspreet cried for hours when the police were unable to find her lost pet.

(d) Jaspreet has barely cried since she was three years of age.

2.   **[Delhi 2019; U]**

The baker usually collected his bills at the end of the month. Monthly accounts used to be recorded on some wall in pencil. Baking was indeed a profitable profession in the old days. The baker and his family never starved. He, his family and his servants always looked happy and prosperous. Their plump physique was an open testimony to this. Even today any person with a jackfruit-like physical appearance is easily compared to a baker.

(a) Where did the baker record his accounts ?

(b) Why did the baker and his family never starve ?

(c) Which word in the extract is a synonym of 'rich'?

(d) How can a baker be identified in Goa ?

3. Evergreen rainforests cover thirty per cent of this district. During the monsoons, it pours enough to keep many visitors away. The season of joy commences from September and continues till March. The weather is perfect, with some showers thrown in for good measure. The air breathes of invigorating coffee. Coffee estates and colonial bungalows stand tucked under tree canopies in prime corners.

(a) Why is the monsoon season not the best period to visit Coorg? **[All India 2014; U]**

(b) What is the best period for the visitors?

[All India 2014; U]

(c) Which word in the passage means the same as 'starts'? **[All India 2014; U]**

4. Marriage gifts are meaningless without the sweet bread known as the bol, just as a party or a feast loses its charm without bread. Not enough can be said to show how important a baker can be for a village. The lady of the house must preaprare sandwiches on the occasion of the daughter's engagement. Cakes and bolinhas are a must for Christmas as well as other festivals. Thus, the presence of the baker's furnance in the village is absolutely essential..

(a) Why is the baker's furnace essential for the Goan people? **[Delhi 2014; U]**

(b) On which occasions are the cakes and bolinhas necessary? **[Delhi 2014; U]**

(c) Which word in the passage is the opposite in meaning of 'absence'? **[Delhi 2014; U]**

5. Coorgi homes have a tradition of hospitality, and they are more than willing to recount numerous tales of valour related to their sons and fathers. The Coorg Regiment is one of the most decorated in the Indian Army, and the first Chief of the Indian Army, General Cariappa, was a Coorgi. Even now, Kodavus are the only people in India permitted to carry fire arms without a licence.

(i) What kind of stories are the Coorg people always ready to tell? **[All India 2013; U]**

(ii) Who was the first chief of the Indian army?

[All India 2013; U]

(iii) What is the special favour granted only to them even now? **[All India 2013; U]**

(iv) Find a word from the passage which means the same as 'courage and bravery, usually in war.'

[All India 2013; U]

<table><tr><td>**2**</td><td>*Short Answer Type Questions*</td></tr></table>

1. Valour and hospitality are inherent in the people of Coorg. Explain. **[All India, 2023; U]**

2. Who are paders and why are they friends of children?

[Delhi, 2023; U]

3. Why are Kodavus permitted to carry fire arms without licence ? **[All India 2022, T-II; U]**

4. Why is Coorg called the land of rolling hills?

[Delhi 2020; U]

5. What excited Rajvir? Why did Pranjol not share his excitement? **[All India 2018; U]**

6. What do we learn about the financial condition of the bakers of Goa? **[All India 2017; U]**

7. What do the elders in Goa still love to remember?

[Delhi 2017; U]

8. What legends are associated with the origin of tea?

[Delhi 2016; U]

9. How can you say, 'bread-baking is still popular in Goa'?

[All India 2014; U]

10. Why was Rajbir excited to see the tea-garden?

[Delhi 2014; U]

11. Baking was considered essential in a traditional Goan village. What reasons does the writer give to support his point? **[All India 2013; U]**

12. How are the tea pluckers different from the other farm labourers? **[All India 2013; U]**

3 ┊ *Long Answer Type Questions* ┊

1. Pranjol and Rajvir discuss their next vacation destination. They shortlist Coorg and Goa. **[All India 2013; U]** Rajvir is keen on Coorg and tries to convince Pranjol. Develop a conversation between the two, based on your understanding of Glimpses of India.

You may begin like this: 4

Rajvir: Hey Pranjol! I think we should be visiting Coorg. It is a beautiful place with coffee plantations. I can smell the aroma already!

Pranjol: I gave you the opportunity to explore a tea plantation last year, in Assam; I want to…

┊ *6. Mijbil the Otter* ┊

1 ┊ *Extract Based Questions* ┊

1. Read the extracts given below and answer the questions that follow :

When I casually mentioned this to a friend, he casually replied that I had better get one in the Tigris marshes, for there they were as common as mosquitoes, and were often tamed by the Arabs. We were going to Basra to the Consulate-General to collect and answer our mail from Europe. At the Consulate-General we found that my friend's mail had arrived but that mine had not.

(a) What was 'they'? **[All India 2019; U]**

(b) Where could the author get 'one'?

[All India 2019; U]

(c) Find the exact word from the extract which means 'domesticated.' **[All India 2019; U]**

(d) What did the author find at the Consulate-General?

[All India 2019; U]

2 ┊ *Short Answer Type Questions* ┊

1. What game did Mij invent? **[All India 2016; U]**

2. What special characteristic of Mijbil did Maxwell learn after he took him to the bathroom? **[Delhi 2015; U]**

3. Give an example from the text to show that Mijbil is an intelligent animal. **[All India 2014; U]**

4. What happened when Maxwell took Mijbil to the bathroom? **[Delhi 2014; U]**

5. What happened when Maxwell took Mijbil to the bathroom? What did Mijbil do two days after that?

[All India 2013; U]

3   *Long Answer Type Questions*

1. Mijbil and the Tiger, both were looked after by humans. Assume they both meet each other in the zoo and have a conversation about their lifestyle and feelings.

Write this conversation as per your understanding of Mijbil the Otter and A Tiger in the Zoo.

You may begin like this

Tiger: Thanks for visiting me, though I don't usually like visitors.

Mijbil: Oh? I would love visitors, I think.

[CBSE Sample 2022-23; **U**]

---

7. Madam Rides the Bus

---

1   *Extract Based Questions*

1. Read the extract given below and answer the questions that follow :

"Don't you want to have a look at the sights, now that you're here?

"All by myself? Oh, I'd be much too afraid."

Greatly amused by the girl's way of speaking, the conductor said, "But you weren't afraid to come in the bus."

"Nothing to be afraid of about that," she answered.

(a) Who is the 'girl' mentioned in the passage?

[Delhi 2015; **U**]

(b) Why didn't she get off the bus when she reached her destination? [Delhi 2015; **U**]

(c) Write the meaning of the word, "amused."

[Delhi 2015; **U**]

---

2   *Short Answer Type Questions*

1. How did Valli save money to travel by bus?

[Delhi, 2023; **U**]

2. Valli's unique maiden bus ride experience could be possible because she belonged to a small village. Do you agree? Why? /Why not? (2 reasons)

[CBSE Sample 2022-23; **U**]

3. What was the most fascinating thing that Valli saw on the street? [All India 2019; **U**]

4. How did Valli react when she saw the dead cow by the roadside? [Delhi 2016; **U**]

5. Why didn't Valli want to go to the stall and have a drink? What does it tell you about her?

[All India 2015; **U**]

6. Give examples from the text to show that Villi was a meticulous planner. [Delhi 2014; **U**]

7. Why does Valli stand upon the seat? What does she see now? [All India 2013; **U**]

3 | *Long Answer Type Questions*

1. The people and surroundings are a great book to learn from. Valli in the lesson 'Madam Rides the Bus' learns a lot from others. Mention the traits of her character which help her to learn from people and her surroundings.

   [All India, 2023; U]

2. As Valli, make a diary entry about your experience of riding the bus alone for the first time.

   [All India 2022, T-II; U]

3. Whenever we want to achieve something, difficulties always come in our way. What did Valli have to do to go and ride in a bus?   **[All India 2020; Delhi 2017 U]**

4. Once we decide to achieve something, so many difficulties come in our way. With focused attention we can make that achievement. How did Valli succeed in fulfilling her desire of riding a bus? **[All India 2017; U]**

5. "Never mind," she said, "I can get on by myself." "You don't have to help me," said Valli to the conductor. She shows extraordinary courage in making the bus journey all alone. Taking inspiration from Valli's character, write how ability and courage to take risk are essential to fulfil one's dream.   **[Delhi 2015; U]**

6. Behaviour of the conductor in 'Madam Rides the Bus' is an example of good manners. Mention the instances of good manners shown by the conductor in the story, write

how you can make your life happy by observing good manners.   **[All India 2014; U]**

---

8. The Sermon at Benares

1 | *Extract Based Questions*

1. At about the age of twenty-five, the Prince, heretofore shielded from sufferings of the world, while out hunting chanced upon a sick man, then an aged man, then a funeral procession and finally a monk begging for alms.

   (a) Name the Prince.   **[All India 2016; U]**

   (b) What are the sights of sufferings that the Prince saw?   **[All India 2016; U]**

   (c) Give the meaning of the word, 'shielded'.

   [All India 2016; U]

2 | *Short Answer Type Questions*

1. What did Siddhartha Gautama come across by chance when he was about twenty-five years old?

   [All India, 2023; U]

2. What is the significance of the Buddha's request for a handful of mustard seeds and the addition of a condition to it?

3. What lesson on death and suffering did the Buddha teach Kisa Gotami in the chapter, "The Sermon At Benares"?

   [All India 2020; U]

4. How did Kisa Gotami realise that life and death is a normal process? **[All India 2019; U]**

5. Why did the Buddha choose Benares to preach his first sermon? **[All India 2015; U]**

6. Why was Kisa Gotami sad? What did she do in her hour of grief? **[Delhi 2015; U]**

7. How did the Buddha teach Kisa Gotami the truth of life? **[All India 2014; U]**

3   *Long Answer Type Questions*

1. 'As ripe fruits are in danger of falling early, so mortals when born are always in danger of death'. With this statement of the Buddha find out the moral values that Kisa Gotami learnt after the death of her child. **[Delhi, 2023; U]**

2. "Not from weeping nor from grieving will anyone obtain peace of mind'.

If you had to use the message of the given quote from the Buddha's sermon (The Sermon at Benares) to help the boy cope with the loss of his ball and what it signifies (The Ball Poem), what would you include in your advice? Also, evaluate why it might be difficult for him to understand the notion. **[CBSE Sample 2022-23; U]**

3. How does Buddha bring about a different perspective in Kisa Gotami's understanding of life ? **[All India 2022, T-II; U]**

4. Describe the journey of Sidhartha Gautama becoming the Buddha.

5. Why did Gotami go to the Buddha ? What lesson did he teach her ?

6. What lesson on death and suffering did the Buddha teach Gotami in the chapter, 'The Sermon at Benaras? **[All India 2018; U]**

7. "The life of mortals in this world is troubled and brief and combined with pain.... ." With this statement of the Buddha, find out the moral value that Kisa Gotami learnt after the death of her child. **[Delhi 2016; U]**

8. The Buddha said, "The world is afflicted with death and decay, therefore the wise do not grieve, knowing the terms of the world." Do you think the statement is appropriate even for today's life? Write your views in the context of the above statement. **[Delhi 2014; U]**

9. Life is full of trials and tribulations. Kisa Gotami also passes through a period of grief in her life. How does she behave in those circumstances? What lesson does a reader learn from the story of her life? Give any two points how you would like to act in the midst of adverse circumstances. **[All India 2013; U]**

9. The Proposal (Play)

1   **Extract Based Questions**

1.   LOMOV : It's cold... I'm trembling all over, just as if I'd got an examination before me. The great thing is , I must have my mind made up. If I give myself time to think, to hesitate, to talk a lot, to look for an ideal, or for real love, then I'll never get married. Brr...It's cold! Natalya Stepanovna is an excellent housekeeper, not bad-looking, well-educated. What more do I want? But I'm getting a noise in my ears from excitement. (Drinks) And it's impossible for me not to marry. In the first place, I'm already 35— a critical age, so to speak. In the second place, I ought to lead a quiet and regular life. I suffer from palpitations, I'm excitable and always getting awfully upset; at this very moment my lips are trembling, and there's a twitch in my right eyebrow.

[CBSE Sample 2023-24; U]

(i)   Which of the following is NOT a reason why Lomov thinks he must marry?

    (a) He is already 35 years old.

    (b) He suffers from palpitations.

    (c) He is excitable and easily upset.

    (d) He is in love with Natalya.

(ii)   Why is it fair to say that Lomov's tone, when he says "What more do I want?", is uncertain and questioning? Answer in about 40 words.

(iii) Read the following descriptions (a)-(c) and identify which one correctly corresponds to the extract.

    (a) A debate is a formal discussion on a particular topic, usually with two or more people presenting different viewpoints and arguments.

    (b) A soliloquy is a speech given by a character alone on stage, which reveals their innermost thoughts and feelings to the audience.

    (c) An aside is a brief comment or remark made by a character directly to the audience, which is not intended to be heard by other characters on stage.

iv   If an actor were to enact this extract, what would he be required to focus on, while modulating his voice?

2.   Lomov : But you can see from the documents, honoured Natalya Stepanovna. Oxen Meadows, its true were once the subject of dispute, but now everybody knows they are mine. There's nothing to argue about. You see my aunts grandmother gave the free use of these Meadows in perpetuity to the peasants of your father's grandfather, in return for which they were to make bricks for her. The peasants belonging to your father's grandfather had the free use of Meadows for forty years, and had got into the habit of regarding them as their own, when it happened that ....

Natalya : No, it isn't at all like that! Both grandfather and great grandfather reckoned that their land extended to Burnt Marsh – which means Oxen Meadows were ours. I don't see what there is to argue about, its simply silly.

(i) The subject of dispute was regarding

[Delhi, 2023; U]

(a) free use of Meadows.

(b) making of bricks.

(c) peasants using Meadows.

(d) ownership of Meadows.

(ii) Find the word from the extract which means 'continuance': **[Delhi, 2023; U]**

(a) dispute (b) perpetuity

(c) belonging (d) reckoned

(iii) Lomov's aunt's grandmother gave Oxen Meadows to Natalya's father's grandfather in lieu of ....

[Delhi, 2023; U]

(iv) According to Natalya why did Oxen Meadows belong to them? **[Delhi, 2023; U]**

(v) Fill in the blank with ONE WORD only:

The peasants had free use of Meadows for .... years. **[Delhi, 2023; U]**

3. Read the extract given below and answer the questions that follow :

"But, please, Stephen Stepanovitch, how can they be yours? Do be a reasonable man !

My aunt's grandmother gave the Meadows for the temporary and free use of your grandfather's peasants. The peasants used the land for forty years and got accustomed to it as if it was their own, when it happened that ....

(a) Who is the speaker of the above lines?

[All India 2018; U]

(b) Why did his aunt's grandmother give the meadows?

[All India 2018; U]

(c) Why did the peasants treat the land as their own?

[All India 2018; U]

(d) What light do these lines throw on the speaker's character? **[All India 2018; U]**

4. "Why, you're in evening dress ! Well, I never ! Are you going to a ball or what? Though I must say you look better ...."

(a) Who is speaking and to whom?

[All India 2017; U]

(b) Why is the person spoken to in an evening dress?

[All India 2017; U]

(c) What does the word, 'ball' mean here?

[All India 2017; U]

5. "Please don't shout ! You can shout yourself hoarse in your own house but here I must ask you to restrain yourself !" **[Delhi 2017; U]**

(a) Who is speaking and to whom?

(b) What is the dispute over?

(c) What does the word, 'restrain' mean?

6. These meadows aren't worth much to me. They only come to five dessiatins, and are worth perhaps 300 roubles, but I can't stand unfairness. Say what you will, I can't stand unfairness.

(a) Who speaks the above lines and to whom?

[Delhi 2016; U]

(b) How much are the meadows worth?

[Delhi 2016; U]

(c) Find a word in the extract that means 'not based on what is just.' **[Delhi 2016; U]**

7. I'm off my balance with joy, absolutely off my balance ! Oh, with all my soul ... I'll go and call Natasha, and all that.

(a) Who is the speaker? **[All India 2014; U]**

(b) Why is he so very happy? **[All India 2014; U]**

(c) Why is he going to call Natasha?

[All India 2014; U]

8. **[Delhi 2014; U]**

Don't excite yourself, my precious one. Allow me. Your Guess certainly has his good points. He's purebred, firm on his feet, has well-sprung ribs, and all that. But, my dear man, if you want to know the truth, that dog has two defects; he's old and he's short in the muzzle.

(a) Who is the speaker here? Who is the speaking to?

[Delhi 2014; U]

(b) According to the speaker what is the truth about Guess? **[Delhi 2014; U]**

(c) What is the adjectival form of 'truth'?

[Delhi 2014; U]

9. **[All India 2013; U]**

Chubukov : [*aside*] He's come to borrow money. Shan't give him any!

[*aloud*] What is it, my beauty?

Lomov : You see, Honoured Stepanitch _______ I beg pardon Stepan Honouritch _____ I mean, I'm awfully excited, as you will please notice _____. In short, you alone can help me, though I don't deserve it, of course ____ and haven't any right to count on your assistance ______.

(i) Why does Chubukov suspect Lomov of coming to borrow money? **[All India 2013; U]**

(ii) Why is Lomov not able to answer properly?

[All India 2013; U]

(iii) What purpose has he come for?

[All India 2013; U]

(iv) Which word in the passage means the same as 'very much'? **[All India 2013; U]**

2   *Short Answer Type Questions*

1. How can we say that Natalya was continuously successful in maintaining an upper hand during her arguments with Lomov? (Any one example)

2. Why did Chubukov misunderstand the purpose of Lomov's visit ? (The Proposal)

   [All India 2022, T-II; U]

3. Which two issues about himself convinced Lomov of his decision to get married?

4. Why does Chubukov suspect Lomov when he comes to his house?   **[All India 2016; U]**

3   *Long Answer Type Questions*

1. Farce is a kind of comedy which includes situations and dialogues that are ridiculous, exaggerated and even absurd. Evaluate the play, The Proposal, as a farce.

2. Neighbours must have a cordial relationship which Lomov and Natalya do not have. Describe the first fight between them.   **[All India 2016; U]**

3. Chekov has used humour and exaggeration in the play to comment on courtship in his times. Illustrate with examples from the lesson, 'The Proposal.' Also mention the values, you think, any healthy relationship requires.

   [All India 2015; U]

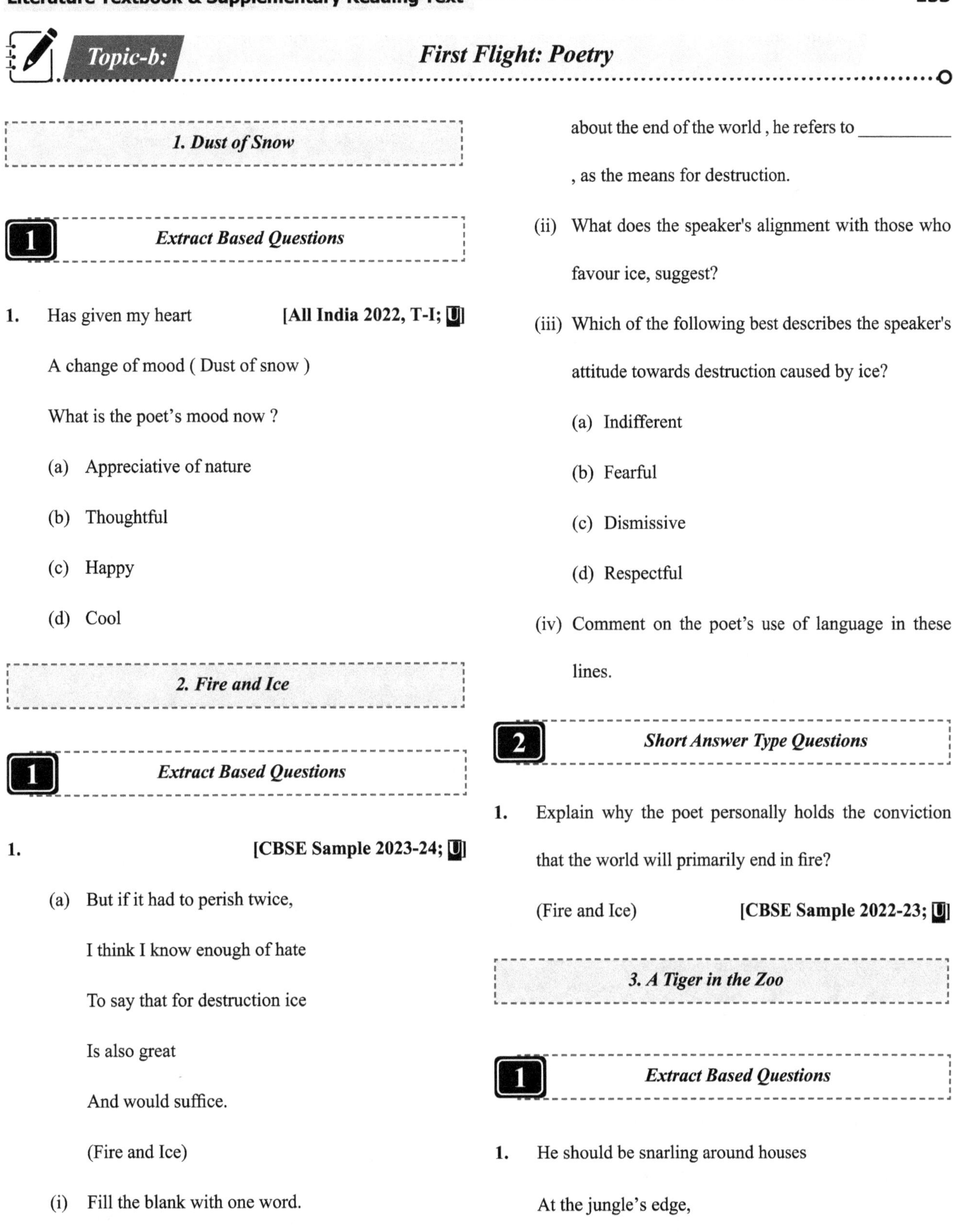

Topic-b: *First Flight: Poetry*

---

1. Dust of Snow

1   *Extract Based Questions*

1. Has given my heart   [All India 2022, T-I; **U**]

A change of mood (Dust of snow)

What is the poet's mood now ?

(a) Appreciative of nature

(b) Thoughtful

(c) Happy

(d) Cool

---

2. Fire and Ice

1   *Extract Based Questions*

1.   [CBSE Sample 2023-24; **U**]

(a) But if it had to perish twice,

I think I know enough of hate

To say that for destruction ice

Is also great

And would suffice.

(Fire and Ice)

(i) Fill the blank with one word.

When the speaker says that ice could also bring about the end of the world , he refers to ___________

, as the means for destruction.

(ii) What does the speaker's alignment with those who favour ice, suggest?

(iii) Which of the following best describes the speaker's attitude towards destruction caused by ice?

(a) Indifferent

(b) Fearful

(c) Dismissive

(d) Respectful

(iv) Comment on the poet's use of language in these lines.

2   *Short Answer Type Questions*

1. Explain why the poet personally holds the conviction that the world will primarily end in fire?

(Fire and Ice)   [CBSE Sample 2022-23; **U**]

---

3. A Tiger in the Zoo

1   *Extract Based Questions*

1. He should be snarling around houses

At the jungle's edge,

Baring his white fangs, his claws,

Terrorizing the village !

But he's locked in a concrete cell,

His strength behind bars,

Stalking the length of his cage,

Ignoring visitors.

(i) Study the following statements :

[All India 2022, T-I; U]

(A) The villagers don't feel happy that the tiger is caged.

(B) We feel sad that the tiger is caged.

(C) The tiger is happy that he doesn't have to hunt for his food.

(a) (A) is right and (B) is wrong

(b) (B) is right and (A) is wrong

(c) (C) is right and (A) is wrong

(d) (A) is wrong and (C) is right

(ii). We should protect the tigers as :

[All India 2022, T-I; U]

(a) they are majestic to look at.

(b) they attract visitors to the zoo.

(c) they are ferocious.

(d) they are part of our environment.

(iii) The tiger terrorizes the villagers as;

[All India 2022, T-I; U]

(a) by killing their cattle

(b) as he does not like to be hunted

(c) as they have cleared his habitat.

(d) as he has got tired of being in the forest.

(iv) 'A tiger in the zoo ignoring visitors' is an example of **[All India 2022, T-I; U]**

(a) Metaphor

(b) Simile

(c) Irony

(d) Personification

(v) The tiger is reacting to his imprisonment in the zoo by : **[All India 2022, T-I; U]**

(a) quietly walking in the cage

(b) showing his anger openly

(c) stalking in the cage

(d) ignoring visitors

2. He hears the last voice at night. **[All India, 2023; U]**

The patrolling cars,

And stares with his brilliant eyes

At the brilliant stars.

He stalks in his vivid stripes

A few steps of his cage.

(i) Whose is the last voice heard by the tiger?

[All India, 2023; U]

    (a) police jeep

    (b) patrolling cars

    (c) watchmen

    (d) roar of lion

(ii) Complete the sentence appropriately.

[All India, 2023; U]

It is clear that 'Repetition' is the poetic device used for 'his brilliant eyes at the brilliant stars' because __________.(Clue: explain how repetition applies here)

(iii) The main contrasting ideas in this extract are

[All India, 2023; U]

    (a) tiger and deer

    (b) cruelty and sympathy

    (c) confinement and freedom.

    (d) master and slave.

(iv) The use of the word 'stalks' creates an image of

[All India, 2023; U]

    (a) cowardice

    (b) frustration

    (c) lethargy

    (d) purposefulness.

(v) State whether the following statement is True or False: **[All India, 2023; U]**

The poem uses 'staring at the sky' to symbolize the freedom 'he' yearns for.

3. He stalks in his vivid stripes

The few steps of his cage,

On pads of velvet quiet,

In his quiet rage.

He should be lurking in shadow,

Sliding through long grass

Near the water hole

Where plump deer pass.

(i) 'Quiet rage' refers to the tigers ......

[Delhi, 2023; U]

    (a) helplessness

    (b) he has not been able to hunt

    (c) his prey has not come to the water hole

    (d) he is not free

(ii) He is lurking in shadows because ....

[Delhi, 2023; U]

(iii) Complete the sentence appropriately:

It is clear that metaphor is the poetic device used for 'pads of velvet' because .... (clue–explain how metaphor applies here).

[Delhi, 2023; U]

(iv) Find a word from the extract which means – to walk with measured, stiff or haughty strides:

[Delhi, 2023; U]

(a) steps

(b) lurking

(c) pads

(d) stalk

(v) State whether the following statement is TRUE or FALSE: **[Delhi, 2023; U]**

The tiger is stealthily waiting for the deer to come to the water hole.

2   *Short Answer Type Questions*

1. How does Leslie Norris use vivid imagery and metaphorical language in A Tiger in the Zoo, to effectively depict the confinement and oppression, experienced by the captive tiger. **[CBSE Sample 2023-24; U]**

3   *Long Answer Type Questions*

1. Mijbil and the Tiger, both were looked after by humans. Assume they both meet each other in the zoo and have a conversation about their lifestyle and feelings.

Write this conversation as per your understanding of Mijbil the Otter and A Tiger in the Zoo.

You may begin like this

Tiger: Thanks for visiting me, though I don't usually like visitors.

Mijbil: Oh? I would love visitors, I think.

[CBSE Sample 2022-23; U]

---

4. How to Tell Wild Animals

1   *Extract Based Questions*

1. **[All India, 2023; ]**

Or if some time when roaming round,

A noble wild beast greets you,

With black stripes on a yellow ground,

Just notice if he eats you.

This simple rule may help you learn

The Bengal Tiger to discern.

(i) Who is the 'noble wild beast' in the above lines?

[All India, 2023; U]

(a) Zebra

(b) Asian Tiger

(c) Asian Lion

(d) Bengal Tiger

(ii) Complete the sentence appropriately.

It is clear that 'Alliteration' is the poetic device used for 'roaming round' because _______. (Clue : explain how alliteration applies here)

[All India, 2023; U]

(iii) State whether the following statement is True or False: **[All India, 2023; U]**

The extract helps to identify a Royal Bengal Tiger.

(iv) In the given lines, what effect does the poet create?

[**All India, 2023;** ]

'Just notice if he eats you.

This simple rule may help you learn

The Bengal Tiger to discern.'

(a) irony

(b) terror

(c) sympathy

(d) criticism

(v) Which word in the extract tells you that you have recognised the 'noble beast'?

[**All India, 2023;** ]

(a) rule

(b) discern

(c) roaming

(d) notice

1. The loss of a possession should make one feel :

[**All India 2022, T-I;** ]

(a) angry

(b) responsible

(c) sad

(d) careless

2   *Short Answer Type Questions*

1. Why does the poet not offer the boy money to buy another ball?   [**Delhi 2020;** U**, All Inid 2020;** U]

2. 'He senses first responsibility' – What responsibility is referred to here?   [**All India 2018;** U]

3   *Long Answer Type Questions*

1   "Not from weeping nor from grieving will anyone obtain peace of mind'.   [**CBSE Sample 2022-23;** U]

If you had to use the message of the given quote from the Buddha's sermon (The Sermon at Benares) to help the boy cope with the loss of his ball and what it signifies (The Ball Poem), what would you include in your advice?

[**CBSE Sample 2022-23;** U]

6. Amanda!

1   *Extract Based Questions*

1. Don't eat that chocolate Amanda!

Remember your acne, Amanda!

Will you please look at me when I'm speaking to you

Amanda!

(I am Rapunzel, I have not a care; life in tower is tranquil

and rare, I'll certainly never let down my bright hair)

(i) The Speaker's tone is   [Delhi, 2023; [U]]

    (a) loving

    (b) hopeful

    (c) instructive

    (d) indifferent

(ii) Complete the analogy with a word from the extract:

[Delhi, 2023; [U]]

rare : uncommon :: peace : ....

(iii) State whether the following statement is TRUE or FALSE: [Delhi, 2023; [U]]

Amanda did not want anyone to invade her privacy and silence.

(iv) Select the appropriate option :   [Delhi, 2023; [U]]

Amanda's mother is continuously ....Amanda.

    (a) encouraging

    (b) reprimanding

    (c) motivating

    (d) disappointing

(v) Which word in the extract is opposite in meaning to the word 'dull'?   [Delhi, 2023; [U]]

    (a) dreary

    (b) shady

    (c) bright

    (d) angry

2. (There is a languid, emerald sea,

where, the sole inhabitant is me-a

mermaid drifting blissfully.)

    (a) Who does 'me' stand for?   [All India 2019; [U]]

    (b) How does 'me' feel?   [All India 2019; [U]]

    (c) Who is 'me' compared to?   [All India 2019; [U]]

    (d) Which word in the extract means opposite of 'sorrowfully'?   [All India 2019; [U]]

2   *Short Answer Type Questions*

1. What impression do you form about Amanda in the poem?   [All India, 2023; [U]]

2. Comment on the tone of the speaker when she says 'Will you please look at me when I'm speaking to you, Amanda!'.   **2**

3. As a reader do you identify with Amanda ? How ?

[All India 2022, T-II; [U]]

3   *Long Answer Type Questions*

1. You have been asked to present an evaluation of the approaches of the mothers of both, the baby seagull and Amanda, towards helping their children. Write this presentation draft including your insights, in about 120 words, comparing the approaches of both parents.

You may begin this way:

One acknowledges that both parents, Amanda's mother and the baby seagull's mother both....however, ...

(Reference -Amanda! & His First Flight)

7. The Trees

Extract Based Questions

1 The trees inside are moving out into the forest,

[CBSE Sample 2022-23; U]

the forest that was empty all these days

where no bird could sit no insect hide

no sun bury its feet in shadow the forest that was empty

all these nights

will be full of trees by morning.

(i) Complete the sentence appropriately.

It is clear that Personification is the poetic device used for 'No sun bury its feet....' because_______________. (Clue: explain how personification applies here)

(ii) The poet has used a poetic device in the given lines. What effect does she wish to create by its use?

…no bird could sit no insect hide

[CBSE Sample 2022-23; U]

no sun…

(a) emphasis

(b) comparison

(c) rhyme

(d) humour

(iii) State whether the following statement is TRUE or FALSE: [CBSE Sample 2022-23; U]

The extract uses trees as a symbol for conservative people.

(iv) Select the appropriate option to complete the sentence, according to the extract. The idea of a forest that has been 'empty all these days' is

. [CBSE Sample 2022-2; U]

(a) unnatural

(b) scary

(c) magical

(d) legendary

(v) How does the use of enjambment impact this extract? [CBSE Sample 2022-23; U]

(a) It forces frequent pauses.

(b) It simplifies the meaning.

(c) It builds momentum.

(d) It makes the lines lyrical.

2. The trees inside are moving out into the forest,

[All India 2020; U]

the forest that was empty all these days

where no bird could sit

no insect hide

no sun bury its feet in shadow

the forest that was empty all these nights

will be full of trees by morning.

(a)   What are the trees trying to do?

[All India 2020; U]

(b)   Why was the forest empty?   **[All India 2020 U]**

(c)   All these days, the forest referred to here was

___________ .   **[All India 2020; U]**

    (i)   filled

    (ii)   empty

    (iii) hidden

    (iv) separated

(d)   The figure of speech used in these lines is __________

.   **[All India 2020; U]**

    (i)   Simile

    (ii)   Alliteration

    (iii) Personification

    (iv) Metonymy

2   *Short Answer Type Questions*

1.   In the poem 'Trees', where are the trees? What are their roots, twigs, etc trying to do?

[All India 2017; U]

3   *Long Answer Type Questions*

1.   You have been chosen to address a student gathering from the neighbourhood schools, to speak on the resilience of human spirit required to transcend discrimination.

Prepare the speech draft in not more than 120 words, with reference to the commonality of themes in Nelson Mandela: Long Walk to Freedom and The Trees by Adrienne Rich.

You may begin this way:

Good morning, everyone. Today, I'd like to discuss two pieces of literature that offer a powerful insight into the resilience of the human spirit required to transcend discrimination.

You may end this way.

To conclude, I'd like to say that ...

Thank you

8. Fog

1   *Extract Based Questions*

1.   **[CBSE Sample 2023-24; U]**

(i)   The fog comes

on little cat feet.

It sits looking

over harbour and city

on silent haunches

and then moves on.

(i)   In what way does the language used in this poem challenge traditional ideas of what poetry should be?

(ii) What is the significance of the use of the word "little" to describe the fog in the poem and how does this word choice contribute to the overall mood and tone of the poem? Answer in about 40 words.

(iii) Complete the sentence with the appropriate option. The lines from the poem tell us that the city is ______.

(a) hilly

(b) coastal

(c) industrial

(d) under-developed

(iv) Identify the type of imagery used in the lines of the poem.

---

9. The Tale of Custard the Dragon

 **1**   *Extract Based Questions*

1. Now the name of the little black kitten was Ink,

[Delhi 2019; U]

And the little gray mouse, she called him Blink,

And the little yellow dog was sharp as Mustard,

But the dragon was a coward, and she called him Custard.

[Delhi 2019; U]

(a) Name the poem and its poet.

(b) What is the colour of Belinda's dog ?

(c) What were the kitten and the mouse called?

(d) Which word in the stanza is the antonym of 'dull'?

2. Belinda tickled him, she ticked him unmerciful,

Ink, Blink and Mustard, they rudely called him Percival,

They all sat laughing in the little red wagon

At the realio, trulio, cowardly dragon.

(a) Who was tickled by Belinda?

[All India 2018; U]

(b) Why did she tickle 'him'?

[All India 2018; U]

(c) Who are Ink, Blink and Mustard?

[All India 2018; U]

(d) Why did they all laugh at 'him'?

[All India 2018; U]

3. Belinda tickled him, she tickled him unmerciful,

Ink, Blink and Mustard, they rudely called him Percival,

They all sat laughing in the little red wagon

At the realio, trulio, cowardly dragon.

(a) Who is Belinda?   **[All India 2014; U]**

(b) How did Belinda and the other pets laugh at the dragon?   **[All India 2014; U]**

(c) Which word in this extract means the same as 'unkind'?   **[All India 2014; U]**

4. Belinda embraced him, Mustard licked him,

No one mourned for his pirate victim.

Ink and Blink in glee did gyrate

Around the dragon that ate the pirate.

(a) Why did Belinda embrace him?

[All India 2013; U]

(i) out of helplessness

(ii) out of gratitude

(iii) out of fear

(iv) out of shock

(b) Why were Ink and Blink happy?

[All India 2013; U]

(i) joy of their victory

(ii) because of the fear of the pirate

(iii) because the pirate was killed

(iv) they were in a good mood

(c) Find a word which means the same as 'move around in circles.'   [All India 2013; U]

(i) mourn

(ii) gyrate

(iii) lick

(iv) embrace

1. How does Ogden Nash's The Tale of Custard the Dragon , challenge the notion that individuals should conform to societal expectations?

[CBSE Sample 2023-24; U]

2. What character trait is revealed of Custard when he accepts that the other animals are braver than him.(The tale of Custard the Dragon)   [Delhi, 2023; U]

3. Give one reason why 'The Tale of Custard the Dragon' is more a fable than a ballad.

[CBSE Sample 2022-23; U]

4. A ballad includes the telling of a tale as well as a surprise ending. Using evidence from the poem, explain how these features are included in 'The Tale of Custard the Dragon'.   2

10. For Anne Gregory

1   *Extract Based Questions*

1. But I can get a hair-dye   [CBSE Sample 2022-23; U]

And set such colour there,

Brown, or black, or carrot,

That young men in despair

May love me for myself alone

And not my yellow hair."

(For Anne Gregory)

(i) What is the poet's tone in the extract?

[CBSE Sample 2022-23; U]

1. thoughtful

2. authoritative

3. agitated

4. insulting

5. argumentative

Select the appropriate option.

(a) 1, 4

(b) 3, 5

(c) 2, 4

(d) 1, 5

(ii) What causes the young men to 'despair', according to the extract?   **[CBSE Sample 2022-23; U]**

(iii) Identify the reason for the speaker's need to colour her hair, as per the extract.

[CBSE Sample 2022-23; U]

(a) Her control over what makes her look beautiful.

(b) Her desire to be loved for inner beauty

(c) Her need to change people's perception about beauty

(d) Her conviction that she is beautiful inside

(iv) Complete the analogy about the speaker's hair.

yellow: blonde :: : carrot

[CBSE Sample 2022-23; U]

(v) Select the sentence in which the word 'set' is used in the similar manner as line 2 of the extract.

[CBSE Sample 2022-23; U]

(a) I want to set him up and get my work done this time.

(b) Do you have another set of the books that I can read?

(c) The dessert needs to set for two hours before being served.

(d) The set for the school play looked quite grand.

2. Read the extract given below and answer the questions that follow :

''Never shall a young man,

Thrown into despair

By those great honey-coloured

Ramparts at your ear,

Love you for yourself alone

And not your yellow hair.''

(a) Whom are these lines addressed to?

[All India 2017; U]

(b) What would throw a young man into despair?

[All India 2017; U]

(c) What does the word, 'ramparts' here mean?

[All India 2017; U]

3.   **[Delhi 2017; U]**

"But I can get a hair-dye

And set such colour there,

Brown, or black, or carrot,

That young men in despair

May love me for myself alone

And not my yellow hair."

(a)   Who is speaking these lines?

(b)   Why are young men in despair?

(c)   What is the antonym of the word, 'despair'?

4.   Read the extract given below and answer the questions
     that follow :

"I heard an old religious man

but yesternight declare

That he had found a text to prove

That only God, my dear,

Could love you for yourself alone

And not your yellow hair."

(a)   What does 'I' refer to here?   [Delhi 2014; ]

(b)   How is God's love different from the love of the
     young lovers?   [Delhi 2014; U]

(c)   Which word in the extract means 'a religious book'?

          [Delhi 2014; U]

3   *Long Answer Type Questions*

1.   The poet in the poem, ' For Anne Gregory' conveys that
     we should give importance to the inner beauty and not to
     the physical appearance. Elaborate with reference to the
     poem.   [All India 2019; U]

Topic-c: *Footprints Without Feet*

---

1. A Triumph of Surgery

1 **Extract Based Questions**

1. For Tricky's present condition :

   [All India 2022, T-I; U]

   A.   Both Mrs. Pumphrey and Tricky are to blame.

   B.   Only Tricky is to blame.

   (a)   (A) is right and (A) is wrong.

   (b)   (B) is right and (A) wrong.

   (c)   Both (A) and (B) are right.

   (d)   Both (A) and (B) are wrong.

2 **Short Answer Type Questions**

1. The story, A Triumph of Surgery is a powerful example of the importance of saying "no". Explain.

   [CBSE Sample 2023-24; U]

2. Why was Mr. Herriot shocked at Tricki's appearance?

   [All India, 2023; U]

3. How did Mrs. Pumphery treat Tricki?

   [Delhi, 2023; U]

4. Dr. Herriot knew his patients as well as their owners really well. Discuss.

   [CBSE Sample 2022-23; U]

5. Why is Mrs. Pumphrcy responsible for Tricki's condition?   **[Delhi 2020; U]**

2. The Thief's Story

1 **Extract Based Questions**

1. It was quite pleasant working for Anil as

   [All India 2022, T-I; U]

   (a)   he was quite rich.

   (b)   he never complained.

   (c)   he was a very simple person.

   (d)   he could be easily fooled.

2 **Short Answer Type Questions**

1. How did Hari Singh justify to himself his stealing Anil's money?   **[All India, 2023; U]**

2. In which queer way did Anil make a living?

   [All India 2020; U]

3. What made Hari Singh come back to Anil?

   [Delhi 2020; U]

4. Why does Anil not hand Hari Singh over to the police?

   [Delhi 2019; U]

5. In which queer way did Anil make a living?

   [All India 2018; U]

3   *Long Answer Type Questions*

1. A character arc is the transformation or development of a character throughout a story and refers to the changes a character undergoes as a result of their experiences, challenges, and interactions with other characters.

In the light of the above information, trace the character arc of the thief in Ruskin Bond's The Thief's Story, in about 120 words.   **[CBSE Sample 2023-24; U]**

2. Trust and compassion can reform a person. Justify this statement in the light of the lesson "The Thief's Story'.

    [Delhi, 2023; U]

3. Fiction writers prefer creating grey characters rather than black and white. Analyse this in detail, with reference to both the characters of The Thief's Story

    [CBSE Sample 2022-23; U]

4. Education, love and sympathy can transform even a thief. How is it true in the case of Hari Singh?

    [All India 2020; U]

3. The Midnight Visitor

1   *Extract Based Questions*

1. And as the light came on, Fowler had his first authentic thrill of the day. For halfway across the room, a small automatic pistol in his hand, stood a man.

    [Delhi 2020; U]

Ausable blinked a few times.

(a) Who was standing in the room with a pistol in his hand?   **[Delhi 2020; U]**

    (i) Ausable

    (ii) Fowler

    (iii) Max

    (iv) A waiter

(b) Ausable blinked because he: **[Delhi 2020; U]**

    (i) was Setting adjusted to the light.

    (ii) got afraid of the man with a pistol.

    (iii) was thrilled to have reached his room.

    (iv) Started thinking of how to get rid of the man.

(c) Fowler was thrilled because what he saw looked like a ....   **[Delhi 2020; U]**

(d) Which word in the extract means the same as 'genuine/real'?   **[Delhi 2020; U]**

2. Ausable was, for one thing, fat. Very fat. And then there was his accent. Though he spoke French and German passably, he had never altogether lost the American accent he had brought to Paris from Boston twenty years ago.

"You are disappointed," Ausable said wheezily over his shoulder.

(a) Who is 'you' here?   **[All India 2020; U]**

    (i) Fowler   (ii) Ausable

    (iii) Waiter   (iv) Max

(b)   Ausable was a native of __________ .

[**All India 2020; U**]

(i)   France

(ii) Germany

(iii) the U.S.

(iv) Sweden

(c)   'You' believed that Ausable was a __________ .

[**All India 2020; U**]

(d)   He spoke French like an __________ .

[**All India 2020; U**]

2   *Short Answer Type Questions*

1.   The various elements of Robert Arthur's writing style work together to create a sense of tension, uncertainty, and suspense, well-suited to the mystery and suspense genre of the story, The Midnight Visitor. Comment, with reference to any one element.

[**CBSE Sample 2023-24; U**]

2.   How did Ausable get rid of Max without using a weapon.

[**Delhi, 2023; U**]

3.   State one likely reason the writer of The Midnight Visitor chose to characterise Ausable as short and fat

[**CBSE Sample 2022-23; U**]

4.   How is Ausable different from other secret agents

[**All India, 2020; U**]

---

4. A Question of Trust

2   *Short Answer Type Questions*

1.   How can you say that Horace Danby was good and respectable but not completely honest?

[**All India 2019; U**]

2.   What was Horace Danby's hobby? How did he manage to fulfill it?   [**All India 2018; U**]

3   *Long Answer Type Questions*

1.   'Honour among thieves' is considered a popular code.

Examine A Question of Trust as a story woven around this code.   [**CBSE Sample 2022-23; U**]

5. Footprints without Feet

1   *Extract Based Questions*

1.   He escaped easily enough from the boys who followed his footprints in London. But his adventures were by no means over. He had chosen a bad time of the year to wander about London without clothes. It was mid - winter. The air was bitterly cold and he could not do without clothes. Instead of walking about the streets, he decided to slip into a big London store for warmth.

(i)   The greatest problem for the invisible man was that :

[All India 2022, T-I; U]

   (a)   being invisible he could do nothing.

   (b)   he could not buy clothes to wear.

   (c)   he was hungry but could not buy food.

   (d)   without clothes he was feeling cold.

(ii) He could escape from the boys as

[All India 2022, T-I; U]

   (a)   the boys were careless.

   (b)   the boys too felt cold in the winter night.

   (c)   the invisible man was cleverer than the boys.

   (d)   he went along a street where there was no mud.

(iii) (A)   It was stupid on his part to come out on a winter night.   **[All India 2022, T-I; U]**

   (B)   He was not completely stupid, though,

   (a)   (A) is right and (B) is wrong.

   (b)   (B) is right and (A) is wrong.

   (c)   Both (A) and (B) are right.

   (d)   Both (A) and (B) are wrong.

(iv) After getting rid of the boys the invisible man felt :

[All India 2022, T-I; U]

   (a) relieved   (b) partly relieved

   (c) anguished   (d) comfortable

(v) The phrase 'slip into' means the same as :

[All India 2022, T-I; U]

   (a) fall into

   (b) enter quietly

   (c) enter boldly

   (d) move out

(vi) Griffin became a homeless wanderer because he :

[All India 2022, T-I; U]

   (a)   was an eccentric scientist.

   (b)   was very greedy.

   (c)   had to go without clothes.

   (d)   had set fire to his landlord's house.

2. His landlord disliked him and tried to eject him. In revenge, Griffin set fire to the house. To get away without being seen he had to remove his clothes. Thus it was that he became a homeless wanderer, without clothes, without money and quite invisible - until he happened to step in some mud, and left footprints as he walked!

(i)   Griffin's landlord tried to eject him because

[All India, 2023; U]

   (a)   he was a lawless person.

   (b)   he had set his house on fire.

   (c)   he didn't like him.

   (d)   he was a drug addict.

(ii) Fill in the blank with one word only.

Griffin deliberately removed his clothes because he wanted to become ______.   [All India, 2023; U]

(iii) Select the option that correctly captures the application of the word 'fire' as used in this extract.

[All India, 2023; U]

(a) Griffin said that he would fire the manager.

(b) The soldiers opened fire at the enemy

(c) His remarks provoked heavy fire from the political opponents.

(d) The Amar palace was completely destroyed by the fire.

(iv) Griffin's presence was felt when

[All India, 2023; U]

(a) he jumped into the water with a splash.

(b) he wore clothes

(c) he left muddy footprints

(d) he stepped in mud

(v) Which of the following is not true with reference to the given extract?   [All India, 2023; U]

(a) Griffin had become penniless.

(b) Griffin promised to behave himself.

(c) Griffin revealed himself by his muddy footprints.

(d) No one could see Griffin when he took off his clothes.

---

3 *Long Answer Type Questions*

1. A brilliant scientist though he was, Griffin misused his scientific discovery. Illustrate this point by giving any two examples from the story.   [All India 2020; U]

2. How did Griffin's invisibility come to his help whenever found himself in trouble?   [Delhi 2020; U]

---

6. The Making of a Scientist

---

1 *Extract Based Questions*

1. The question he tried to answer was simple: What is the purpose of the twelve tiny gold spots on a monarch pupa?   [CBSE Sample 2023-24; U]

"Everyone assumed the spots were just ornamental," Ebright said.

"But Dr Urquhart didn't believe it."

To find the answer, Ebright and another excellent science student first had to build a device that showed that the spots were producing a hormone necessary for the butterfly's full development. This project won Ebright first place in the county fair and entry into the International Science and Engineering Fair. There he won third place for zoology. He also got a chance to work during the summer at the entomology laboratory of the Walter Reed Army Institute of Research.

(i) State any one inference about Dr Urquhart from the given context:

Everyone assumed the spots were just ornamental," Ebright said.

"But Dr Urquhart didn't believe it."

(ii) State TRUE or FALSE.

None of the terms (a) -(d) below, can be applied to the question - What is the purpose of the twelve tiny gold spots on a monarch pupa?

(a) A hypothesis - a proposed explanation for a phenomenon

(b) An assumption - something that is taken for granted or assumed to be true without proof

(c) A premise - a proposition that forms the basis of an argument

(d) A theory - a well-substantiated explanation for a natural phenomenon

(iii) Ebright's approach towards finding the purpose of the gold spots on a monarch pupa was highly effective. Elaborate in about 40 words, with reference to the extract.

(iv) Which phrase would correctly substitute 'a chance', in the given sentence from the extract.

He also got a chance to work during the summer at the entomology laboratory of the Walter Reed Army Institute of Research.

---

2   *Short Answer Type Questions*

1. How did Ebright's mother help him to become a scientist?

[All India, 2023; U]

2. Why did Richard Ebright raise a flock of butterflies?

[Delhi, 2023; U]

3. Validate the importance of small, fun learning tasks towards successful careers, in the context of Richard Ebright in The Making of a Scientist.

[CBSE Sample 2022-23; U]

4. How did Ebright get the idea of his new theory about cell life ? **[All India 2022, T-II; U]**

5. How did Richard Ebright's mother help him?

[All India 2020; U]

6. How did Ebright's mother help him in becoming a scientist? **[Delhi 2019; U]**

7. Which book did Ebright's mother get for him? How did it change his life? **[All India 2017; U]**

8. How did Richard Ebright's mother help him?

[Delhi 2017; U]

9. Why did Richard Ebright raise a flock of butterflies?

[All India 2014; U]

10. How did Richard's mother help him to become a scientist?

[Delhi 2014; U]

11. What lesson did Ebright learn when he did not win anything at a science fair? **[All India 2013; U]**

3 *Long Answer Type Questions*

1. Parents play a crucial role in the upbringing of their children. Critically examine the parents of Bholi and Ebright, highlighting their impact on their children's lives.

---

7. The Necklace

---

2 *Short Answer Type Questions*

1. Why was Matilda unhappy in her early married life?

   [Delhi 2020; U]

2. How did M. Loisel try to make his wife happy?

   [All India 2017; U]

3. Why was Matilda always unhappy after her marriage?

   [Delhi 2017; U]

4. Why was Mme Loisel always unhappy?

   [All India 2016; U]

5. Why was Matilda in a hurry to go to her house after the ball?

   [All India 2015; U]

6. Do you think M. Loisel has an enjoyable evening at the ball? Give reasons for your answer.   **[Delhi 2015; U]**

7. Why did Matilda not want to see her rich friends?

   [Delhi 2016; K, U]

8. Why did Matilda change her lifestyle after the ball?

   [Delhi 2014; U]

3 *Long Answer Type Questions*

1. Imagine that M. Loisel, from The Necklace by Guy de Maupassant, writes a diary entry, exploring the theme of class and social status, and the nature of social mobility, in the context of his own experience.

   [CBSE Sample Paper, 2023-24; U]

   Write this diary entry , as M. Loisel, in about 120 words.

2. Mme Loisel's disposition invites her doom. Elucidate with reference to the text.   **[All India, 2023; U]**

3. Contentment in one's life is very important to lead a peaceful life. We should be happy with what we have and should not crave for what we don't have. Matilda suffered in life because she was not content in her life. Her desires led to her disaster. What do you learn from her mistake in life?   **[Delhi, 2023; U]**

4. As a reader do you sympathise with Matilda ? Give reasons from the text to support your answer. (The Necklace)   **[All India 2022, T-II; U]**

5. We should be happy with what we have and should not crave for what we don't have. Matida suffered in her life because she was not contented. Comment (100-150 words)

6. Mme Forestier proved to be a true friend of the Loisels. Elaborate.   **[Delhi 2019; U]**

8. Bholi

2   *Short Answer Type Questions*

1. How does education play a transformative role in Bholi's life? **[CBSE Sample 2023-24; U]**

2. Why did Bholi dislike Bishambar? **[All India 2020; U]**

3. Why was Sulekha nicknamed Bholi? **[All India 2016; U]**

4. What filled Bholi, a dumb cow, with a new hope? **[All India 2015; U]**

5. For what unusual reasons was Bholi sent to school? **[Delhi 2015; U]**

6. Give examples from the text to show that Bholi was a neglected child? **[Delhi 2014; U]**

3   *Long Answer Type Questions*

1. Bholi was believed to be a 'dumb cow'. What turned her into a fearless, bold and confident girl? **[All India, 2023; U]**

2. How did education change Bholi's personality? **[Delhi 2020; U]**

3. Bholi is a child different from others. This difference makes her an object of neglect and laughter. Elaborate. **[All India 2019; U]**

4. School education turned Bholi from a dumb cow into a bold girl. How did she save her father from a huge expense and become his support in his old age? **[All India 2017; U]**

5. Education is always a great asset in the life of a woman. How did Bholi, an educated girl, face the challenge posed by Bishambar's greed? **[Delhi 2017; U]**

6. "Don't you worry, Pitaji! In your old age I will serve you and mother". Through this statement the narrator wants to highlight the moral values Bholi was imbued with. Based on the reading of the lesson, what made Bholi aware of her rights and how did she use them? **[Delhi 2016; U]**

7. "Put the fear out of your heart and you will be able to speak like anyone else." These words of encouragement from the teacher highlight that change of social attitude and encouragement can help a child like Bholi to become confident and faced the world bravely. Taking help from the lesson, 'Bholi' write how the social attitude towards Bholi made her an introvert. What should be done to help such children to face the world bravely? **[Delhi 2015; U]**

8. What social attitudes are presented in the story, 'Bholi'? How does Bholi's teacher help her overcome these barriers? **[All India 2013; U]**

> ### *9. The Book that Saved the Earth*

> **1**   *Extract Based Questions*

1.B   OMEGA: It shall be done, Sir. Remove vitamins. (Crew takes vitamins from boxes on their belts.) Present vitamins. **[CBSE Sample 2022-23; U]** (They hold vitamins out in front of them, stiffly.) Swallow vitamins. (They pop the vitamins into their mouths and gulp simultaneously. They open their eyes wide, their heads shake, and they put their hands to their foreheads.)

THINK-TANK: Excellent. Now, decipher that code.

ALL: It shall be done, Sir. (They frown over the book, turning pages.) OMEGA: (brightly) Aha!

IOTA: (brightly) Oho!

OOP: (bursting into laughter) Ha, ha, ha.

THINK-TANK: What does it say? Tell me this instant. Transcribe, Omega.

(i) Select the option that correctly captures the usage of the word 'present' from line 1 of the extract.

           [CBSE Sample 2022-23; U]

  (a) Oops received a nice <u>present</u> from Think Tank.

  (b) Iota needs to <u>present</u> his opinion firmly.

  (c) Omega must focus on the <u>present</u> and leave the past behind.

  (d) Oops didn't know anyone even though a crowd was <u>present</u>.

(ii) Complete the analogy by selecting the suitable word from the text   **[CBSE Sample 2022-23; U]**

frown: smile:: gloomily: _______________

(iii) Select the option that displays the reason why all crew members were asked to have vitamins.

In order to -   **[CBSE Sample 2022-23; U]**

  (a) boost their physical energies.

  (b) adapt to their circumstances.

  (c) quickly turn all the pages.

  (d) accomplish a specific task.

(iv) According to the extract, what did THINK-TANK most likely want OMEGA to do when he said 'Transcribe…'?   **[CBSE Sample 2022-23; U]**

  1. read aloud

  2. translate

  3. make notes

  4. interpret

  5. record reactions Select the correct option.

  (a) 1 & 3

  (b) 2 & 4

  (c) Only 3

  (d) 1, 4 and 5

(v) The playwright places certain words and sentences in brackets in the given extract. List any ways these benefit both the director and actors.

[CBSE Sample 2022-23; U]

(i) ___________________

(ii) ___________________

2 *Short Answer Type Questions*

1. What difficulty do the crew of the space probe face on the Earth? [All India 2019; U]

2. What does Noodle tell Think-Tank about the books? [Delhi 2016; U]

3. How did the book change Think-Tank's opinion about the Earthlings? [All India 2014; U]

4. What guesses are made by Think-Tank about the books found on earth? [All India 2013; U]

3 *Long Answer Type Questions*

1. It is morally incorrect to invade another country/planet for one's own benefit. The Martians did not understand the value of peaceful coexistence. How did the book of nursery rhymes save the Earth from the Martian invasion? [All India 2016; U]

Solutions

Topic-a: *First Flight: Prose*

---

1. A Letter to God

1. **(i)** **(b) A, B and C**

Lencho wrote, the second letter because he was 'unhappy' that the God did not give the full amount. He was curious to receive the response and hopeful for getting it.

(ii) **(b) A and B**

The postmaster thought that Lencho was happy from the help of postmaster and his staff and write. The letter to thank his God. So the Postmaster expected these things so option (A) and (B) are correct.

(iii) **(b) dismayed**

On reading the letter the postmaster was disappointed because Lencho was not happy with the given help of Postmaster and his staff.

(iv) **(d) Ironic**

The statement was ironic because employees are very helpful and loyal, they were not brunch of crooks.

Note

Irony is an unusual or unexpected part of a situation etc. that seems strange or amusing.

(v) **(d) asked**

Sanctioned is the synonym of approved and here asked is the synonym of demanded.

2   *Short Answer Type Questions*

1. The description of the devastation caused by the hailstorm reflects the sadness within Lencho. The fact that "not a leaf remained on the trees" and "the flowers were gone from the plants" suggests a sense of emptiness and loss, which mirrors Lencho's feelings of despair and disappointment. **(2 Marks)**

2. Lencho was hoping for a good rain as it was much needed for a good harvest. Lencho's only hope was the help of god. He believed that god sees everything. God can see deep into ones conscience. **(2 Marks)**

3. The night after the rains turned sorrowful for Lencho because the hailstorm had destroyed his entire field of ripe corn, leaving nothing behind. This meant that his family would go hungry that year, as they had no other source of income. Lencho's only hope was the help of God, which he expressed in a letter to Him.

(2 Marks)

4. Lencho's crop was almost ready; it needed just a little shower. At that time it began to rain. Lencho was filled with happiness but it continued for long and turned into snowfall damaging his crop completely. Lencho's happy mood therefore changed into concern.

(2 Marks)

5. Lencho a farmer by profession, got his crops ruined in a hailstorm and he and his family, due to this, suffered from starvation. He therefore, wrote a letter to God to send him 100 pesos. **(2 Marks)**

2. Nelson Mandela - Long Walk to Freedom

1. (b) First to his family and the second to his country.

    According to the lesson, every man has twin obligations. Obligation to his family, to his wife and children, and he has an obligation to his people, his community and his country. So, twin obligations are first to his family and second to his country.

2 *Short Answer Type Questions*

1. On the day of inaugural ceremony. Nelson Mandela remembered his fellow freedom fighters who had sacrificed their lives for the sake of the freedom of the country. **(2 Marks)**

3 *Long Answer Type Questions*

1. Good morning, everyone.

Today, I'd like to discuss two pieces of literature that offer a powerful insight into the resilience of the human spirit required to transcend discrimination. Both works share some of the common themes.

Both Mandela's excerpt and Rich's poem address the issue of discrimination. Mandela speaks of how his own experiences of discrimination made him more determined to fight against it. He emphasizes the need to move beyond the divides created by race, gender, and class. Similarly, Rich's poem acknowledges the discrimination faced by trees, which are often overlooked and undervalued. She argues that these trees deserve to be recognized and appreciated, just as all living beings should be.

To conclude, I'd like to say that the common themes of transcending discrimination and the efforts involved in achieving equality are prevalent in both these pieces of literature and remind us of the strength of the human spirit and the importance of standing up for what we believe in, even when faced with obstacles. By acknowledging and valuing all forms of life and working towards a more just and equal world, we can continue to build a better future for ourselves and for future generations.

Thank you

2. Nelson Mandela referred to the apartheid policy of the white race against the black people "as an extraordinary human disaster" white people snatched freedom from the colored people of South Africa to whom the country really belonged. The blacks were subjected to oppression for long. They were not even allowed to discharge their obligations to their own families, community and their country. White people had no compassion for them and oppressed their own people and put them in prison if they asserted their freedom it was curtailed. The black people lived like slaves. Thus Mandela came to believe that since a system like that apartheid could be based on hate they could definitely a system which could be based on love and respect for each other this convey action was the basic of the long struggle against apartheid.

(6 Marks)

3. I agree with Nelson Mandela that no one is born hating another person because of the colour of his skin, or his background or his religion. We are all born with a capacity for love and compassion, and it is only through our experiences and environment that we learn to hate. We are taught to fear and distrust those who are different from us, and this can lead to hatred and bigotry. We must strive to break down these barriers and teach our children to embrace diversity and to respect and accept those who are different from us. We must strive to create a world where everyone is treated equally, regardless of their race, religion or background. We must strive to create a world where everyone is free to express their beliefs and opinions without fear of judgement or persecution. Only then can we truly create a world of peace and understanding. **(6 Marks)**

4. In his pursuit of independence for the Blacks in South Africa, Nelson Mandela had lost the lives of many of his close friends who laid their lives to make their people independent. On 10th May, the dignitaries from all over the world had gathered there to watch a government which had no considerations for apartheid. Since it was a historic event; Nelson Mandela could not help remembering those martyrs and hence a sense of history dawns on him.

After a reverse struggle and imprisonment for 37 years; Nelson Mandela was able to end apartheid – the most heinous distinction between man and man – from his country. While taking oath as the president; he clearly stated; apartheid on any basis is not going to creep into the South African constitution. And thus he succeeded in ending it altogether. **(8 Marks)**

---

3. Two Stories About Flying

1. (c) (C) and (D)

According to the lesson he had not eaten since the previous night fall and his elder brother caught his first herring and his parents circled around raising a proud cakle. So he felt jealous and hungry.

---

1   *Extract Based Questions*

1. (i) his vision was obstructed.

(ii) stopped responding completely.

(iii) they could not hear him.

(iv) Ragini matched the swimmer as he twisted twice in air before diving into the water.

(v) fear

---

2   *Short Answer Type Questions*

1. The risk here refers to the risk of flying through the storms and black clouds. The narrator took the risk of flying through the black clouds because he wanted to reach his home and meet his family. The desire to meet his family made him take the risk of flying in the dark stormy clouds. **(2 Marks)**

2. The young seagull was terrified when he dived at the fish, his mother was holding, but he soon felt his wings spread outwards and the wind rushing against his feathers. He was no longer afraid and he soared gradually downwards and outwards. He flapped his wings and soared upwards, and soon he was flying with his family, curveting, banking, soaring and diving. He had made his first flight and was filled with joy. **(2 Marks)**

3. The baby seagull could not take his first flight as he was scared that his wings will not support his body weight. He saw his family fly, yet the fear of falling down gripped his mind. He was too scared to even try.

(2 Marks)

4. Afraid of taking a flight on his own the seagull suffered from starvation because one of his family members were ready to come to his rescue. Standing by the edge of the nest, he could see his food-fish in the sea but could not eat because he feared being drowned into the sea.

(2 Marks)

3 *Long Answer Type Questions*

1. In comparison to Amanda's mother, the seagull's mother seems to be more attuned to her child's needs and abilities. She recognizes that the baby seagull is capable of flying and wants to help him achieve his full potential. However, she may not be taking into account his fears and anxieties, which can be just as important to his well-being as his ability to fly. In contrast, Amanda's mother seems to be too focused on correcting her daughter's flaws and may not be paying enough attention to her strengths and abilities. Even though both mothers have good intentions and want to better their children's lives, their methods, in part, may be misguided or ineffective. The seagull's mother could benefit from being more sensitive to her child's emotions, while Amanda's mother could benefit from focusing on her daughter's strengths and building her self-esteem.

---

4. From the Diary of Anne Frank

1. She was very talkative

   Mr. Koesing called Anne, a 'Chatter box' and was annoyed with Anne as. She was very talkative. Option (d) is correct.

2. People have good ears for listening

   Paper has more patience than people because they don't tell any thing to others but a person tells everything to his closest person. So option B is not correct that people have good ears for listening.

1 *Extract Based Questions*

1. (i) Maths Teacher. **(5 × 1 = 5 Marks)**

   (ii) (b) Only II

   Procrastinating - to pull off till another day.

   (iii) Trait

   (iv) (d) She had inherited it.

   (v) (c) Find it difficult to manage.

   'under control' things that can be managed by on its own.

3 *Long Answer Type Questions*

1. Anne was a girl of thirteen years. She was very intelligent and had a sharp brain. She was very different from the other girls of her age. She could think clearly and deeply. She had deep thoughts and ideas that she wanted to share with someone. But she felt lonely in the world. She had

loving parents, an elder sister and a number of friends. But she was not close to anyone. She could talk to them about common everyday matters, but could not pour her heart out to them. She had no one with whom she could share her secrets and the changes she was experiencing. She wanted a patient listener with a sympathetic heart. But she found that people had no patience to listen to her. Thus, Anne decided to write a diary, which she named Kitty, to share her feelings. Even though her diary was not a human being, she felt that it had much more patience than any human could ever have. She made Kitty her friend. She could express herself freely to her. The diary did not get bored listening to her. It was indeed a true friend to her. It never rejected her friendship. As she had never written a diary before, she thought that nobody would be interested in reading her diary. But that did not hold true, as years later, when her diary was published, it became one of the most read chronicles of the World War, one seen through the eyes of a young girl.

(10 Marks)

2. The main theme of 'The Diary of a Young Girl' is loneliness and isolation which life in the annex symbolised and Anne Frank's adolescence heightened. Anne's perpetual feeling of being lonely and misunderstood led her to make diary entries on the many experiences she had. Through her diary, we learn that neither Mrs. Frank nor Margot offered emotional support to Anne. Though Anne felt very connected to her father and derived strength and encouragement from him, he was not a fitting confidant for a thirteen-year-old girl.

3. Anniliese Marie 'Anne' Frank (12 June, 1929 – February March 1945) was German born Jewish girl who wrote while in hiding with her family and four friends in Amsterdam during the German occupation of the Netherlands in World War II. Anne frank, a mere 13 year old girl, wrote her diary because she had no friend with whom she could share her inner feelings and emotions. Throughout her life, the red and white checkered diary redeemed her of the weight of these feelings. As a last resort, she found refuge in her diary and grew so intimate that she gave it a name 'kitty' and treated it as her true friend. She believed truly that paper has more patience than persons. All her feelings – be it personal or public – therefore, have been jotted down in the diary. She never maintained secrecy from it. She recorded even petty issues like her quarrel with her mother or friends. Whatever fear, anger and frustrations, that she came across during the world War II, all have been recorded in the diary with minute details. The whole book that presents the story revolving around the life of Anne Frank is in the form of a diary penned by Anne Frank herself as she had lived her days and nights. The title therefore, stands justified.

4. Anne Frank, like other girls of her age has some deficiencies as well as some plus points in her character. She has a keen sense of humour; she is mature enough to delve deep into any complex incidents. She is intelligent. Her ability to express or record her feelings in crystal clear terms is appreciable. She never lets her writings become boring.

Anne was wiser than......... She sometimes had issues with her mother and friends but she never got violent. Although she had no friend in whom she could confide; she found an amicable solution – to write a diary. Her thoughts expressed in the diary are mature enough to move even the scholars of the field. All the more she is of the strong view that women should be respected at par with their male. She wasn't ready to succumb to any kind of discrimination. She called her diary 'Kitty' and treated it as a friend; and as a true friend never hides anything from a friend, she too never kept anything a secret from her diary. Had she been alive a little longer, she would have become a celebrated writer.

5. Anne's diary was as significant to her as any other character because she did not have any friend to share her feelings and emotions with. She received it as a birthday present when she turned thirteen and named it Kitty. The diary came to her rescue because it was her constant companion in her times of loneliness. She treated it as a dear friend and confided and vented out her feelings in all her entries. She never kept anything away from her diary and wrote down every event in her life including quarrels with her family and neighbours. She wrote down her experiences, the war, the trauma, frustration, anxiety, anger, sadness and concerns over the political and social situations during the war including the mistreatment of Jews by Germans. The diary to Helen was as constant as a soul mate.

---

5. Glimpses of India

Extract Based Questions

1. i. (c) He had grown up in and around tea gardens.

   ii. that the cultivation/harvesting (or any similar suitable word) (of tea) is the highest at one place namely Assam.

   iii. frustration / irritation/ exasperation (or any suitable word) compatible with the exclamation mark in the sentence.

   iv. (b) Traditional tales

   v. (b) Jaspreet cried out loud when she saw a white tiger in the sanctuary.

2. (a) The baker recorded his accounts on some wall in pencil.

    (b) Since baking was a profitable profession, the baker and his family never starved.

    (c) prosperous

    (d) A baker in Goa has a jack-fruit like appearance.

3.   **(1×3=3 Marks)**

    (a) The monsoon season is not the best period to visit Coorg because during this time it pours down heavily.

    (b) The best period to visit Coorg is from the month of September to March, which is also known as the season of joy.

    (c) commences

4.   **(1×3=3 Marks)**

    (a) The baker's furnace is essential for the Goan People because baked delicacies like cakes and bread are an essential part of all their festivities.

    (b) Cakes and bolinhas are a must for Christmas as well as all other festivals.

    (c) presence

5. (a) (i) The Coorgi people are ready to recount stories of valour related to their sons and fathers.

                                                (1 Mark)

        (ii) The first chief of the Indian army was General Cariappa.   **(1 Mark)**

(iii) The special favour granted to the people of Coorg is that they are permitted to carry fire arms without a licence.   **(1 Mark)**

(iv) valour   **(1 Mark)**

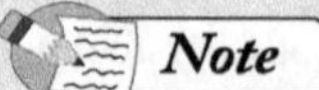

Note

a. While answering a question based on an extract from the textbook, you should be mindful to present the exact idea contained in the passage has without altering it in any way. In case your opinion is asked, don't hesitate to present it reasonably.

b. So far as question on vocabulary is concerned, you should take care to find the exact word from the passage that matches the meaning given.

2   *Short Answer Type Questions*

1. Coorgis are a proud race of martial men and beautiful women. They are very hospitable and entertain their guests relating stories of their fathers and sons. Coorgi soldiers are brave. Coorgi regiment is one of the most decorated regiments of the Indian army.

    Coorgis are the only people in India who can carry firearms without license.   **(2 Marks)**

2. Paders are the makers of the famous Portuguese loaves of bread. They are friends of children because they provide them with delicious and nutritious bread. The loaves of bread are a source of comfort and joy for children, and the paders are a reminder of the good old Portuguese days.   **(2 Marks)**

3. Kodavus are a martial race and have been bearing arms for 1000 of years. They are permitted to carry fire arms without licence because firearms have become a part of their tradition over the years.   **(2 Marks)**

4. Mid way between Mysore and the coastal town of Manglore, Coorg is situated; it appears as if it has drifted from the kingdom of God. This appearance makes the writer call it a land of rolling hills.   **(2 Marks)**

5. (a) Rajvir was excited about the trip to his friend's house which had a tea garden and he had never seen a tea garden. On the other hand, Pranjol was not as excited as him because he lived amongst this lush greenery.

                    (2 Marks)

6. The financial condition of the bakers was that they were prosperous and well off, since baking was a profitable profession and bread was loved by all the people. Their families were never starved.   **(2 Marks)**

7. The elders in Goa still love to remember the good old days when the Portuguese settlers were part of their lives. They are nostalgic and grateful that though the eaters of the bread have vanished, the mixers and the mould remained.   **(2 Marks)**

8. Tea originated in China as far back as 2700 B.C. Legend states that the Chinese emperor while taking a walk paused to rest under a tree to boil himself cup of water. Some leaves fell into the water. These were tea leaves

                    (2 Marks)

(a) *Since these are questions pertaining to the texts you have studied as part of the syllabus here you are at liberty to add some new information from your side, if required, but only in reference to what you have read in the texts.*

(b) *Mind the word limit and incorporate your ideas in precise sentences.*

(c) *In questions beginning with 'why', try to give all the reasons given in the text, unless the question mentions a required number, but in case they are too many, write only two or three and add 'etc' at the end.*

9. The family tradition is still carried on even today by the new generation of bakers or pads in Goa. Even now marriage gifts are meaningless without the sweet bread or the bol, and a party or a feast loses its charm without Goan bread.   **(2 Marks)**

10. Rajbir had never seen so much greenery before as the soft green paddy fields gave way to tea bushes. Against the densely wooded hills, tea bushes stretched as far as the eyes could see. Rajbir was really excited to see the magnificent view.   **(2 Marks)**

11. Baking was essential in Goa because Marriage gifts were incomplete without these sweetbreads. Sandwiches, cakes and bolinhas were a must for Christmas as well as other festivals. **(2 Marks)**

12. The tea pluckers are different from other farm labourers. The women plucking tea leaves in the tea gardens look like dolls. They wear plastic aprons and carry baskets at their backs to put tea leaves in them. **(2 Marks)**

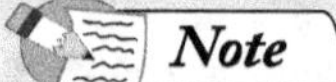

Note

a. *While answering long answer type questions, you must adhere to the word limit given. Take care that you neither exceed nor fall short by more than 5 words.*

b. *In support of your answer, you may quote from the text but misquoting can mar the wholesomeness of your answer. So be careful.*

c. *In a question like 'Why does Valli stand upon the seat', don't fail to mention the value points like*

   1. *Her height was short. So she could not look through the window.*

   2. *It was her first bus ride. So she wanted to enjoy it to the full.*

   3. *She was a curious girl. She had meticulously planned for the ride and succeeded. So she did not want to miss any beauty connected with the ride.*

3   *Long Answer Type Questions*

1. **Rajvir:** There is a lot more to do in Coorg than smelling the coffee! The place has rainforests, so the megafauna will be worth watching. Not just this, Coorg provides opportunities to indulge in adventure sports like river rafting, rappelling, and mountain biking, to name a few.

   Pranjol: That sounds interesting, but I would prefer some serene moments, too, away from this post-pandemic hustle-bustle.

   Rajvir: Believe me, I am. Coorg is the place. It has beautiful natural walking trails, and Brahmagiri hills offer a panoramic view. I read that the place has the largest Tibetan settlement, so the environment will reflect peace and spirituality, I'm sure.

   Pranjol: I have to say, you've presented a fine case in favor of Coorg and convinced me. Let's plan to leave for Coorg next Wednesday!

6. Mijbil the Otter

1   *Extract Based Questions*

1. (a) 'They' refers to the otters. **(1×4=4 Marks)**

   (b) The author could get an otter from the Tigris marshes.

   (c) Tamed

   (d) At the Consulate-General, the author found that his friend's mail had arrived whereas his mail hadn't.

 **Short Answer Type Questions**

1. The game Mij had invented was played with a ping-pong ball. He would put the ball at one end of a sloping lid and then grab it as it ran to the other end.

(2 Marks)

2. When Maxwell first took the otter into the bathroom, he discovered that Mijbil liked playing with water. He would jump and roll in water like a hippopotamus did. This was because otters generally get infuriated with still water. **(2 Marks)**

3. Mijbil was a smart and friendly animal. He invented ping-pong game and he could splash in the water. He also enjoyed playing with marbles and other kind of games which shows him as an intelligent otter. **(2 Marks)**

4. When Maxwell took Mijbil to the bathroom, it was filled with joy and went wild in the water for half an hour. It was shooting up and down the bathtub, plunging and rolling in it, and making enough splash like a hippo.

(2 Marks)

5. He went wild with joy in the water in the tub. Two days later, Mijbil went to the bathroom. He got into the bathtub and turned the tap on. He was happy under the running water. **(2 Marks)**

3 **Long Answer Type Questions**

1. **Tiger:** Why would you say that? How can you like these annoying humans who are responsible for me being in this cage?

Mijbil: I feel safe like this. That is why I don't hate them and believe that I am protected this way.

Tiger: How can you feel protected not being in your habitat- the jungles?

Mijbil: I believe that I will not be able to survive like you because I am not big and scary like you. Any predator can easily harm me in the wild.

Tiger: True, but they can learn to co-exist. It is their harmful activities, such as hitting us with stones, etc., that make us attack them. If they learn how to behave, we will stay out of their way.

Mijbil: I get your point and feel sad about your situation. But please be cheerful, dear Tiger.

Tiger: It is easier said than done, but I will try my best.

---
7. Madam Rides the Bus

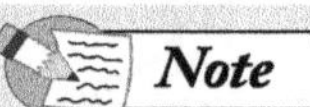
Extract Based Questions

1. (a) The girl mentioned in the passage is Valli.

   (b) Valli did not get off the bus when she reached her destination because she was afraid of getting down alone. Though bold, she was afraid of getting down at a place unknown to her.

   (c) To finding something funny or entertaining.

> **Note**
>
> a. *Extract based questions contain only 1 mark and usually require exact answers.*
>
> b. *Be careful not to exceed 2 sentences even while answering 'why' questions. Be precise and to the point.*
>
> c. *In case of MCQs, sometimes, the correct option is not obvious; but, it is relatively easy to see which ones are incorrect. So, you should eliminate the incorrect ones to get the correct answer.*

2 ***Short Answer Type Questions***

1. Valli saved money by resisting the temptation to buy peppermints, toys, and balloons, and instead thriftily saving whatever stray coins came her way. She eventually saved a total of sixty paise, which was enough to pay for her bus fare. **(2 Marks)**

2. **Value Points**

   - A bus ride seemed like a fascinating means of recreation and adventure ---unlike cities and bigger towns

   - She could travel alone safely –unfortunately, not recommended in larger townships or cities

   - There was only one bus that Valli observed several times – cities have varied means of transport that might seem mor adventurous

   Disagree:

   - Fascination for riding a bus or an automobile can exist in children of Valli's age even in big cities.

   - Travelling unnoticed is easier in large cities than in small towns or villages due to familiarity.

   - Cities would offer more opportunities for a bus ride due to availability and frequency of several buses on the same route. **(2 Marks)**

3. The most fascinating thing that Valli saw on the streets was the bus that travelled between her village and the nearest town. **(2 Marks)**

4. Valli became very sad after seeing the dead cow. The beautiful creature that had been full of life on her way to the town now looked horrifying. It was covered with blood and its eyes were lifeless. **(2 Marks)**

5. Valli didn't want to go to the stall and have a drink because she didn't have money for it. This shows that Valli had a strong will power and pride. **(2 Marks)**

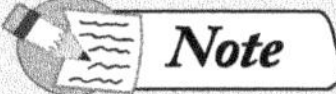

Note

a. To answer questions carrying 2 marks only, remember not to elongate the relevant points; and rather to be as brief as possible.

b. Express your points in clear terms, within the prescribed word limit, without leaving out any relevant information.

c. Remember, a 'why' question must contain reasons for the concerned issue; while a 'what' question should be answered by providing the fact asked.

6. Valli listened carefully to the conversations between her neighbours and people who regularly used the bus and also asked discreet questions. She gathered all the necessary details about the fare, distance and time, and then planned her trip. **(2 Marks)**

7. Valli stood up on her seat because her view of the beauty of nature was being obstructed by a canvas blind. She had to stand on her seat to look over the blind to relish the scenic beauty. **(2 Marks)**

3   *Long Answer Type Questions*

1. Valli used to listen to her neighbours about the ride of the bus, She dreamt of riding on the bus. Her passion to fulfill her dream fired her curiosity. This curiousness made her listen to the conversations of people going on the bus ride and asking questions about their experience of the bus so, she could gather information regarding the bus journey.

On the bus journey, Valli acted confidently and behaved maturely. She did not consider herself to be any less than an adult. She was focused on fulfilling her dream and did not get tempted to go outside the bus and she was being observant and explored the town when the bus reached the town.

On the return journey, she was sad as she learns about the death of a cow. This made her aware of the fact that death is a part of life and should be accepted as it is a natural phenomenon. Thus, the bus journey taught her a lot of things. Mandela said "People must learn to hate, and if they can learn to hate, they can be taught to love."

2. Date : 1st July 20XX

Time: 8:00 pm

Dear Diary,

Today, I would like to tell you a story of valli and her experience of riding the busalone for first time.

Valli was a small girl who lived near a bus stop and wanted to take a bus ride.

She discovered that the fare was 30 paise for one half and it would take 45 mins. She knew about all these things from the talks of her neighbours.

One fine overwhelmed spring day Valli rode the bus. She overcame her shyness, and sat quickly on a empty seat.

She saw plam trees, grass lands mountains and green fields outside.

Then she saw a terrified cow running for her life in the middle of the rood. The cow had been killed in an accident. Vally got sad after seeing this accident and stayed silent along the entire way to home.**(4 Marks)**

Bye Diary

3. Valli was a girl of poor family; she saw a bus passing by the road daily. The bust went to a nearby town which was around 30 kms away from her village. Since she saw the bus daily; there grew a strong desire in her heart that she will one day take a ride on that. For this, she started

collecting money for the to and journey ticket; she avoided buying toffees on ice-crea. She also collected information about the bus like — how much time it took to reach the town and how much time to come back. She also learnt at what time it began its journey and it came back. After that she observed closely her mother who took a rap in the noon. She slept around 2.3 hrs. During this period she decided to take a ride to the town and the was successful in her attempt because of reserved nature and meticulous planning.

> *Note*
>
> a. *These long answer questions are value based. They are designed to test your awareness of human values.*
>
> b. *Your answer should show that you know the story well and have learnt the moral lesson and value conveyed by it.*
>
> c. *These questions have different parts. Your answer should be written in different paragraphs for each part.*

4. Eight- year old Valli lived in a remote village. She wished to ride on a bus that plied through her village. This desire became stronger with every passing day. How was she going to do this? She started planning. These were the preliminary difficulties that she faced. The little girl

overcame them and set out on her journey, which she thoroughly enjoyed. It was because of her meticulous planning and determination that the little girl was able to achieve success with regard to satisfying her one and only burning desire of riding on a bus. **(4 Marks)**

5. Valli lived in a remote village. She was fascinated by a bus that would come to her village every hour. She developed a keen desire to ride the bus. She began planning meticulously started saving money for the bus journey. Eventually she travelled all alone, confidently and independently and finally returned home safely. She enjoyed her journey, did not succumb to any temptations, did not accept any favours from the conductor and she exercised extreme caution throughout the journey. Valli's efforts at achieving her goal in life, is a lesson, we all should imbibe in our lives. **(4 Marks)**

6. Yes, the bus conductor shows an example of courtesy and good manners. The bus conductor was a jovial and good-hearted person. He gave his hand to Valli to help the kid climb on the bus. He was amused to see the behaviour of the kid and treated Valli with respect and called her 'madam'. He also thought that she might be hungry and offered her the cold drink. He was concerned towards her throughout the journey.

Note

a. *Mind the word limit.*

b. *The question demands critical appreciation of the given statement. Give your views emphatically supported by strong pleas.*

c. *Use your best diction to express your opinion.*

---

8. The Sermon at Benares

1   *Extract Based Questions*

1. (a) The name of the prince was Siddhartha Gautama

    (b) The sights of suffering that the Prince saw, while out hunting was a sick man and an aged man

    (c) Protected

2   *Short Answer Type Questions*

1. When he was at the age of twenty-five while hunting one day, he saw a sick man, an aged man, then a funeral procession, and finally, a monk begging for alms. Thus he was exposed to the sufferings of the world. These sights moved him such a lot that he went out into the world to seek enlightenment. **(2 Marks)**

2. Buddha wanted to teach Kisa Gotami a life lesson. Through his request for a handful of mustard seeds from a household where no one had ever died, Buddha wanted to make her realize the universal nature of death.

(2 Marks)

3. The Buddha tanght Kisa gotami that death and suffering were inevitable no human can escape death for what is teach wil die one day. One has to accept to line with suffering and pain. **(2 Marks)**

4. Buddha asked Kisa Gotami to fetch a handful of mustard seeds from a house where none had died. She could not understand that initially. When she saw the city lights flicker up and extinguish, that's when she realised that death was inevitable. **(2 Marks)**

5. The Buddha gave his first sermon at Benares because he considered it to be the holiest of places on the banks of the Ganges. His first sermon reflected his wisdom about one kind of suffering i.e. death. **(2 Marks)**

> **Note**
>
> a. To answer questions carrying 2 marks only, remember not to elongate the relevant points; and rather to be as brief as possible.
>
> b. Express your points in clear terms, within the prescribed word limit, without leaving out any relevant information.
>
> c. Remember, a 'why' question must contain reasons for the concerned issue; while a 'what' question should be answered by providing the fact asked.

6. Kisa Gotami was sad, because she had lost her only son. The grief-stricken lady then carried her dead son to the houses of the neighbours begging for medicines, in a bid to restore his life. **(2 Marks)**

7. Buddha changed Kisa's thinking of her child's death with the help of a simple act. He asked her to procure a handful of mustard seeds from that house where no one had ever died. **(2 Marks)**

3   *Long Answer Type Questions*

1. Kisa Gotami learnt that death is an inevitable part of life and is common to all. She realised that no matter how much one grieves, it will not bring the dead back. She also realised that life is short and fleeting, and that one should not be too attached to material things. She also learnt that one should not be too consumed by grief, as it will only lead to further suffering. Lastly, she learnt that the path to peace and freedom from suffering lies in overcoming sorrow and surrendering all selfishness. Through her experience, Kisa Gotami learnt the importance of accepting death and the impermanence of life.

2. The learning from the referenced quote of Buddha is that loss of irreplaceable things brings grief and sorrow, but one needs to be calm and understanding about the perishable nature of things. This approach would help the boy cope with the loss of his ball. He would realize that loss is an important part of life. It is necessary to learn from experience, adapt and move on.

The boy is too young to understand the depth of these words. He is alone in his loss. He has no one to explain and must learn from his experience painstakingly. He requires time to cope. It is easy to feel disheartened at that age.

3. Kisa Gautami was devastated by the death of her son and she went from door to door, seeking help. Some one told her to talk to Buddha, who then asked her to procure a handful of mustard seeds. This raised hope in Gautami's heart that person could be revived. But the condition imposed by Sakyamuni was that the seeds should be brought from a house where the family has not lost a loved one to death. She went from door to door in search of mustard seeds. Everyone was ready to offer. But the condition forfeited them from doing any service. All the efforts of Kisa Gautami went in vain. The futile search of Kisa Gautami mode her realize that sorrows are a past of life and one can attain peace only by acceptance.

Kisa Gautami comprehended that she was being egoistic in her distress as death saves nobody. It is normal for everyone that there does not exist any individual who has not lost a darling. Indeed this was the very ting that the Buddha believed she should comprehend. **(4 Marks)**

4. Born and brought up as a prince, Siddhartha Gautama studied sacred scriptures for 4 years and when he came back; he was married to a princes from whom he had a son. They lived together for 10 years. confined in the royal palace for so long; he wanted to go out and see the common people. Unfortunately when he went out of the palace; he came across successively an old man; a siek man and a corpse.

Puzzled over the state he renounced his place and wandered for 7 years aimlessly. And he then sat under a peepal tree for enlightenment which he got there after 7 days. Thereafter he spent rest of his days sharing his knowledge with others and begging for money and food.

5. As her son had died; somebody advised Kisa Gotami to meet Buddha who possibly could bring him back to life. With thin view in mind, Kisa Gotami approached him and asked Buddha to inject life in her son's dead body. Buddha asked her bring a handful of mustard seeds from a house in which nobody had ever died. Kisa Gotamic went door to door with the request but to her bad luck; she could not get such a house. Disappointed, she came back to Buddha and he preached then ____ life and death

are preconceived part of thin world; nothing can change life rule. The one who has been born; has to die one day. There in no escape from this rule. **(8 Marks)**

6. At the death of her only son, Kisa Gotami was so aggrieved that she began to talk and behave nonsense. She approached each of the persons in the village with a request to bring back her son to life again. One of the persons suggested her to see Buddha. Buddha knew that she won't understand things if told in plain terms. He asked her to bring a handful of mustard seeds from a house in the village where nobody had ever died. In her excitement, she approached every door but found no such house. Distressed, she returned to Budha who preached that the life of mortals in this world is troubled, brief and combined with pain. For, there is not any means by which those who have been born can avoid dying.

7. After the death of Kisa Gotami's only child, she became very sad and she was unable to accept the fact that her child had expired. It was then that someone advised her to meet Gautama Buddha. When she met Gautama Buddha, he gave her an exercise to do. She was asked to collect mustard seeds from a house, where there has never been a death. She went from one house to another but was unable to find a single house where no death had occurred. Thus, Kisa realised that death is imminent and everyone who is born is bound to die one day. Buddha

changed her understanding of death, by this exercise and she could come to terms with reality. She understood that the life of human beings who are mortals, was indeed troubled, brief and combined with pain.

(a) These questions are based on the prescribed short stories or extracts but require long comprehensive answers.

(b) These questions usually state some commonly observed fact and then ask a related question in context of a prescribed chapter. So, you should first elaborate on the stated truth and then illustrate with quotes and incidents from the text.

(c) Take care to organize your ideas logically as well as chronologically.

8. Yes, the statement is appropriate even for today's life. According to Buddha, death is inevitable. Everyone must die and that's the way of life. Those who fail to understand this cannot accept death when it comes to their loved ones. In the story "The Sermon at Benares", a mother is unable to accept her son's death and thus goes in search for a way to bring him back to life. Buddha, with his wisdom, finds a way to teach her this important truth of life.

9. After the death of Kisa Gotami's only child, she became very sad. She carried her dead child to her neighbours in order to get medicine to bring him to life. She was unable to accept the fact that her child had expired. It was then that someone advised her to meet Gautama Buddha. When she met Gautama Buddha, who was asked to collect mustard seeds from a house where no one has ever died. She was unable to find a single house where no death had occurred, and realised that death is imminent. Every individual has his or her way of dealing with tragedy. I would perhaps have crumbled under the loss, unable to deal with the fact of not being able to see the person again. After eventually accepting the loss, I'd choose to take care of a child who is as alone in the world as I am and find some meaning in l.   **(5 Marks)**

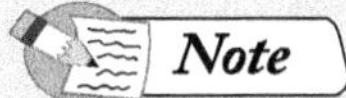

Note

a. *While answering such questions, word limit should not be ignored*

b. *When there are two or more questions in one, give your answer to each in different paragraphs. For instance, to answer Q. 16, in the first paragraph, you may describe what the people in general will draw from this story ; in the second, you may give a personal account of what you would learn. from it; and in the third, you may write how you would act in a similar circumstance.*

c. *While giving your own opinion, it is advised that the action or reaction that you propose to present must be optimistic. Pessimistic views can annoy the examiner.*

---
9. The Proposal (Play)
---

1    *Extract Based Questions*

1. (i) (d) He is in love with Natalya

(ii) Lomov's tone when he says "What more do I want?" is uncertain and questioning because he is trying to convince himself that Natalya Stepanovna is a suitable match for him, but at the same time, he seems to be struggling with doubts and fears. His tone suggests that he is trying to reassure himself that he has made the right decision, but he is not entirely convinced.

(iii) (b) A soliloquy is a speech given by a character alone on stage, which reveals their innermost thoughts and feelings to the audience.

(iv) The actor would be required to convey Lomov's nervousness and excitement through his voice modulation.

2. (i)   ownership of meadows.

    (ii) Perpetuity.

    (iii) making bricks.

    (iv) Both grandfather and great grandfather reckoned that their land extended to burnt march which include Oxen meadows.

    (v)   Forty.   **(1×4=4 Marks)**

3. (a) The speaker of the above lines is Ivan Vassilevitch Lomov.

    (b) His aunt's grandmother gave the free use of Oxen meadows to Natalya's grandfather's peasants.

    (c) The peasants began to treat the land as their own as they had started making bricks there.

    (d) These lines show that the speaker had a bad sense of social behaviour which seems inappropriate to the place and person.

4. (a) These words are being spoken by Natalya to Lomov in the play 'The Proposal"

    (b) Lomov is in an evening dress because he had come over to ask Natalya's hand in marriage.

    (c) 'Ball' refers to a dance form.

> **Note**
>
> *(a) These are 1-mark questions. So, write exact and factual answers only. Resist writing information that is not asked.*
>
> *(b) Answer in concise sentences containing multiple information. Too many small sentences with*

5. (a) Natalya is speaking to Lomov.

    (b) The dispute is over the ownership of the Oxen Meadows.

    (c) The word 'restrain' means 'keep under control or within limit'.   **(1×3=3 Marks)**

6. (a) Natalya speaks the above lines to Lomov

    (b) The meadows are worth five dessiatins, and are worth about 300 roubles.

    (c) unfairness

7.   **(1×3=3 Marks)**

    (a) The speaker of these lines is Chubukov.

    (b) He is happy because his friend Lomov had come to meet him to request for his daughter's hand in marriage for his son.

    (c) He is going to call Natasha to find out her opinion on the matter.

8.   **(1×3=3 Marks)**

(a) These words are being spoken by Chubukov to Lomov

(b) According to the speaker, the guest certainly has his good points. He is pure bred, firm on his feet, has well-sprung ribs, and all that. But the truth is that dog has two defects: he is old and short in the muzzle.

(c) truthful

Note

a. *While answering questions of this type, be as brief as possible but also see the main points are not left out.*

b. *To answer such questions, the student is not expected to write the answer in full sentences, a phrase or sometimes a single word or two will serve the purpose.*

c. *While writing the answer of a vocabulary question, mind the number, gender, tense, person etc of the given word and answer accordingly e.g., synonym for pain is grieve (not grieved).*

9. (b) (i) Chubukov anticipates that he must have come to ask for money which he doesn't intend on giving.   **(1 Mark)**

(ii) Lomov is a 35 year- old gentleman who suffers from palpitations, gets upset very easily and doesn't sleep well. He is therefore not able to answer properly.   **(1 Mark)**

(iii) He has come with the intention of asking Chubukov's daughter's hand in marriage.

          (1 Mark)

(iv) Awfully   **(1 Mark)**

2   *Short Answer Type Questions*

1.   Value Points

Upper hand –

• She was able to answer every query and present an argument defeating the one presented by Lomov.

Arguments –

• Argument about ownership of Oxen meadows – Natalya argued that it is a matter of principle and not greed.

• She showed conviction and belief while arguing.

OR

• Argument about dogs – Natalya argued that her dog was cheaper, was of better breed and could run faster.

• Never lost cool while presenting her arguments.

          (2 Marks)

2. Chubukov misunderstood the purpose of Lomovs visit because he thought that Lomov came to borrow money. Lomov did not reveal the purpose of his coming.

(2 Marks)

3. Lomov was expected to marry and could not have stayed unmarried. He believed that he ought to lead a quiet, settled, and regular life at his critical age of thirty-five.

(2 Marks)

4. Chubukov suspects Lomov since he thinks Lomov has come to borrow money from him. But Lomov is unable to express his desire to marry Chubukov's daughter. This increases Chubukov's suspicion. **(2 Marks)**

3   *Long Answer Type Questions*

1. The play 'Proposal' is a farce because of its exaggerated and absurd dialogues and situations. The characters behave oddly and childishly. They argue and quarrel and make a mountain out of a molehill. They insult and hurl accusations at each other. Instead of solving the problems maturely, they fight again on another topic. Lomov's nerve problems, Chubukov's theatrical statements, and Natalaya's impulsive and belligerent remarks all add to the farcical nature of the play. Additionally, how the final proposal is made amidst all the chaos is the ultimate depiction of farce.

2. Neighbours must have a cordial relationship, which Lomov and Natalya do not have. It was unfortunate that they could not extend common courtesies to each other. In the story The Proposal, Lomov had gone over to Chubukov's house to ask Natalya's hand in marriage. Very soon he started fighting with her over a small piece of land. This land adjoined her land and his oxen meadows touched her birch woods. Natalya told Lomov that the tried meadows belonged to her but Lomov claimed that the oxen meadows were his. Both threatened each other. The situation might be different if both the parties had followed the right approach. **(4 Marks)**

3. The Proposal' is a satirical one-act play written by Anton Chekov in 1888-89. The Proposal as its name suggests speaks about an expression of the desire of one protagonist wanting to marry another. The play, wright reveals that the thought behind wealthy families seeking matrimonial ties, is to increase their estates and landed properties.

The author has used humour and exaggeration to highlight the issue at hand. It is not an unknown fact that big businesses and families indulge in this form of extending family holdings under the garb of matrimony. Speaking about values required for a relationship to be healthy, one has to be accommodating and reasonable rather than being quarrelsome and covetous. Love and understanding are the stronghold of every relationship.

Note

a. For these questions that require long answers, you should organise all your thoughts in mind and express them in sequence in clear terms.

b. Unnecessary ideas you have had through other sources should not be included.

c. Be alert always to keep your answers not only concise but also wholesome.

d. Do not forget to read and edit your answer after having finished writing it.

Topic-b: **First Flight: Poetry**

---

1. Dust of Snow

1. Happy

The poet was sad. Then his mood changed and poet was happy. So the option happy is correct.

Note

In this poem, Robert Frost wants to signify that every big change or revolution is initiated from a very small change. In the poem, crow's way changed the stressful sad mood into happy one.

---

2. Fire and Ice

1 **Extract Based Questions**

1. (i) Hatred/ indifference / bitterness / apathy / detachment / rigidity

(ii) The speaker's alignment with those who favour ice suggests that they have seen the destructive consequences of a lack of empathy and emotional connection.

(iii) d- Respectful

(iv) The language used in these lines is simple and straightforward. The words and phrases are easy to understand and the poem is written in a conversational tone. Despite its simplicity, however, the poem carries a profound message about the destructive power of both fire and ice, and the inevitability of destruction. The use of simple language in this context makes the message more accessible to a wider audience and adds to the poem's overall impact.

2 **Short Answer Type Questions**

1. Value Points

- He was a victim of the fiery aspect of desire.

- By his own admission, (From what I've tasted ......) he had experienced its destructive effects in his life.   **(2 Marks)**

---

3. A Tiger in the Zoo

 **Extract Based Questions**

1.. (i) (B) is right and (A) is wrong.

   The stanza is from poem "A tiger in the Zoo', and villagers feel safe when tiger is caged and in the zoo. We don't feel happy to see him like this.

   (ii) They are part of our environment.

   According to the poem we should protect tigers and save them because they are part of our environment.

   (iii) by killing their cattle

   According to poem tiger snarls around houses and kills their cattle and terrorizes the villagers.

   (iv) Personification

   Personification means when we attribute human qualities to non-human entities 'Tiger' is performing humanly activity of ignoring.

   (v) Ignoring visitors

   According the poem tiger locked in the cage and ignored visitors.

2. (i) (b) Patrolling cars

   (ii) The word 'Brilliant' has been repeated here(used twice).

   (iii) (c) Confinement and freedom.

   (iv) (b) Frustration

   (v) true.

3. (i) helplessness.

   (ii) It is his natural conduct and it is hiding behind tall grasses in the shadow of the trees and bushes of the forest while waiting for its pray.

   (iii) pads are soft just like velvet fabric.

   (iv) stalk.

   (v) True.

3 **Long Answer Type Questions**

1. **Tiger:** Why would you say that? How can you like these annoying humans who are responsible for me being in this cage?

   Mijbil: I feel safe like this. That is why I don't hate them and believe that I am protected this way.

   Tiger: How can you feel protected not being in your habitat- the jungles?

Mijbil: I believe that I will not be able to survive like you because I am not big and scary like you. Any predator can easily harm me in the wild.

Tiger: True, but they can learn to co-exist. It is their harmful activities, such as hitting us with stones, etc., that make us attack them. If they learn how to behave, we will stay out of their way.

Mijbil: I get your point and feel sad about your situation. But please be cheerful, dear Tiger.

Tiger: It is easier said than done, but I will try my best.

---

4. How to Tell Wild Animals

1   *Extract Based Questions*

1.   (i)   (d)   Bengal tiger.   **(5 × 1 = 5 Marks)**

    (ii)   The first letter (a consonant) in both the words is same.

2.

(iii) True

(iv) (b)   terror

(v) (b)   Discern

---

5. The Ball Poem

1.   (b)   Responsible

    According to the poem loss of possessions should make one feel responsible and people will take. Balls means responsibilities.

2   *Short Answer Type Questions*

1. There are many reasons why the poet does not offer money to the boy to buy a new ball – (i) He wanted him to learn the lesson of separation from loved ones (ii) The attachment of the boy with the lost ball can not be replaced with the purchase of a new ball (iii) The ball was a symbol of his sweet memories etc.   **(2 Marks)**

2.   **(2 Marks)**

Topper's Answer

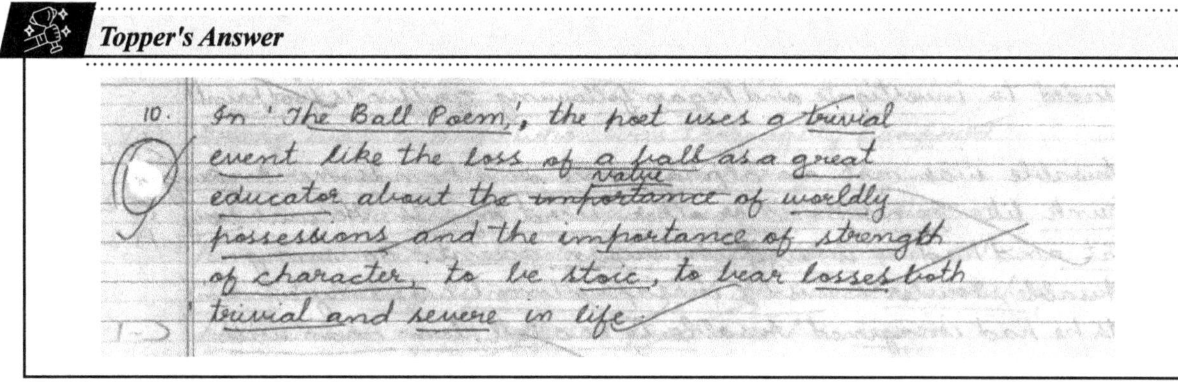

2. The poet doesn't want to intervene or console the boy because he knows that in this world people are always running after acquiring and owning things. He realises that this first responsibility in such a world.

(2 Marks)

3   *Long Answer Type Questions*

1. The learning from the referenced quote of Buddha is that loss of irreplaceable things brings grief and sorrow, but one needs to be calm and understanding about the perishable nature of things. This approach would help the boy cope with the loss of his ball. He would realize that loss is an important part of life. It is necessary to learn from experience, adapt and move on.

The boy is too young to understand the depth of these words. He is alone in his loss. He has no one to explain and must learn from his experience painstakingly. He requires time to cope. It is easy to feel disheartened at that age.

6. Amanda!

1   *Extract Based Questions*

1. (i) Instructive.   **(5 × 1 = 5 Marks)**

(ii) tranquil.

(iii) True.

(iv) reprimanding.

(v) bright.

2. (a) 'Me' stands for Amanda.

(b) Amanda feels suffocated at the fact that her parents constantly nag her.

(c) Amanda compares herself to a beautiful mermaid who lives all alone.

(d) Blissfully

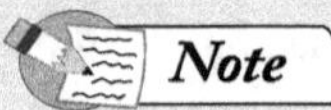

Note

(a) Extract based questions follow a specific pattern. Remember to answer in the very style of the question.

(b) Very often, a question asks' What or who does 'X' refer to?

Your answer should be 'X' refers to ....

(c) Students generally falter in constructing their answer appropriately to a question framed as 'What is/are 'X' referred to in the extract above?' Your answer in such a case should be, 'X' referred to in the extract above is/are.......

(d) Part (a) of the above question asks 'What does 'me' stand for?' So, your answer should be, ''Me' stands for Amanda' rather than ''Me' refers to Amanda.'

2　　　　　　*Short Answer Type Questions*

1. Amanda feels suffocated because she is controlled and instructed not to do one thing or the other. She feels that her freedom is curtailed. But Amanda wishes to be free to live in her own world. She is a very sensitive girl who indulges in daydreaming quiet often. She highly valves silence and freedom. **(2 Marks)**

2. The speaker of the lines is exasperated and irritated. The tone is that of frustration and annoyance. The exclamation mark is suggestive of the inherent emotion.

(2 Marks)

3. Yes, as a reader I identify with Amanda because like Amanda I am a day dreamer. I have my fantasy world where I am often lost.

Like her mother, my mother also keeps on nagging me to be more attentive and look after myself.

(2 Marks)

3　　　　　　*Long Answer Type Questions*

1. In comparison to Amanda's mother, the seagull's mother seems to be more attuned to her child's needs and abilities. She recognizes that the baby seagull is capable of flying and wants to help him achieve his full potential.

However, she may not be taking into account his fears and anxieties, which can be just as important to his well-being as his ability to fly. In contrast, Amanda's mother seems to be too focused on correcting her daughter's flaws and may not be paying enough attention to her strengths and abilities. Even though both mothers have good intentions and want to better their children's lives, their methods, in part, may be misguided or ineffective. The seagull's mother could benefit from being more sensitive to her child's emotions, while Amanda's mother could benefit from focusing on her daughter's strengths and building her self-esteem.

7. The Trees

1　　　　　　*Extract Based Questions*

1. (i) the sun, which is non-human, is attributed the human feature of having feet.

(Accept any synonyms giving the similar/ correct meaning)

(ii) (a) emphasis

(iii) FALSE

(iv) (a) unnatural

(v) (c) It builds momentum

2. (a) The trees are trying to move out into the forest

   (b) Because thed trees and plants had been confined into houses

   (c) (ii) empty

   (d) (iii) personification.

 **Short Answer Type Questions**

1. The poet is referring to the decorative trees and indoor plants. Their roots feel cramped and are trying to free themselves, the twigs are stiff and the boughs are like the newly discharged patients coming out of clinic doors. **(2 Marks)**

3 **Long Answer Type Questions**

1. Good morning, everyone.

   Today, I'd like to discuss two pieces of literature that offer a powerful insight into the resilience of the human spirit required to transcend discrimination. Both works share some of the common themes.

   Both Mandela's excerpt and Rich's poem address the issue of discrimination. Mandela speaks of how his own experiences of discrimination made him more determined to fight against it. He emphasizes the need to move beyond the divides created by race, gender, and class. Similarly, Rich's poem acknowledges the discrimination faced by trees, which are often overlooked and undervalued. She argues that these trees deserve to be recognized and appreciated, just as all living beings should be.

   To conclude, I'd like to say that the common themes of transcending discrimination and the efforts involved in achieving equality are prevalent in both these pieces of literature and remind us of the strength of the human spirit and the importance of standing up for what we believe in, even when faced with obstacles. By acknowledging and valuing all forms of life and working towards a more just and equal world, we can continue to build a better future for ourselves and for future generations.

   Thank you

8. Fog

1 **Extract Based Questions**

1. (i) Unlike traditional poetry that often relies on complex rhyme schemes and metaphors, this poem uses simple, everyday language to create a vivid picture in the reader's mind to create a powerful and evocative mood.

(ii) The word "little" used to describe the fog in the poem suggests the subtle and quiet nature of the fog. The word "little" also evokes a sense of innocence and vulnerability, as if the fog is a harmless creature moving through the city.

(iii) b- coastal

(iv) visual/animal imagery

---

9. The Tale of Custard the Dragon

 **Extract Based Questions**

1. (a) The poem is 'The Tale of Custard the Dragon' and the poet is Ogden Nash.

   (b) Yellow is the colour of Beinda's dog.

   (c) The kitten and the mouse were called Ink and Mustard respectively.

   (d) Sharp.

2. (a) The dragon Custard was tickled by Belinda.

   (b) She tickled him in order to make him laugh a little, as the cage looked very scary and it was making the dragon sad and anxious.

   (c) Ink is a little kitten; Blink is a grey mouse and Mustard is a yellow dog.

   (d) They all laughed at the dragon because he was looking like a coward.

3. (1×3=3 Marks)

   (a) Belinda is the name of the girl in the poem 'Custard the Dragon'.

   (b) She taunted him for his cowardice and was quite merciless in tickling, taunting and troubling him. She and her other pets called him Percival and laughed at him.

   (c) unmerciful

4. (a) (ii) Out of gratitude.

   (b) (i) joy of their victory

   (c) (ii) Gyrate

 **Short Answer Type Questions**

---

1. Ogden Nash's Tale of Custard the Dragon can be interpreted as a subversion of societal expectations. The poem presents Belinda as a brave and independent female character (described as brave as a barrel full of bears, a trait that is stereotypically associated with masculinity), while the male characters (Ink, Blink, Mustard) are portrayed as weaker and less courageous. Moreover, when faced with danger, Custard, the dragon, labelled a coward, is the one who steps up to defend Belinda and her household. **(2 Marks)**

2. Custard's character trait of humility is revealed when he accepts that the other animals are braver than him. He didn't contradict anyone who called him a coward rather coyly begged to be kept safe in a cage. **(2 Marks)**

3. **Value Points**

- Fable is fictitious narrative usually with animals, birds etc as characters and shares a strong message whereas a ballad is narrative verse that can be silly or heroic.

- The Tale of Custard the Dragon includes animals, is surely fictitious and shares a meaningful message.

- Hence, better qualifies as a fable. **(2 Marks)**

4. 'The Tale of Custard the Dragon' is a poem told in the form of a story with a plot and resolution. It portrays Custard's life with Belinda and other pets. In the end, Custard rose to the occasion and proved his bravery by gobbling the pirate. **(2 Marks)**

---

10. For Anne Gregory

 **1**   *Extract Based Questions*

---

1. (i) (c) 3, 5 (agitated and argumentative)

(ii) Beinghopelessly in love / the uncertainty in love/ Unsurity of the return of their affections

(iii) (d) Her conviction that she is beautiful inside.

(iv) yellow: blonde :: orange /red : carrot (either one can be accepted for full one mark)

(v) (c) The dessert needs to set for two hours before being served.

2. (a) These lines are being addressed to the woman with the yellow hair.

(b) Young men are in despair because they fall in love with Anne Gregory's yellow hair, and not her. Therefore, they are not able to acquire her.

(c) In these lines 'ramparts' means that her hair stood round her ear like 'the outer walls around a castle.'

3. (a) Anne Gregory is speaking these lines.

(b) Young men are in despair because they fall in love with Anne Gregory's yellow hair, and not her. Therefore, they are not able to acquire her.

(c) Hopeful, eager

4.   **(1×3=3 Marks)**

(a) 'I' refers to the poet.

(b) Young lovers love for her yellow hair represents the love for physical beauty whereas God loves an individual for being himself/herself.

(c) A text.

3   *Long Answer Type Questions*

1.   In the conversation that takes place between Anne Gregory and another speaker, the poet has tried to show that inner beauty is the real beauty, whereas physical appearance is changeable and hence, unimportant. The speaker says to Anne that young men love her for her beautiful yellow hair and may never love her for her what she really is. To this, Anne replies that her hair-colour can be changed into black, brown or carrot, meaning that external beauty is all superficial and men should not love her for that. Through Anne's reply, the poet has made clear his preference for internal beauty over physical appearance.

Topic-c: *Footprints Without Feet*

1   *Extract Based Questions*

1.   (a)   (A) is right and (B) is wrong

For trick's present condition Mrs. Pumphrey and Tricky both are responsible. So option (A) is right and (B) is wrong.

2   *Short Answer Type Questions*

1.   Mrs. Pumphrey's love and indulgence for her dog, Tricki, leads to the dog becoming severely overweight, unhealthy and ill. Despite Herriot's advice to put Tricki on a diet and exercise regimen, Mrs. Pumphrey is unable to say 'no' and abstain from overfeeding the dog. The story , thus, highlights the fact that sometimes, the best way to help someone is to say no and steer them towards a better path.   **(2 Marks)**

2.   Mr. Herriot was a veterinary doctor and Tricki was a little dog. But tricky was hugely fat. It looked like a bloated sausage with a leg at each corner. Its eyes were bloodshed and rheumy. Seeing all that, Mr. Herriot was shocked.

(2 Marks)

3.   Mrs. Pumphery treated Tricki with excessive love and affection. She presumed that he was suffering from malnutrition as he seemed listless, so she gave him extra between meals to build up his strength, like malt, cod liver oil and a bowl of Horlicks at night to make him sleep. She continued to feed him cream cakes and chocolates as she didn't have the heart to refuse him.

(2 Marks)

4.   Dr. Herriot could understand the problems of his patients (dogs) just by observing them. He saw Tricki in the market and understood that the dog required help. He also understood the owner (Mrs. Pumphrey) well and never spoke any harsh and advising words on the seriously obese dog, knowing very well that she was responsible for his condition.   **(2 Marks)**

5. Mrs. Pumphrey was a rich lady who loved his dog Tricki more than enough. She pampered him and gave him snacks in between his meals. The dog became lazy and began to suffer from indigestion due to his inactivity. Mrs. Pumphrey, in this way was responsible for Tricki's bad condition. **(2 Marks)**

---

2. The Thief's Story

1   *Extract Based Questions*

1. (c) He was a very simple person

   Anil never complained even when 'I' did not know how to cook.

   > **Note**
   >
   > The story reveals that Anil was not as dumb as 'I' felt. Anil know about the theft, but still he remained silent.

2   *Short Answer Type Questions*

1. Hari Singh justified his action of robbing Anil by saying that he had robbed a person who was not attentive. Also, he told himself that stealing was his habit and regular practice of stealing has made him rob Anil. **(2 Marks)**

2. Anil income was irregular. We did some freelance work in publishing houses. His income was meagre but he was able to pull on his life. We had no permanent source of income. **(2 Marks)**

3. Hari Singh had realised the importance of education that he was getting from Anil. He thought education would open up a lot of opportunities for him to lead a relaxed life in future. Hence the stolen money in hand appeared to be an hindrance in the path of his bright future. He, therefore. went back to Anil. **(2 Marks)**

4. Repentance is the first step towards reformation. Had Anil sent Hari Singh to the police, he might have been converted into a seasoned criminal. To see Hari Singh as an improved human being, Anil did not hand him over to the police. **(2 Marks)**

5. Anil used to make his living by writing, other irregular sources and start-ups. He kept worrying about his next payment. But when he got the money he would blow it up without a care. **(2 Marks)**

Note

(a) These 2-mark questions generally require textual answers straight from the text. You should be able to answer these if you have read the text thoroughly.

(b) However, occasionally, questions like (d) What does it show about her (Matilda's) character?' appear. To answer these, you need to make your own assessment based on the events and incidents that unfold in the story. So, you must have a good vocabulary as well as style of expression to convey your ideas as required.

---

3   *Long Answer Type Questions*

---

1. The thief's character arc in the story shows a transformation from a career criminal to a person who learns to trust and work hard for a living. At the beginning of the story, the thief is portrayed as an experienced criminal who is focussed on staying ahead of the law. He is initially attracted to Anil because he believes he can exploit the young man's trusting nature. As the story progresses, the thief begins to develop a friendship with Anil, who teaches him how to cook, write and read.

    This transformation of the thief's character reaches a climax when he is presented with an opportunity to steal money from Anil, but instead chooses to resist the temptation and considers the consequences of his actions. The story implies that the thief has realized that a life of crime is not fulfilling and that he is now open to exploring new opportunities for a better life.

2. The lesson 'The Thief's Story' is a testament to the power of trust and compassion to reform a person. The protagonist, Hari Singh, is a thief who meets Anil, a kind and trusting man. Anil takes Hari in and teaches him to cook and write, despite the fact that Hari cannot pay him. Through Anil's trust and compassion, Hari is able to see a different way of life and is inspired to change his ways. Anil's kindness so moves him that he cannot bring himself to rob him, despite having the perfect opportunity. This shows that trust and compassion can be powerful tools in reforming a person and inspiring them to make positive changes in their life.

3. Both characters in the story The Thief's Story are neither completely black (negative) nor white (ideal). They have redeeming qualities as well as those that need improvement. Their personas are grey. Hari Singh, the thief, is artful and too smart for his age. He fooled his victims and the police. He wasn't ashamed of lying and stealing. He made no effort to confess that he had stolen the notes. However, he changed due to Anil's love, affection, and trust. While Anil is helpful and simple, he is easily trusting. He never uttered a word despite

knowledge of the theft. However, he is casual about his money and ignores Hari's pilfering. Both characters are not flat. They present a sense of unpredictability and present a moral challenge.

4.

Topper's Answer

Hari Singh was a fifteen-year-old orphan and a seasoned con-artist. He was left to fend for himself and adopted the wrong approach to do so by engaging in thievery. On meeting Anil, a tall, lean and easy-going boy, Hari manages to worm his way through to Anil's heart. He offers to work for Anil but his real intention is to decamp with Anil's money. When Anil offers to educate him, Hari is delighted as he feels he can widen his dragnet to the high income group.

However, as the story proceeds, we see Anil's trusting manners and candid deportment having a positive impact on Hari's heart and mind. Even after stealing Anil's money, Hari returns it as his conscience is wide-awake and he realises that breaking Anil's trust in him would cost him dearly. He realises the importance of education in a man's life and now wants to be educated and live a respectful life in society. He now has an admirable aim and returns to Anil to fulfil it.

Thus, Anil's trust in Hari thaws his hardened heart and transforms him from a thief to a boy with his own admirable dream. The education, love and sympathy that Anil gives him makes him use his discretion between right and wrong. We can therefore conclude that education, love and sympathy can undoubtedly transform even a thief.

3. The Midnight Visitor

1   *Extract Based Questions*

1. (a) (iii) Max

   (b) (iv) started thinking of how to get rid of the man.

   (c) a movie scene

   (d) authentic

2. (a) (ii) Fowler

   (b) (iii) the U.S.

   (c) Slim trim and smart guy full of energy and dynamism.

   (d) amateur

2   *Short Answer Type Questions*

1. The author creates mystery and suspense by skilful use of language to create tension. Throughout the story, he employs short, punchy sentences that create a sense of urgency and a feeling that events are unfolding quickly and unpredictably.

   This helps to build momentum and keep the reader engaged, while also conveying a sense of unease and urgency. **(2 Marks)**

2. Ausable tricked Max into thinking that the police were at the door, when in reality it was just a waiter bringing a drink that Ausable had ordered. Max then panicked and tried to escape by climbing out the window, only to discover that there was no balcony. Ausable then used this opportunity to get rid of Max without using a weapon. **(2 Marks)**

3. Ausable was characterized as short and fat as the writer wanted to draw attention to and emphasize his wit and mental ability to handle any grave situation. He wanted to establish the point that brain power is far more potent than muscle power. **(2 Marks)**

4.   (2 Marks)

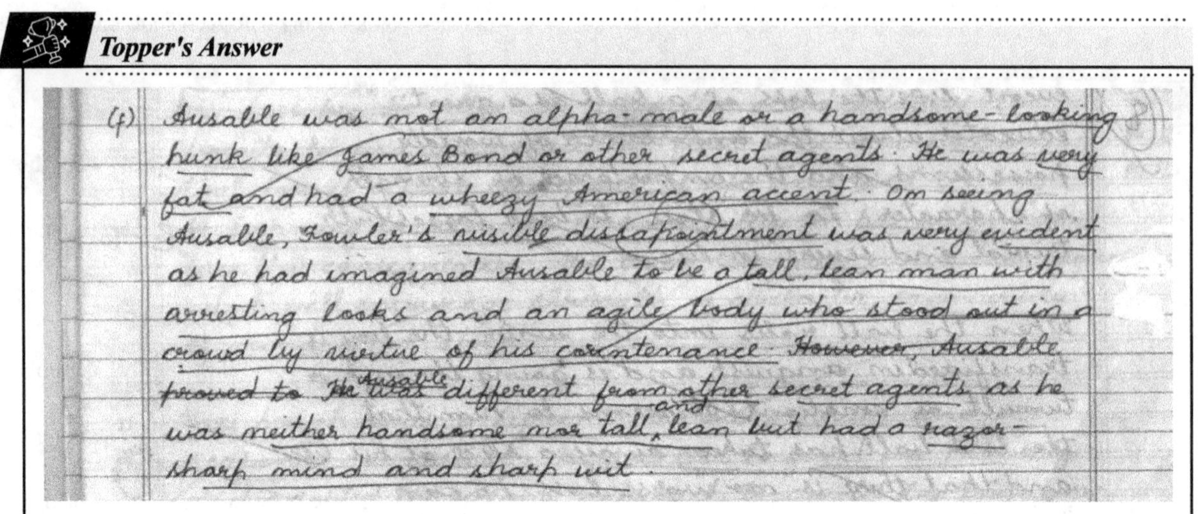

Topper's Answer

---

4. A Question of Trust

3   *Long Answer Type Questions*

2   *Short Answer Type Questions*

1. Horace's habits were not typical of a thief. He was fond of books. He used to steal only once a year, and he never stole more than his needs. However, an act of theft is a crime, no matter how well a thief behaves; so this description is apt for Danby. He cannot be categorised as a typical thief because he is not a regular offender like the other thieves. **(2 Marks)**

2. Horace Danby's hobby was to collect rare and expensive books. He managed to fulfil his hobby by stealing such books once in every year. Each year he robbed secretly and safely to collect and read them. **(2 Marks)**

1. It is believed that thieves never double-cross each other or commit crimes against each other. They would be inclined to help rather than betray each other. The protagonist Horace Danby was careful and meticulous in his theft which he conducted once a year. He didn't anticipate the role of the lady in red.

The Lady in red made a fool of him. Despite being a thief herself, she did not follow the code of honor normally existing between two thieves. This resulted in Horace Danby going to prison for the first time in his life. He felt betrayed.

---
5. Footprints without Feet

 **1** *Extract Based Questions*

---

1. (i) (d) Without clothes he was feeling cold.

This passage is from lesson, "foot prints without feet". Griffin, the scientist, carried out experiments to prove that the human body could become invisible. It was mid-winter and he was feeling cold without clothes.

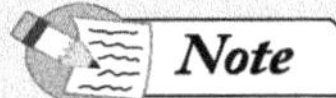 *Note*

This chapter is an excerpt taken from "The Invisible Man" written by H.G. Wells.

(ii) (d) He went along a street where there was no mud.

He could escape from the boys as he went along a street where there was no mud according to the lesson.

(iii) (c) Both (A) and (B) are right.

He had chosen a bad time of the year. It was mid-winter. So, the statement A is right, but it is the part of his experiment. Hence the statement A and B both are right.

(iv) (b) Partly relieved

According to lesson his adventures were by no means over means invisible man felt partly relieved.

(v) (b) Enter quietly

The phrase "slip into" is the same as enter quietly according to the passage Griffin quietly entered the store. For warmth.

(vi) (d) Bad set fire to his land lord's house

According to the lesson Griffin had set fire to his land lord's house because his land lord disliked him and tried to throw him out. In Revenge Griffin set fire to the house.

2. (i) (c) He did not like him.

(ii) Invisible.

(iii) (d) The Amar palace was completely destroyed by the fire.

(iv) (c) He left muddy imprints.

(v) (b) Griffin promised to behave himself.

---
3 *Long Answer Type Questions*

---

1. Griffin was undoubtedly a brilliant scientist who had invented a formula with which he could become invisible. No one in this world has achieved so far this wonderful know how. But he used it for his benefit and to loot others due to which he met with his death.

Remaining invisible, he murdered his own father and fled away from there. Since he was invisible the police would not catch him. Later in the town, he commits a theft in the house of the Vicar. There also he employs his formula to stay invisible.

Apart from these he steals clothes from a shop and runs away. Had he employed his invisibility for the welfare of the society, he would have been honoured suitably.

Note

a. *To answer these LA questions based on the prescribed novel, you must have read the novel completely at least once.*

b. *Often, new questions not discussed before are asked. If you have read the complete novel, you will find it easy to frame your answer to such a question.*

c. *You should know the theme and moral values and lessons conveyed in the novel to answer these questions well.*

2. Although Griffin had a criminal bent of mind; he had the power to become immersible. Whenever he wanted to escape being caught, he used it and saved himself. Utilizing the same capability, he first escaped from the two keen boys' observation; then entered unseen into a big store to get warm. Again when he was located and chased by the boys in the morning; he puts off his clothes and flees becoming immersible. In iping too, he robs a clergyman remaining invisible. Again when Jaffers wanted to catch

him; he knocked him unconscious. Thus invisibility is what he resort to whenever he is in trouble.

---

6. The Making of a Scientist

1   *Extract Based Questions*

1. (i) (Any one)

   We can infer that -

   • Dr Urquhart was a scientist who questioned assumptions

   • He was willing to investigate alternative explanations for phenomena

   • Dr Urquhart was a curious / open-minded scientist

   • He was not content to simply accept conventional wisdom

   (ii) True

   (This statement would not be called a hypothesis, assumption, premise, or theory. It is simply a statement of the question that Ebright was trying to answer.)

   (iii) Ebright's approach was highly effective in finding the purpose of the gold spots on a monarch pupa. By building a device that showed that the spots were producing a hormone necessary for the butterfly's full development, he was able to provide evidence that contradicted the prevailing assumption that the spots were purely ornamental. This earned him recognition in science fairs and provided him with opportunities to work at research laboratories.

(iv) an opportunity

2 ┆ *Short Answer Type Questions*

1. Richard Ebright's mother helped him by encouraging his interest and helped him enhance his knowledge and learning. She took him on trips bought him telescopes microscopes cameras mounting materials and other equipment and helped him in every possible way. If he did not have anything to do she found things for him to learn. Even the book that became a turning point in his life was given to him by his mother. Hence it can be rightly said that his mother played a crucial role in the making of a scientist. **(2 Marks)**

2. Richard Ebright raised a flock of butterflies in order to increase the number of butterflies he could tag for research by Dr. Frederick A. Urquhart of the University of Toronto, Canada. He would catch a female monarch, take her eggs, and raise them in his basement through their life cycle, from egg to caterpillar to pupa to adult butterfly. Then he would tag the butterflies' wings and let them go. **(2 Marks)**

3. Richard Ebright started the collection and breeding of butterflies as a fun activity. He got curious about the gold spots and the secretions. He was successfully able to develop a theory of cell structure and DNA because of it. Fun activities turned into the making of a renowned scientist. **(2 Marks)**

4. During the junior year, ebright got the idea for his new theary about cell life. He was looking at X-ray photos of the chemical structure of a hormone. Seeing the photos he believed that the photos gave him answer to his puzzle how the cells can read the blue print of its DNA? **(2 Marks)**

5. Dichard Ebright's mother was always there with him; she gossiped about scientific discoveries/inventions; she also brought him books on science and encouraged him to experiment. Thus she was a great help to him. **(2 Marks)**

6. From the very beginning, Ebright had driving curiosity alongwith a bright mind. Her mother encouraged his interest in learning. She took him on trips; bought telescopes, microscopes, cameras, books, etc., to support him. **(2 Marks)**

7. One day Ebright's mother gifted him, 'The Travels of Monarch X', that had the description of how monarch butterflies migrate to Central America. He devoted his time to the study of butterflies and won many prizes. In this way, this book changed his life. **(2 Marks)**

8. Richard Ebright's mother encouraged his intense interest in learning. She recognised the intellectual capacity of her son and therefore always found him something interesting to do, and learn from. She took him on trips and bought equipment to help him learn. **(2 Marks)**

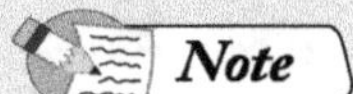 *Note*

(a) Word limit for such questions is 30-40; so, you contain all your ideas in response to the question asked within this only.

(b) In most cases, the answer is to be written in full sentences ; so, you need to exercise the skill of expressing all your relevant ideas concisely so as to avoid losing marks for crossing the word limit. It is a skill you must acquire with dedicated practice.

9. Richard Ebright raised a flock of butterflies because she was very much interested in collecting things. Besides his mother asked him to read a book named 'The Travels of monarch X' which inspired him to raise butterflies.

(2 Marks)

10. Richard Ebright's mother exposed him to the world around him by taking him on field trips, bought him books, telescope, microscope, cameras, mounting materials and other equipment. This helped him in becoming a famous scientist. **(2 Marks)**

11. When Richard Ebright did not win anything at the science fair, he realized that the winners had tried to conduct real experiments unlike him. He realized that a mere display of something that is not challenging, does not help you qualify to be a winner. It was necessary for him to work towards presenting real experiments. **(2 Marks)**

 **3**   *Long Answer Type Questions*

1. In the chapters, Bholi and The Making of a Scientist, parents play a crucial and indelible role as models, teachers, friends, and guides. They influence the children implicitly and explicitly. Richard Ebright's mother was a caring and loving companion to her son. She invested time and energy in making her son successful. On the other hand, Bholi's parents were indifferent, insensitive, and had a patriarchal mindset. They did not believe in the education of girls and did not bother to groom Bholi. Despite their prosperity, they left Bholi to her misery and decided to get her married off to Bishamber.

The contribution and companionship of parents cannot be denied. Love, care, and guidance from parents make a difference, sculpt children, and shape their futures.

---

7. The Necklace

 **Short Answer Type Questions**

1. Born in the family of clerks, Matilda Loisel was married to a clerk but she had high ambitions to lead a luxurious life. She could not afford it in the salary of her husband. Hence her early married life was unhappy.   **(2 Marks)**

2. Mr M. Loisel had to buy a suitable dress for his wife to enable her attend the party that was being hosted by the minister. He was short of money, so he sacrificed the 400 francs that he had saved to buy a gun to buy her a new party dress.   **(2 Marks)**

Note

(a) These SA questions require thinking and planning on your part. Try to remember the relevant details pertaining to the question asked and organise your ideas in concise sentences.

(b) These are 2-mark questions and the word limit is 30-40 only. So, plan out beforehand and answer to the point refraining from including any extra information whatsoever.

(c) Despite containing only 2 marks, some of these questions often have two or more questions in one. Be careful not to miss out any keeping within the word limit.

(d) Sometimes, questions like (c) How did it(the book) change his life?' is asked. Students often find it difficult to adhere to the word limit in such cases. So, you need to practice providing multiple information in concise sentences to answer such questions.

3. Matilda Loisel was unhappy with her circumstances virtually since the time she was born. She wanted to belong to the rich and affluent section of the society. Her desire failed as she married a man who was of the same social status.   **(2 Marks)**

4. Mme Loisel was always unhappy because of her social status. She wanted to be a very wealthy person and be surrounded by servants. But she was not able to attain such social standard.   **(2 Marks)**

5. Matilda, left the ball in a hurry because her husband threw the modest wraps around her shoulders and its lack of richness and glamour clashed with the elegance of the ball costume. She did not want to be noticed.

     (2 Marks)

 **Note**

a. *To answer questions carrying 2 marks only, remember not to elongate the relevant points; and rather to be as brief as possible.*

b. *Express your points in clear terms, within the prescribed word limit, without leaving out any relevant information.*

c. *Remember, a 'why' question must contain reasons for the concerned issue; while a 'what' question should be answered by providing the fact asked.*

6. No. No, M. Loisel had not enjoyed the evening at the ball. He was quite bored with the ball, and he had been half asleep in one of the little salons since midnight with three other gentlemen whose wives were enjoying themselves very much. **(2 Marks)**

7. Matilda didn't want to see her rich friends because she got jealous of all the luxuries, dresses and jewels that they had. She felt miserable and hopeless because she couldn't have any of it. **(2 Marks)**

8. Matilda had to replace the necklace she had lost the cost of which was 36,000 Francs. She and her husband had to struggle hard to repay the debt that was taken to buy a new necklace. **(2 Marks)**

3 *Long Answer Type Questions*

1. It's been a tough the past few years, for my wife, Matilda, and me. As I reflect on our experience, I can't help but think about the broader societal issues that have contributed to our predicament. It's clear to me now that our society is structured in a way that makes upward mobility difficult, if not impossible. The rich get richer, while the rest of us struggle to make ends meet.

We live in a world where social status is determined by the amount of wealth one possesses, rather than by one's character or virtues. This narrow view of success has led many people, including Matilda, to pursue material possessions at the expense of their own happiness. The loss of the borrowed necklace was a painful lesson for both of us. It reminded us that the pursuit of social status and upward mobility can be a trap, leading people to sacrifice their happiness and well-being in the pursuit of an unattainable dream.

2. Mme Loisel belongs to a family of clerks. Her existence is quite average. They live on meagre income, enough for basic needs but not to fulfil aspirations. She gets married to a clerk and is so caught up with her dreams of wealth and pleasure that she is out of touch with the truths of her real life. In order to keep up appearances just to flatter her pride, she blows up four hundred francs on a gorgeous dress. And, not contented, she goes on borrowing a necklace from her friend. And, all of this is just to impress the wealthy and the rich with her beauty and glamour (even if on loan). No doubt, her pride is flattered and her wish of fine dining, expensive dresses and jewels got satisfied but at a great price. Unfortunately, the necklace was lost and the couple has to cough up their entire inheritance and borrow as well to replace it. Repayment of the debt eats away the next ten years of their youth. They live poor. All the house hold chores and cares of a life of poverty visit them. Hence, her disposition invites her doom.

3. Matilda's mistake in life serves as a lesson to us all about the dangers of discontentment and unbridled desires. Her desire for luxury and extravagance led her to borrow a diamond necklace from her friend, and when she lost it, she and her husband had to spend ten years of their lives paying off the debt. This teaches us that contentment is key to a happy life, and that we should be careful not to let our desires get the better of us. We should be mindful of our spending and not let our wants and needs get out of control. Matilda's mistake also serves as a reminder to be grateful for what we have and to not take our blessings for granted.

4. Matilda haisel was a pretty and charming lady but she felt she took birth into a family of unfavourable economic conditions. She was married off to a clerk in the ministry of education who can afford to provide her only with a modest though not comfortable life style. She felt the burden of the poverty intensly. She regretted a lot in the life and spent endless hours imaging a more odogrant existence. While her husband expressed his pleasure at the small modest supper she has prepared for him. She dreamt eloborate feast served on fancy China and eaten in the company of wealthy friends. She possessed no fancy jewelery or clothing, yet those were the only things lived for.

She borrowed a jewellery from Me Loisel for the party. While relurning home, she lost it. She and her husband worked day and night to by another diamond necklace. The new diamond necklace would cost them 500 frances.

As a reader I sympathise with Mathilde because without any help of servants, she cooked, cleaned and dealt with the help of merchant and butcher to save each penny for simple enduance. The spouse worked in the evening and night to pay their obligation.   **(4 Marks)**

5. Being gorgeous and beautiful Matida thought that she was made to enjoy all the comforts of the world but she belonged to poor family and was married to a clerk. Her husband was already ready to fulfill her wishes but she was not satisfied. Once her husband brought passes for the party and asked her to get ready. Matilda borrowed a necklace from her friend and attended the party but the necklace was unluckily lost. For 10 years to come, she and her husband worked hard to buy that kind of necklace and sacrificed all their happiness. Matilda's friend told that the necklace was an imitated one. Anyway life span was gone. Thus they suffered because they were not contented with what they possessed. **(8 Marks)**

6. The Loisels were a well-to-do family but they lacked luxurious items like expensive jewellery or crockery. Once Mrs. Loisel was expected to attend a dance ball with some high profile people. Since she had no suitable jewellery for the purpose, she called upon her childhood friend, Mme forestier. She open-heartedly welcomed her and lent her, her choicest diamond necklace. Mrs Loisel attended the dance ball but she unfortunately lost the necklace. To repay for this, she and her husband toiled hard for 25 years and bought a necklace of the same kind. When she took it to Mme Forestier, she told her plainly that the necklace, she had lent was not so expensive and returned it back to her. Thus we see,

Mme forestier not only helps Mrs Loisel in times of need but also exhibits her honesty by not accepting the diamond necklace. It was indeed a true friendship.

(8 Marks)

8. Bholi

2 *Short Answer Type Questions*

1. Education helped Bholi to gain confidence and self-esteem, enabling her to stand up for herself and challenge societal norms. It empowers her to break free from the chains of patriarchy and choose her own path. It also enables her to recognize and resist oppression and inequality, making her an agent of change in her community. **(2 Marks)**

2. Although Bholi was not good to look at; she was young and educated. For the sake of her parents, she consented to marry 55 year old Bishambhar but Bishambhar put a condition that he will take ` 5000/- to marry Bholi. Bholi could not tolerate him and protested. She therefore; did not like him. **(2 Marks)**

3. Some part of Sulekha's brain was damaged as a result of a fall when she was just a few months old. She remained intellectually backward in comparison to her siblings. Therefore, she was called Bholi, the simpleton.

(2 Marks)

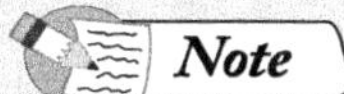

Note

(a) Word limit for these SA questions is 15 to 20 only; so, you should contain all your ideas regarding the answer within 20 words only. However, exceeding or falling short by 5 words is permissible.

(b) You should try to write the full sentences in such questions but short and wholesome answer is appreciated.

(c) Take only the relevant quotations from the story and relate them to arrive at your answer.

4. Bholi, the dumb cow, with the encouragement and help she got from her teacher could pronounce her name and say, Yes, without stammering. This made her heart-throb with new hope and new life. **(2 Marks)**

5. Bholi was sent to school because she had an ugly face. She lacked sense, therefore, the chance of getting married was less. These were the unusual reason why Bholi was sent to school. **(2 Marks)**

6. Bholi was neglected and considered a dumb cow by her family. She was sent to school by her parents against social norms, as they believed that no one would seek her hand in marriage as she had a slow brain and pomarked ugly face. **(2 Marks)**

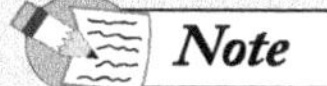

Note

a. Since the word limit for these 2 mark questions is 15 -20 only, you must be very precise including all your ideas regarding the answer within 20 words only.

b. In most cases, the answer is to be written in full sentences but very concisely.

c. Take only the relevant quotations from the story of Bholi to write the answer of Question 15(f), for example, and justify them using your reasoning.

3 *Long Answer Type Questions*

1. **Value Points:**

Bholi stammered -had pock marks on her face was ill treated by everyone -was sent to school as she supposedly had no future -teacher's love and affection moulded her -became confident, bold, didn't accept to marry lame, old, greedy Bishamber.

Such children should be made aware of their rights though they should equally be aware of their duties. There should be no discrimination among girls and boys as providing good education to the sons and ordinary to the daughters. The society should not treat such children as inferior. Society should follow the example of Bholi's teacher who encouraged her with great love and affection and made her stand on her own legs to face the life bravely and with confidence.

2.   **(8 Marks)**

Bholi alias Sulekha at the outset of the story in a sharp contrast to Bholi alias Sulekha by the end of the story. Under the marks left by chicken pox; she looked ugly and since she wasn't taken care of properly by her parents; she hesitated to speak and stammersed in case she spoke ever. But by the end of the story she becomes so bold and brave that she stands up against the oppressive approach of her would be groom-Bishambhar and refuses to marry him. Such a stark change in her character is in fact the cause and effect of education and the sympathetic attitude of her teacher. When education is complete; she stammers no more and takes the bull by its horn. This indomitable attitude is instilled in her through education only.

3.   Bholi was the fourth daughter of Ramlal. She suffered brain damage when she was only ten months old. At the age of two, she had small pox which left permanent pox marks on her body. She also stammered while speaking because of which she became a laughing stock among people. She was a neglected child of the family. Nobody took care of her and nobody had any expectation from her. Her parents called her a dumb cow and considered her so. Her sister's old dresses were passed on to her. No one cared to wash or mend her clothes. No one oiled her hair or tried to teach her anything. Luckily, she went to school and her teacher was a gentle lady who changed her life completely. She later turned out to be a learned girl. When her parents decided to marry her off to Bishamber, a fifty year old lame and greedy man, she did not protest. But later, when he insulted her parents and demanded 5000 rupees, she refused to marry him and declared that she would always serve her parents in their old age. Thus, in spite of being a neglected child, Bholi turns out to be very responsible indeed.   **(8 Marks)**

4.   Bholi, was a young girl who had contracted small pox at a young age and had started looking ugly. She also stammered while speaking and was shy by nature. When she got admitted to school, her teacher encouraged her to succeed and helped her gain confidence. After a while, her parents decided to marry her off to a man twice her age. She agreed as an ideal daughter would. However when the greedy groom demanded a hefty dowry she rebelled and refused to marry him. Education transformed the dumb cow into a bold girl. She saved her father from a huge expense. By teaching to earn a living she began supporting him in his old age.

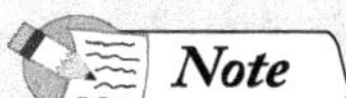

Note

(a) *These are value-based questions aimed at testing your awareness of human values as well as social values.*

(b) *To answer these questions, you not only need to be well-versed with the prescribed texts but also be a good human being so that your answer reveals your good values.*

(c) *Ideas expressed should be clear and precise. Avoid writing the idea you are not sure of. Illustrate your statements with quotations/incidents from the story.*

(d) *Write your answer in an organized and logical way.*

Note

(a) *These value based questions generally state a worldly observation or universal truth before the actual question. You are expected to present your views on the same before answering the actual question.*

(b) *In the above question, you should first support 'Whenever we want to achieve...' OR 'Education is an asset in....' with examples or your own experiences and thereafter answer the textual question.*

(c) *Ideas expressed should be clear and precise. Avoid writing the idea you are not sure of. Illustrate your statements with quotations/incidents from the story.*

5. Education is one of the greatest assets of a human being. People can steal your money; they cannot steal your knowledge. Education is more important for girls, as they can use this to avoid being exploited in a patriarchal world. This is exactly what happened with Bholi. At first, to save her family's honour, she agreed to marry an old and ugly man. However, she broke off the agreement later when she saw how greedy and despicable, he was. He demanded a hefty dowry, which was the main reason Bholi rejected him.

6. Bholi was a very shy and cowardly child because she had marks on her face and stammered. But when she was admitted to school, her teacher encouraged her to speak up and gain more knowledge. Bholi became aware of her rights and abilities through schooling. On the day of her marriage, the groom demanded a high dowry from her father because she was ugly. She spoke up then and refused to marry such a person. She saved her parents' money and gave an apt answer to the shameless bridegroom. **(4 Marks)**

 *Note*

(a) *Although this is a long answer type question, unnecessary number of words is not to be inserted into it.*

(b) *Use simple diction, make correct and meaningful sentences, express your ideas concisely and do not forget to mind the word limit.*

(c) *At the same time no fact pertaining to the question should be left out.*

7. Bholi was the youngest of Ramlal's four daughters. Unlike her sisters, Bholi suffered from ill-health, resulting in her falling short of societal norms with regard to intellect and looks. Society is sometimes very cruel to "differently endowed" people. But Bholi's teacher at the village primary school changed her life. She told Bholi, "Put the fear out of your heart and your will be able to speak like anyone else." In her teaching, she found a kind and helpful human being. She gave Bholi all the confidence and encouragement that she needed so badly.

 *Note*

a. *In such value based questions, your opinion is asked to test your understanding of human values. You should use your awareness of social and human relations to answer them.*

b. *Give an honest opinion and positive views.*

8. Ramlal and his wife did not believe in the ideology of sending girls to school as it would be difficult to find a good match for them. Bholi was Ramlal's youngest daughter. Unfortunately, due to a fall and an attack of small pox as a child, she became intellectually and physically a different child was sent to school. This changed her life totally changed. Her teacher encouraged and inspired her to rise higher in life. Being educated and confident now, Bholi refused to marry a mean and greedy man. She decided to serve her old parents and her village by teaching other girls. **(4 Marks)**

9. The Book that Saved the Earth

1 *Extract Based Questions*

1. (i) (b) Iota needs to present his opinion firmly.

(ii) frown: smile: gloomily: brightly

(iii) (d) accomplish a specific task.

(iv) (b) 2 & 4

(v) • Help actors and director gain clarity about the emotions and gestures required while performing / directing

• Helps with understanding stage setting and movements.

 **2** | *Short Answer Type Questions*

1. Earth was the only planet with books. The Martians had never seen books before. Moreover, they could not understand the Earth's language and transcription. So, they felt that the books were vitamins and had to be eaten. **(2 Marks)**

2. Noodle told Think-Tank that he had seen films about the books that the Earthlings used them for communication and not eating. Then Noodle added that they opened and watched the books... **(2 Marks)**

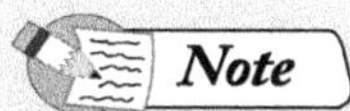 *Note*

(a) Since these are questions pertaining to the texts you have studied as part of the syllabus here you are at liberty to add some new information from your side, if required, but only in reference to what you have read in the texts.

(b) Mind the word limit and incorporate your ideas in precise sentences.

(c) In questions beginning with 'why', try to give all the reasons given in the text, unless the question mentions a required number, but in case they are too many, write only two or three and add 'etc' at the end.

3. When Martian commander Think-Tank saw the book full of nursery rhymes, he thought that it must be a book of Earthlings in which they've written about attacking the mars. So, he changed his idea of invading the earth and commanded his army to return back to their planet. **(2 Marks)**

4. After seeing the books, Think Tank jumped to a strange conclusion. He said that books are sandwiches. Then he refers to it as communication sandwiches and tries hard to instruct his team to identify how it is used for communication. Noodle then solved the issue when he suggested that they are perhaps for eye-communication and not for ear-communication. **(2 Marks)**

Note

a. To answer this question, thorough reading of the text is a must because this calls for understanding of the incidents and the characters involved therein.

b. Adhere strictly to the word limit; exceeding or falling short by not more than 5 words is permissible.

c. As far as possible, don't give details which you are not sure of.

<table><tr><td>**3**</td><td>*Long Answer Type Questions*</td></tr></table>

1. It is morally incorrect to invade another country or planet for one's own benefit. The Martians did not understand the value of peaceful coexistence. In the play, 'The Book that Saved the Earth', a science fiction, the author describes how a book of nursery rhymes, 'Mother Goose', is responsible for stopping the Martian invasion on Earth. Think-Tank, the ruler of Mars plans to invade Earth before lunch and sends Probe One, to get more information about the Earthlings. They begin reading the rhymes from 'Mother Goose'. Think-Tank misinterprets the rhymes, takes them as threats to him

and Mars. Scared, he calls back Probe One, drops the idea of invading the earth.

> ### Note
>
> *(a) As a rule, the student is supposed to stick to the word limit given therein, any violation may lead to deduction of marks. It is, however, permissible to exceed or fall short by 5 words.*
>
> *(b) Ideas expressed should be clear and precise. Avoid writing the idea you are not sure of. Illustrate your statements with quotations/incidents from the story.*
>
> *(c) Write your answer in an organized and logical way.*

CBSE Competency Focused Practice Questions

 **Topic-a:**   *First Flight*

HIS FIRST FLIGHT

1. **Read the given extract and answer the questions that follow.**

But he kept calling plaintively, and after a minute or so he uttered a joyful scream. His mother had picked up a piece of the fish and was flying across to him with it. He leaned out eagerly, tapping the rock with his feet, trying to get nearer to her as she flew across. But when she was just opposite to him, she halted, her wings motionless, the piece of fish in her beak almost within reach of his beak. He waited a moment in surprise, wondering why she did not come nearer, and then, maddened by hunger, he dived at the fish. With a loud scream he fell outwards and downwards into space. Then a monstrous terror seized him and his heart stood still. He could hear nothing. But it only lasted a minute.

A. Which of these shows the shift in emotion the seagull experiences from the beginning to the end of the extract?

          [CFPQ, CBSE 2022]

  (a) from calm to fearful

  (b) from anxious to nervous

  (c) from mournful to petrified

  (d) from joyous to depressed

B. Re-arrange the following events in the sequence that they occur in the extract.   **[CFPQ, CBSE 2022]**

  (I) The seagull lost control.

  (II) The seagull jumped towards the food.

  (III) The seagull's mother flew towards him.

  (IV) The seagull's mother refused to go nearer.

  (a) (IV) - (III) - (I) - (II)   (b) (III) - (IV) - (II) - (I)

  (c) (II) - (I) - (IV) - (III)   (d) (I) - (II) - (III) - (IV)

C. Which of these is true about the seagull and his mother?

          [CFPQ, CBSE 2022]

  (a) They disrespected each other but pretended to love one another.

  (b) They mocked each other but helped one another when it was needed.

  (c) They had different thoughts about their family but cared for each other.

  (d) They felt differently about the goal but wanted to achieve the same result.

D. How did the seagull cope with his fear of flying?

[CFPQ, CBSE 2022]

(a) He distracted himself by closing his eyes.

(b) He blocked out his fear and willed himself to be strong.

(c) He felt challed by the other seagulls and acted in a fit of rage.

(d) He realised that flying came naturally to him by diving unknowingly.

E. Which of these factors were NOT responsible for the young seagull learning to fly? **[CFPQ, CBSE 2022]**

(a) the continuous efforts of his mother and father

(b) the depth and vastness of the ocean beneath him

(c) the hunger and weakness that was maddening him

(d) the success of his siblings in diving and catching prey

F. Select the option that shows the correct relationship between the following statements. **[CFPQ, CBSE 2022]**

(1) The young seagull overcomes his fear and learns to fly.

(2) The fear of firsts vanishes when one takes the leap sometimes.

(a) (1) is a supporting detail for (2).

(b) (1) and (2) are unrelated.

(c) is true but (2) is false.

(d) (1) contradicts (2).

BLACK AEROPLANE

2. **Read the extract given below and answer the questions that follow.**

I saw the clouds. Storm clouds. They were huge. They looked like black mountains standing in front of me across the sky. I knew I could not fly up and over them, and I did not have enough fuel to fly around them to the north or south. "I ought to go back to Paris," I thought, but I wanted to get home. I wanted that breakfast. 'I'll take the risk,' I thought, and flew that old Dakota straight into the storm. Inside the clouds, everything was suddenly black. It was impossible to see anything outside the aeroplane. The old aeroplane jumped and twisted in the air. I looked at the compass. I couldn't believe my eyes: the compass was turning round and round and round. It was dead. It would not work! The other instruments were suddenly dead, too. I tried the radio. "Paris Control? Paris Control? Can you hear me?"

A. *They looked like black mountains standing in front of me across the sky.*

Which sentence uses the same figure of speech as used in the above lines from the extract? **[CFPQ, CBSE 2022]**

(a) My friend told me that his father could paint like Picasso.

(b) The garage looked like it had not been cleaned in a long time.

(c) Like any good cook will tell you, don't let the milk boil for too long.

(d) am a big fan of Sachin Tendulkar and would like to be a cricketer one day.

B. *Storm clouds. They were huge... It was dead. It would not work!*

In the extract, why has the author used short and abrupt sentences as shown above?   **[CFPQ, CBSE 2022]**

(a) to emphasise the narrator's reckless nature

(b) to convey the narrator's sense of urgency

(c) to move easily from one topic to another

(d) to make the text easier to read

C. Which of these best describes the narrator's decision to fly into the storm clouds?   **[CFPQ, CBSE 2022]**

(a) mysterious and thrilling

(b) selfish and uninformed

(c) hasty and emotional

(d) lazy and absurd

D. Read what four students said about the narrative style of the author.   **[CFPQ, CBSE 2022]**

Arjun: The first person narration of the story maintains an objectivity about the events as it forces the narrator to be neutral.

Bijoy: The first person narration of the story maintains a sense of mystery as we follow along with the narrator's thoughts instead of knowing everything beforehand.

Lucy: The first person narration of the story allows us to relate with the narrator as we are forced to look at the events through his perspective only.

Adiba: The first person narration of the story allows us to form a vivid picture of the events as if it is happening in real time.

With reference to the extract, which of the opinions mentioned above is NOT valid?

(a) Arjun's

(b) Bijoy's

(c) Lucy's

(d) Adiba's

E. Select the option that shows the correct relationship between (1) and (2).   **[CFPQ, CBSE 2022]**

(1) The narrator might have been able to fly through the storm if he was in a new aeroplane.

(2) Instruments in the narrator's aeroplane that were working well suddenly stopped functioning in the storm.

(a) (1) is the result of (2).

(b) (1) is the explanation for (2).

(c) (1) is an inference based on (2).

(d) (1) and (2) are independent of each other.

F. Which of these lines from the story supports the opinion stated below? **[CFPQ, CBSE 2022]**

The story 'The Black Aeroplane' is a mystery.

(a) "DS 088, I can hear you. You ought to turn twelve degrees west now, DS 088. Over."

(b) I knew I could not fly up and over them, and I did not have enough fuel to fly around them to the north or south.

(c) 'He knows that I am lost,' I thought. 'He's trying to help me.'

(d) So who helped me to arrive there safely without a compass or a radio, and without any more fuel in my tanks?

HOW TO TELL WILD ANIMALS

3. Choose the option that best shows the similarities among the animals in 'How to Tell Wild Animals'.

[CFPQ, CBSE 2022]

(1) They all live in the east.

(2) They all have swift movements.

(3) They all are two-eared mammals.

(4) They all have their unique qualities.

(a) (1) and (2)

(b) (2) and (3)

(c) (3) and (4)

(d) (4) and (1)

4. If when you're walking round your yard

You meet a creature there,

Who hugs you very, very hard,

Be sure it is a Bear.

If you have any doubts, I guess

He'll give you just one more caress.

Which of these best describes the poet's tone in the above lines from 'How to Tell Wild Animals'?

[CFPQ, CBSE 2022]

(a) It is cautionary as the bear might attack anytime.

(b) It is humorous as he compares a deadly attack to a hug.

(c) It is analytical as he compares the bear to other animals.

(d) It is full of wonder as he observes the bear in its natural habitat.

5. And if there should to you advance

A large and tawny beast

Which sentence uses the word 'advance' in the same way as used in the above lines from the poem 'How to tell Wild Animals'? **[CFPQ, CBSE 2022]**

(a) Alexander's army made an advance towards the fort.

(b) Juno will advance in his learning, little by little, every day.

   (c) Cynthia asked for an advance payment for the work done.

   (d) Freddie wants to make a scientific advance that will change the world.

6. Which of these best describes the Bal Tiger from 'How to Tell Wild Animals'? **[CFPQ, CBSE 2022]**

   (a) It is loving and affectionate.

   (b) It is energetic and beautiful.

   (c) It is gigantic and leaps with grace.

   (d) It is hungry and craves human flesh.

7. *If there is nothing on the tree,*

   'Tis the chameleon you see.

   What does the poet imply about the chameleon in the above lines from 'How to Tell Wild Animals'?

   [CFPQ, CBSE 2022]

   (a) it moves swiftly

   (b) it only lives on trees

   (c) it has the ability to camouflage

   (d) it does not have ears and wings

THE BALL POEM

8. *No use to say 'O there are other balls'*

   Which of these is the poet conveying in the above line from 'The Ball Poem'? **[CFPQ, CBSE 2022]**

   (a) There multiple choices in life.

   (b) What is lost is often irreplaceable.

   (c) Collecting things is a sign of greed.

   (d) Grown-ups can cope with loss easily.

9. Which of these best describes the poet's tone in 'The Ball Poem'? **[CFPQ, CBSE 2022]**

   (a) It is rational as he analyses the incident like an experienced adult.

   (b) It is regretful as he is not able to console the boy even though he wants to.

   (c) It is indifferent as he says that one must not console the boy who is crying.

   (d) It is full of wonder as he observes the boy closely to discover the nature of loss.

10. Select the option that shows the correct relationship between (1) and (2) from 'The Ball Poem'.

   (1) The poet chooses not to intrude on the boy.

   (2) The poet believes loss to be permanent and irreparable. **[CFPQ, CBSE 2022]**

   (a) (2) is the meaning of (1)

   (b) (2) is the opposite of (1)

   (d) (2) is a fact and (1) is an opinion

   (c) (2) explains the reason for (1)

A BAKER FROM GOA

11. Read the extract and answer the questions that follow.

In our childhood we saw bakers wearing a shirt and trousers which were shorter than full-lth ones and longer than half pants. Even today, anyone who wears a half pant which reaches just below the knees invites the comment that he is dressed like a pader! The baker usually collected his bills at the end of the month. Monthly accounts used to be recorded on some wall in pencil. Baking was indeed a profitable profession in the old days. The baker and his family never starved. He, his family and his servants always looked happy and prosperous. Their plump physique was an open testimony to this. Even today any person with a jackfruit-like physical appearance is easily compared to a baker.

A. The author mainly focuses on the physical appearance of the baker in the above extract.

Which of these lines from the extract justifies the above opinion? **[CFPQ, CBSE 2022]**

(a) *The baker and his family never starved.*

(b) *The baker usually collected his bills at the end of the month.*

(c) *Monthly accounts used to be recorded on some wall in pencil.*

(d) *He, his family and his servants always looked happy and prosperous.*

B. Monthly accounts used to be recorded on <u>some wall</u> in pencil.

Which of these best explains the author's purpose for using 'some wall' in the above line? **[CFPQ, CBSE 2022]**

(a) to convey that bakers were very organised in their job

(c) to show that bakers were not very worried about their income

(c) to indicate that bakers had more customers than they could service

(d) to show that bakers were not too advanced in the systems they used

C. Select the option which best describes the relationship between the following statements from the extract.

[CFPQ, CBSE 2022]

(1) *He, his family and his servants always looked happy and prosperous.*

(2) *Their plump physique was an open testimony to this.*

(a) (2) gives a summary of (1)

(b) (2) explains the meaning of (1)

(c) (2) is an inference drawn from (1)

(d) (2) supports the point made in (1)

D. *Even today, anyone who wears a half pant which reaches just below the knees invites the comment that he is dressed like a pader!*

Which of these best describes the author's tone in the above line? **[CFPQ, CBSE 2022]**

(a) neutral

(b) playful

(c) reflective

(d) welcoming

E. Based on the extract above, what type of text is 'A Baker from Goa'? **[CFPQ, CBSE 2022]**

(a) a factual essay on past practices

(b) a diary entry about one's life events

(c) a research article which analyses a concept

(d) a historical account written based on personal knowledge

F. Which of these best explains why the author chose 'A Baker from Goa' as the title for the text?

[CFPQ, CBSE 2022]

(a) The author discusses his journey as a baker to describe the cuisines of Goa.

(b) The author details the adventures of a baker to explore the cultural issues of Goa.

(c) The author narrates the life of a baker to paint a vivid picture of Goa's cultural history.

(d) The author recounts his childhood memories of home-baking to show Goa's rich traditions.

MIJBIL THE OTTER

12. Read the given extract and answer the questions that follow.

I made a body-belt for him and took him on a lead to the bathroom, where for half an hour he went wild with joy in the water, plunging and rolling in it, shooting up and down the lth of the bathtub underwater, and making enough slosh and splash for a hippo. This, I was to learn, is a characteristic of otters; every drop of water must be, so to speak, extended and spread about the place; a bowl must at once be overturned, or, if it will not be overturned, be sat in and sploshed in until it overflows. Water must be kept on the move and made to do things; when static it is wasted and provoking.

A. Which of these best describes the narrator's tone in the extract? **[CFPQ, CBSE 2022]**

(a) tired and exhausted

(b) fascinated and playful

(c) doubtful and surprised

(d) informative and objective

B. *...and making enough slosh and splash for a hippo.*

In the above line, why does the narrator compare Mijbil to a hippo? **[CFPQ, CBSE 2022]**

(a) to show how much water a small creature like Mijbil can displace

(b) to note the similarity between the appearance of Mijbil and a hippo

(c) to condemn the water wastage that happens due to an otter's actions

(d) to give information on the natural behaviours of various water animals

C. Which of these shows the usage of <u>'must'</u> as it has been used in the extract?   **[CFPQ, CBSE 2022]**

  (a) It is a must for all students to follow the rules set by the principal.

  (b) Our host must be wondering where we are because we are quite late.

  (c) You must brush your teeth everyday if you want them to stay white and hygienic.

  (d) She plays these odd games where she must eat only even number of vegetables.

D. How has the author learnt about the behaviour of otters?   **[CFPQ, CBSE 2022]**

  (a) He has used his bookish knowledge of otters to understand Mijbil better.

  (b) He has noted Mijbil's actions and compared them to those of other otters.

  (c) He has had past experiences with other otters and knows what Mijbil is likely to do.

  (d) He has observed Mijbil's actions and used that to understand what otters generally do.

E. *Water must be kept on the move and made to do things;* <u>*when static it is wasted and provoking*</u>.

The underlined part of the above line is the narrator's __________ of Mijbil's reason for moving water.

                           [CFPQ, CBSE 2022]

  (a) factual description

  (b) scientific explanation

  (c) practical demonstration

  (d) subjective interpretation

MADAM RIDES THE BUS

13. **Read the given extract and answer the questions that follow.**

The bus slowed down to a crawl, and the conductor, sticking his head out the door, said, "Hurry then! Tell whoever it is to come quickly." "It's me," shouted Valli. "I'm the one who has to get on."

By now the bus had come to a stop, and the conductor said, "Oh, really! You don't say so!"

"Yes, I simply have to go to town," said Valli, still standing outside the bus, "and here's my money." She showed him some coins. "Okay, okay, but first you must get on the bus," said the conductor, and he stretched out a hand to help her up.

"Never mind," she said, "I can get on by myself. You don't have to help me." The conductor was a jolly sort, fond of joking. "Oh, please don't be angry with me, my fine madam," he said. "Here, have a seat right up there in front. Everybody move aside please - make way for madam."

A. *"Hurry then! Tell whoever it is to come quickly."*

What is the conductor's assumption while saying the above line? **[CFPQ, CBSE 2022]**

(a) The child is trying to catch the bus for her own self.

(b) The passers in the bus are getting extremely impatient.

(c) The child is trying to stop the bus for an adult family member.

(d) The adults who should be supervising Valli are being very irresponsible.

B. *"Oh, really! You don't say so!"*

The above line conveys the conductor's ___________.

[CFPQ, CBSE 2022]

(a) definite refusal to give a ticket to Valli to board the bus

(b) total surprise on learning that Valli will be travelling alone

(c) serious command to Valli to not say such things as a child

(d) excited exclamation over the money that he will earn from Valli

C. Which of these can we say about Valli after reading the extract? **[CFPQ, CBSE 2022]**

(a) She wants to change how adults view children.

(b) She wants to save money to seem responsible.

(c) She wants to be seen as an independent person.

(d) She wants to rebel against everyone who questions her.

D. When the conductor calls Valli 'madam', he is being __________ her. **[CFPQ, CBSE 2022]**

(a) a bully to

(b) helpful to

(c) formal with

(d) playful with

E. *..."and here's my money." She showed him some coins.*

Why does Valli show the conductor the money at this moment in the extract? **[CFPQ, CBSE 2022]**

(a) to show-off the money she saved so painstakingly

(b) so that the conductor does not think that she is poor

(c) to prove to the conductor that she can afford the ticket

(d) so that she is called 'madam' by all the adults in the bus

14. **Read the given extract and answer the questions that follow.**

Day after day she watched the bus, and gradually a tiny wish crept into her head and grew there: she wanted to ride on that bus, even if just once. This wish became stronger and stronger, until it was an overwhelming desire. Valli would stare wistfully at the people who got on or off the bus when it stopped at the street corner. Their faces would kindle in her longings, dreams, and hopes. If one of her friends happened to ride the bus and tried to describe the sights of the town to her, Valli would be too jealous to listen and would shout, in lish: "Proud! proud!" Neither she nor her friends really understood the meaning of the word, but they used it often as a slang expression of disapproval.

A. Which of these best describes Valli's desire to ride the bus in 'Madam Rides the Bus **[CFPQ, CBSE 2022]**

B. Which of these is true about Valli and her friends?

[CFPQ, CBSE 2022]

(a) They have all travelled in a bus.

(b) They are not very fluent in lish.

(c) They all want to ride the bus together.

(d) They do not go to any school for education.

15. *'The Tale of Custard the Dragon' is a fantasy ballad.* Which of these options supports the above statement?

[CFPQ, CBSE 2022]

(a) that Belinda has a pet dragon

(b) that everyone mocked custard

(c) that the pirate was loaded with weapons

(d) that Mustard vanishes at the sight of danger

16. Re-arrange the following events as they occur in the poem 'The Tale of the Custard Dragon'.

[CFPQ, CBSE 2022]

(I) Belinda's house is attacked by a Pirate.

(II) Belinda and the animals make fun of Custard.

(III) The animals are frightened beyond their wits.

(IV) Mustard justifies why he was unable to be brave.

(a) (II) - (IV) - (III) - (I)

(c) (III) - (IV) - (I) - (II)

(b) (I) - (II) - (IV) - (III)

(d) (II) - (I) - (III) - (IV)

17. Which of these can be concluded about Ink, Blink and Mustard after reading 'The Tale of Custard the Dragon'?

[CFPQ, CBSE 2022]

(a) They were boastful creatures.

(b) They were courageous warriors.

(c) They were obedient towards Belinda

(d) They were kidnappers sent by the pirate.

18. *...And Ink and Blink <u>chased lions down the stairs</u>* What does the underlined phrase from 'The Tale of Custard the Dragon' convey about Ink and Blink?

[CFPQ, CBSE 2022]

(a) how fast they were

(b) how loyal they were

(c) how large they were

(d) how brave they were

19. Why do you think Lencho from 'A Letter to God' is able to predict the forthcoming rainfall even before the clouds appear? Answer in 20-30 words. **[CFPQ, CBSE 2022]**

20. In 20-30 words, compare the theme of the poem 'Fire and Ice' with the poet's tone. **[CFPQ, CBSE 2022]**

21. In the poem 'Fire and Ice', which literary device are fire and ice examples of? In 40-50 words, explain why the poet uses them. **[CFPQ, CBSE 2022]**

22. In 30-40 words, describe the mood of 'His First Flight' towards the end of the chapter. Support the answer with an example from the text. **[CFPQ, CBSE 2022]**

23. *His father and mother had come around calling to him shrilly, upbraiding him, threatening to let him starve on his ledge unless he flew away.*

In the above line from 'His First Flight,' do you think the seagull's parents took the right approach to make him fly? In 100-120 words, justify your stance with two reasons, **[CFPQ, CBSE 2022]**

24. *I was very happy to go behind the strange aeroplane like an obedient child.*

In 20-30 words, explain why the narrator said the above line in the story 'The Black Aeroplane'.

[CFPQ, CBSE 2022]

25. *The pilot in the black aeroplane was an illusion created by the narrator's own mind.*

Justify the above opinion with reference to the story 'The Black Aeroplane'. In 100-120 words, mention two reasons why you think the narrator's mind may have played this trick. **[CFPQ, CBSE 2022]**

26. In 20-30 words, describe your reaction if you were to come across one of the animals in 'How to Tell Wild Animals' in real life? **[CFPQ, CBSE 2022]**

27. In 40-50 words, mention two of your favourite animals from 'How to Tell Wild Animals' with a reason supporting each choice. **[CFPQ, CBSE 2022]**

28. If you were to compare the animals from the poem 'How to Tell Wild Animals' to people, what personalities would these people have? Pick any two animals from the poem and describe their human counterparts in 100-120 words. **[CFPQ, CBSE 2022]**

29. *He senses first responsibility*

In a world of possessions.

In the above lines from 'The Ball Poem', what does the poet mean when he says that the boy senses 'first responsibility' after losing the ball? Answer in 20-30 words. **[CFPQ, CBSE 2022]**

30. What is the boy's loss of his ball used as a metaphor for in 'The Ball Poem'? Support your answer with one point of evidence from the poem in 40-50 words.

[CFPQ, CBSE 2022]

31. Identify and explain the literary devices in this poem.

What is the boy now, who has lost his ball,

What, what is he to do? I saw it go

Merrily bouncing, down the street, and then

Merrily over- there it is in the water...

In the above lines from 'The Ball Poem', the poet uses imagery and repetition. In 100 words, identify both these literary devices and the effect of each one on the reader.

[CFPQ, CBSE 2022]

32. Who would Anne consider a real friend based on 'The Diary of Anne Frank'? Describe in 20-30 words.

[CFPQ, CBSE 2022]

33. How does Anne Frank's writing age readers? Comment on any one aspect with evidence from 'The Diary of Anne Frank' in 40-50 words. **[CFPQ, CBSE 2022]**

34. In 'The Diary of Anne Frank', how does Anne Frank feel about Mr Keesing's essay assignments and what is her purpose for writing them? Describe what this tells us about her in 100-120 words. **[CFPQ, CBSE 2022]**

35. How does the author establish that the *pader* is an important part of Goan society? Support your answer with one example from 'A Baker from Goa' in 40-50 words. **[CFPQ, CBSE 2022]**

36. How does the author create a sense of nostalgia in the story 'A Baker from Goa'? Support your answer with one piece of evidence from the story in 40-50 words.

[CFPQ, CBSE 2022]

37. With reference to 'A Baker from Goa', describe any two aspects of Goan lifestyle which [4] show Portuguese influence. In 100-120 words, support each aspect with evidence from the text. **[CFPQ, CBSE 2022]**

38. *I do, however, prefer to step aside for wild elephants.*

What is the tone of the above line from the text 'Coorg'? What does the author want to indicate in this line? State your response in 20-30 words. **[CFPQ, CBSE 2022]**

39. Which time of the year would you recommend someone to visit Coorg? Justify your answer with details from the text 'Glimpses of India: Coorg' in 40-50 words.

[CFPQ, CBSE 2022]

40. Which aspects of Coorg does the author explore from a historical perspective? **[CFPQ, CBSE 2022]** Describe any two aspects in detail in 40-50 words.

41. *The text 'Glimpses of India: Coorg' is only a factual description of the place and its culture.*

In 100-120 words, state your opinion on the above statement and justify it with any two points about the author's writing style and its effects on the reader.

[CFPQ, CBSE 2022]

42. Briefly describe any one event from the story 'Mijbil the Otter' that shows that otters are intelligent creatures. Answer in 20-30 words. **[CFPQ, CBSE 2022]**

43. How does Mijbil's behaviour change after a few days as compared to the night when he's first brought home by the narrator in 'Mijbil the Otter'? Why do you think this change happens? Answer in 40-50 words.

[CFPQ, CBSE 2022]

44. *It is, in effect, a thraldom to otters, an otter fixation, that I have since found to be shared by most other people, who have ever owned one.*

What does the narrator mean to convey in the above statement? Explain any two pieces of evidence from 'Mijbil the Otter' that support this statement in 100-120 words. **[CFPQ, CBSE 2022]**

45. *Her first journey - what careful, painstaking, elaborate* *plans she had had to make for it!*

The above is a line from 'Madam Rides the Bus'. Why do you think Valli put in so much effort in planning for this journey? State a reason in 20-30 words. **[CFPQ, CBSE 2022]**

46. The boy in 'The Ball Poem' loses his ball and Valli in 'Madam Rides the Bus' encounters the death of a cow. What is similar about what the two characters learn from these experiences? State your response in 40-50 words.

[CFPQ, CBSE 2022]

47. In the story 'Madam Rides the Bus', the elderly woman in the bus keeps enquiring after Valli because she is a child. What assumptions could she have about children? Do you think these assumptions are justified when applied to Valli? State why or why not in 100- 120 words.

[CFPQ, CBSE 2022]

48. Read the line given below from the poem 'The Tale of Custard the Dragon'. What effect do the words 'realio, trulio' have on the poem? **[CFPQ, CBSE 2022]**

Custard the dragon had big sharp teeth,

And spikes on top of him and scales underneath,

Mouth like a fireplace, chimney for a nose,

And realio, trulio, daggers on his toes.

49. *Custard was not treated properly by Belinda and his fellow animals.*

Justify the above statement in 20-30 words with an example from 'The Tale of Custard the Dragon'.

[CFPQ, CBSE 2022]

50. In 40-50 words, analyse any one of Custard's qualities with an example from 'The Tale [3] of Custard the Dragon'. **[CFPQ, CBSE 2022]**

51. *Imagery and Personification are used abundantly in 'The Tale of Custard the Dragon'.*

State one evidence each for their usage and analyse the author's purpose behind it in 100-120 words.

[CFPQ, CBSE 2022]

52. The play 'The Proposal' highlights the social and practical necessities of marriage. Support this statement in about 120 words with reference to each character.

[CFPQ, CBSE 2022]

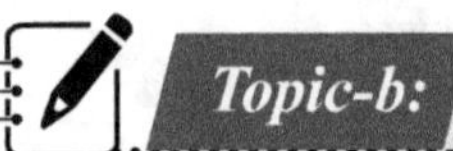

Topic-b: *Footprints without Feet*

THE MIDNIGHT VISITOR

1. **Read the given extract and answer the questions that follow.**

    "Instead, you have spent a dull evening in a French music hall with a sloppy fat man who, instead of having messages slipped into his hand by dark-eyed beauties, gets only a prosaic telephone call making an appointment in his room. You have been bored!" The fat man chuckled to himself as he unlocked the door of his room and stood aside to let his frustrated guest enter. "You are disillusioned," Ausable told him. "But take cheer, my young friend. Presently you will see a paper, a quite important paper for which several men and women have risked their lives, come to me. Some day soon that paper may well affect the course of history. In that thought is drama, is there not?"

    A. Which of these best describes what Ausable is doing in the extract?   **[CFPQ, CBSE 2022]**

    (a) He is relating to Fowler and attempting to change his view.

    (b) He is justifying his appearance to Fowler as that of a real spy.

    (c) He is summarising events to help Fowler make sense of them.

    (d) He is shaming himself so that Fowler's disappointment reduces.

    B. If someone is 'disillusioned', it means that they   **[CFPQ, CBSE 2022]**

    (a) have become angry at someone for having unrealistic ideas

    (b) have disappointed someone with how they are in real life

    (c) have created fantasies to make it easier to accept reality

    (d) have gotten a reality check that has disappointed them

    C. According to the extract, which elements are expected to be present in the life of a spy?   **[CFPQ, CBSE 2022]**

    (I)   attractive women who deliver information

    (II)   discreet phone calls from other famous spies

    (III) dramatic events that involve guns and action

    (IV) an athletic body that moves in an agile manner

    (a) Only (I)

    (c) Only (III) and (IV)

    (b) Only (I) and (IV)

    (d) Only (I), (II) and (IV)

D. Why does Ausable refer to Fowler as 'my young friend'?

[CFPQ, CBSE 2022]

(a) to make a sarcastic comment about Fowler's childishness

(b) to remind Fowler that young people are usually cheerful

(c) to reassure Fowler that they are indeed friends

(d) to highlight how naive and innocent Fowler is

E. *"In that thought is drama, is there not?"*

Which of these would be the most suitable response from Fowler if Ausable is successful in helping him 'take cheer'? [CFPQ, CBSE 2022]

(a) No, there is no drama in a mere piece of paper.'

(b) Now I am intrigued; please tell me more about it.'

(c) Yes, we should take action to mark our names in history.'

(d) Is it? I am very disappointed that I came all the way for this.'

FOOTPRINTS WITHOUT FEET

2. Which option best describes Mrs Hall from 'Footprints Without Feet'? [CFPQ, CBSE 2022]

(a) hospitable but firm

(b) scared and superstitious

(c) accommodating but curious

(d) opportunistic and insensitive

3. *The two boys started in surprise at the fresh muddy imprints of a pair*

of bare feet. What was a barefooted man doing on the steps of a house, in the middle of London? And where was the man?

Why does the author begin 'Footprints Without Feet' with these questions? [CFPQ, CBSE 2022]

(a) to seek answers to the queries

(b) to spark curiosity about the story

(c) to show a lack of knowledge about the plot

(d) to highlight the unusual reaction of the characters

4. In 'Footprints Without Feet' Griffin's invisibility causes ____________ among the people around him.

[CFPQ, CBSE 2022]

1. jealousy and hatred 2. crime and bloodshed

3. awe and amazement 4. chaos and destruction

(a) (1) and (2) (b) (2) and (3)

(c) (3) and (4) (d) (4) and (1)

5. Based on your reading of 'Footprints Without Feet', how would Griffin most likely react if he were to be captured by constable Jaffers? [CFPQ, CBSE 2022]

(a) surrender quietly

(b) resort to violence

(c) argue his way out

(d) plead with his captor

THE MAKING OF A SCIENTIST

3. **Read the extract given below and answer the questions that follow.**

Then in the seventh grade he got a hint of what real science is when he entered a county science fair - and lost. "It was really a sad feeling to sit there and not get anything while everybody else had won something," Ebright said. His entry was slides of frog tissues, which he showed under a microscope. He realised the winners had tried to do real experiments, not simply make a neat display.

Already the competitive spirit that drives Richard Ebright was appearing. "I knew that for the next year's fair I would have to do a real experiment," he said. "The subject I knew most about was the insect work I'd been doing in the past several years."

A. Which of these could be one of the winners' projects for the county science fair? **[CFPQ, CBSE 2022]**

(a) a diagram of human cheek cells under a microscope

(b) a model of the water cycle with miniature water bodies

(c) a study on mint leaves that shows how light affects its growth

(d) a summary of past research on how caterpillars become butterflies

B. Which of these best summarises Ebright's reaction to losing at the county science fair in the seventh grade?

[CFPQ, CBSE 2022]

(a) He felt discouraged but was happy about his efforts.

(b) He felt dejected but was motivated to do better next time.

(c) He felt defeated but accepted that others were better than him.

(d) He felt hopeless but became aggressive about winning next time.

C. Why does the author quote Ebright at several points in the above extract? **[CFPQ, CBSE 2022]**

(a) to prove that his account of Ebright is authentic

(b) to support the statements he is making about Ebright

(c) to show examples that contradict Ebright's arguments

(d) to reveal how Ebright truly felt about his achievements

D. What changed for Ebright after he lost at the county science fair? **[CFPQ, CBSE 2022]**

(a) his interest in studying the science of insects

(b) his notion of what the field of science truly is

(c) his understanding of his own scientific abilities

(d) his fascination with scientific instruments like microscopes

E. Which of these best captures how the word 'real' has been used in the extract? **[CFPQ, CBSE 2022]**

(a) something that is natural and organic

(b) something that can be seen and touched

(c) something that shows results or proves a theory

(d) something that shows one's intelligence and hard work

4. In 'The Thief's Story', why did Hari believe that friends were more trouble than help? In 20-30 words, state your opinion with one reason. **[CFPQ, CBSE 2022]**

5. According to you, why didn't Anil confront Hari about stealing his money in 'The Thief's Story'? Explain in 20-30 words. **[CFPQ, CBSE 2022]**

6. Was Anil from 'The Thief's Story' good at managing his money properly? Justify your answer in 40-50 words.

[CFPQ, CBSE 2022]

7. Imagine you are Hari from 'The Thief's Story'. After not getting on the train, you sit on the bench in the maidan, drenched in the rain. In 40-50 words, write about your thoughts that led you back to Anil.**[CFPQ, CBSE 2022]**

8. *The greedy man showed fear; the rich man showed anger; the poor man showed acceptance.*

With reference to the above line from 'The Thief's Story, explain why different people react differently when their money is stolen. Answer in 40-50 words.

[CFPQ, CBSE 2022]

9. State any one way in which Ausable or Max from 'The Midnight Visitor' are different from the usual portrayal of spies in movies and books. Why do you think the author has portrayed the characters in this way? Answer in 40-50 words. **[CFPQ, CBSE 2022]**

10. What could be a reason for Fowler to visit Ausable in 'The Midnight Visitor'? Support your answer with details from the story in 40-50 words. **[CFPQ, CBSE 2022]**

11. What makes Ausable a good spy? Explain any one quality with close reference to the story 'The Midnight Visitor' in 40-50 words. **[CFPQ, CBSE 2022]**

12. *Griffin had shaken himself free, and no one knew where to lay hands on him.*

In 20-30 words, give one example from 'Footprints Without Feet' to describe the price Griffin had to pay for his freedom. **[CFPQ, CBSE 2022]**

13. In 40-50 words, state any two features that make 'Footprints Without Feet' an adventure story.

[CFPQ, CBSE 2022]

14. In 'Footprints Without Feet', Griffin the scientist is disliked by most people. In 100-120 words, state any one reason why he is widely disliked and suggest one action he can take to reform himself. **[CFPQ, CBSE 2022]**

15. What is common about the role that Dr Urquhart and Mr Weiherer played in Richard Ebright's life? Describe any one commonality with evidence from the text 'The Making of a Scientist' in 20-30 words. **[CFPQ, CBSE 2022]**

16. *"Richard was competitive," Mr Weiherer continued, "but not in a bad sense."*

How would you describe a person who is competitive 'in a bad sense'? How is Richard Ebright different from such a person? Answer with reference to the text 'The Making of a Scientist' in 40-50 words. **[CFPQ, CBSE 2022]**

17. The text 'The Making of a Scientist' reveals Richard Ebright's many interests outside science as well. Do you think the saying, 'jack-of-all-trades, master of none' applies to Ebright? Justify your opinion with any two pieces or textual evidence in 100-120 words.

[CFPQ, CBSE 2022]

Solutions

Topic-a: *First Flight*

1.

| A | (c) | B | (b) | C | (d) | D | (d) | E | (b) |
| F | (a) | | | | | | | | |

2.

| A | (a) | B | (b) | C | (c) | D | (a) | E | (c) |
| F | (d) | | | | | | | | |

3. (d) **4.** (b) **5.** (a) **6.** (d) **7.** (c)

8. (b) **9.** (a) **10.** (c)

11.

| A | (d) | B. | (b) | C. | (d) | D. | (b) | E. | (d) |
| F. | (c) | | | | | | | | |

12.

| A. | (b) | B. | (a) | C. | (d) | D. | (d) | E. | (d) |

13.

| A. | (c) | B. | (b) | C. | (c) | D. | (d) | E. | (c) |

14.

| A. | (b) | B | (a) |

15. (d) **16.** (a) **17.** (d) **18.** (d)

19. Lencho is able to predict the forthcoming rainfall as he is a farmer and his livelihood depends on the weather. He is in touch with nature and can read Its signs well.

20. The theme of the poem is that of destruction and the end of the world, which is a grim subject. The tone of the poem however, does not reflect this seriousness and is conversational and assertive.

21. In the poem, fire and ice are examples of symbolism. The poet uses them as they paint a vivid picture of destruction in our minds. We can easily imagine humanity being destroyed by raging fires as well as extreme winters. The symbols help the poet to create a lasting impression of emotions like desire and hate which are difficult to visualise by themselves.

22. When the young seagull finally takes his first flight, the mood is one of celebration. The seagull's family stops threatening him and instead praise him for his first flight by giving him scraps of food and shouting with happiness.

23. No, I believe that their approach was incorrect because they let their anger take the decision for how to teach the young seagull. This might have made him feel abandoned and unsupported. The parents should have accepted his fear instead of threatening him and let his siblings tease him for it. Rather, they taunted him with his cowardice and Isolated him. This added to his fear which affected his confidence and discouraged him. He quietly hid inside the little hole under the ledge. This made him feel that he would never be able to fly like his brothers and sister.

24. The narrator's aeroplane's systems started malfunctioning inside the storm clouds. So, when the pilot of the black plane signalled to him, he was happy to follow because he had no other way out.

25. When the narrator landed at the airport, he went to the woman in the control tower to ask for the other pilot. He was told that there was no other flight in the area apart from the one in which he came. Moreover, the other airplane itself did not have any lights on it's wings and seemed to mysteriously appear beside him.

I think that the narrator's mind must have created this illusion so that he could calmly get himself out of the situation without panicking. Since all the systems in the plane had stopped working, he needed to rely on his instincts to survive. This may have happened because it was a life-or-death situation in which his mind must have been in a heightened state.

26. If I were to come across the lion, I would be excited to see them from a safe distance because it is hard to find wild animals in the city.

27. Two of my favourite animals from the poem are the Chameleon and the Asian Lion. The Chameleon's ability to camouflage itself and attain a colour similar to its background, fascinates me. Moreover, the Lion's mighty roar and tawny coat make it one of my favourites.

28. The leopard can be a parallel for someone who will cause harm. Just like a leopard will not stop attacking even after one cries for help, a person with such leopard-like tendencies will possibly cause more damage than good. They will try to hurt others around them and cause pain. Further, an animal like a hyena may be a metaphor for a person who pretends to harbour good intent and 'smile' on the outside. However, like the hyena, they may prey on others and use them for their gain. Innocent people may not be able to sense their duplicity and may fall prey to their underhanded ways.

29. The boy learns that he must be responsible for the things that he owns as they can be lost or taken away from him easily.

30. The boy's loss of his ball has been used as a metaphor for the painful transition into adulthood. The poet states that the child is learning about the nature of loss that he will have to deal with at many points in life.

31. The poet uses repetition in the poem, emphasising 'what' thrice in the first two sentences. This helps him draw attention to the boy's loss and the feelings of anger and sadness this has caused. On a deeper level, repetition helps him show the loss of purpose and emptiness which accompanies loss in life. He uses repetition in the word 'merrily' which helps highlight the ball's movement, 'bouncing, down the street.' This allows an emphasis on the sudden nature of loss which happens when one least expects it. Thus, the literary devices enable the poet to highlight the seriousness of loss. He also explores the nature and impact of loss through these devices.

32. Anne would call someone a real friend if she could share whatever is in her heart and confide in him or her. She would be able to get very close to such a person.

33. I think Anne Frank's writing ages readers because it is easy for readers to understand her story. For instance, before she starts her first entry, she gives a brief sketch of her life. This background information helps the reader to understand her context.

34. Anne takes Mr Keesing's essay assignments as a challenge. She thinks Mr Keesing is either trying to teach her a lesson or make fun of her by doing so. Therefore, for the first essay, her purpose is to convince Mr Keesing of the importance of talking and why it is impossible for her to talk less. For her third essay, she tries to be inventive and composes a poem to humour Mr Keesing. Both these incidents show us that Anne is a creative person who takes challes in her stride. After the submission of all her essays, she is also successful in being permitted to talk in class. This also shows that she is a good writer.

35. Bread i an Integral part of the Goan society. It is essential to weddings and celebration of festivals like Christmas, in Goa. For instance, a wedding gift In Goa is 'meaningless without the sweet bread 'bol'. Therefore, the baker of the bread, the pader, is important in Goan society.

36. The author creates a sense of nostalgia in the story by talking fondly of his childhood in Goa. He recollects his childhood memories of the pader. He revisits the joyous days when they would eagerly await bread bangles and peep into the pader's basket the slightest opportunity.

37. Portuguese influence finds its way into many aspects of Goan life. In particular, it can be observed in the age-old baking practices and cultural traditions. The narrator mentions that even today, the mixers, moulders, and makers of loaves are carrying forward the Portuguese legacy of bread baking in Goa. They still use the old furnaces and go on rounds with a bamboo, selling their bread. These bakers are still known as 'pader' in Goa, which is originally a word, used in Portuguese language. The culture around bread also spreads to marriages and other ceremonies. The Goans gift the sweet bread called 'bol' during weddings.

38. The tone of this line is humourous. The author is saying that wild elephants can be dangerous.

39. September to March is considered the most pleasant months of Coorg as the weather is cool with light rain. Any time in these months would be recommended to visitors as they can explore Coorg. It rains heavily during the months of monsoon during which time, it is difficult to go outside.

40. The author explores the history of the cultural descent of the Coorgi people, their traditional wear called Kuppia and mentions General Cariappa of the army. Regarding the traditional dress Kuppia, the author traces its origins to the Arab dress Kuffia which looks like a long coat, worn with a belt.

41. I disagree that Coorg as a text only deals with factual descriptions. While it does give the reader Information on the climate, flora, fauna and culture of Coorg, the author's description also romanticises Coorg.

After reading the text, one can imagine what Coorg looks like and could feel like to a visitor. The author makes use of imagery to describe the landscape and climate of Coorg. The reader also feels more connected to the various animals that can be found in Coorg. This could be because the author personifies the animals to describe them.

42. Mijbil runs to the bathtub and is able to open the tap with his paws. This shows that otters are intelligent because Mijbil would have learnt from observation that turning the tap makes water come out.

43. On the first night, Mijbil was indifferent and distant from the author. However, after a few days, he started showing a lot of interest and curiosity in his surroundings. I think this shift happened because Mijbil started feeling more comfortable around the narrator. Also, with the opportunity and freedom to explore the surroundings and not be caged.

44. In the stated line, the narrator meant to convey that he became very attached to Mijbil and almost obsessed with what he did. His own life started revolving around Mijbil. The entire story describes Mijbil's actions in deep detail. The narrator also lemans many things about Mijbil and knows about his habits. This suggests that while he observes Mijbil, he also takes a great Interest to understand why Mijbil does certain actions. For Instance, when the narrator describes what he lemans about otters and water, he mentions some very specific actions that Mijbil does with water.

45. Valli made elaborate plans because this would be the first time that she would take a bus and travel outside town by herself. Being well-prepared probably gave her the confidence to do something so scary.

46. With the loss of his ball, the boy learns that while loss is painful, one learns to deal with it. For Valli, while the death of the cow initially saddens her, she doesn't let it continue to make her sad. Both experience loss as painful but understand it as something that one eventually has to cope with.

47. The adults around Valli are watchful of her. The elderly woman in the bus keeps asking her where she is going and if there is an adult accompanying her. This shows that she believes children should not travel alone as they are not very aware of their surroundings and may get lost easily.

I think this assumption is not justified because Valli does not lose her way at any point. She knows exactly where she is going and how much time the journey will take. She successfully travels alone in the bus and comes back home safely as well. Therefore the old woman's assumption about children is not justified in Valli's case.

48. The words realio' and 'trulio' refer to 'really and 'truly', respectively. They have been Invented by the poet and repeated in different stanzas to enhance the rhythm and lyrical quality of the poem. Also, adds to the light-heartedness and comical quality of elements.

49. Custard was laughed at by Belinda and his fellow animals. Despite proving to be the bravest when the time came, he was mockingly called 'Percival' for being a coward.

50. One of the qualities of custard that stands out is fearlessness. He shows courage when a pirate armed with weapons attacks the house, while everyone else flees, he attacks the pirate and gobbles him up in order to protect Belinda and his animal friends.

51. In 'The Tale of Custard the Dragon' the poet uses imagery to show Custard's strth by describing in detail his physical characteristics. He writes of his razor-like teeth scales, spikes, pointy toes and fire spouting mouth. The poet also does this while describing the pirate, making him appear scarier by talking about how he was armed with pistols and a cutlass. With a wooden leg and a black beard, he instilled fear in Belinda and the animals. The poet uses personification to enhance the impact created by his words and gives Belinda's pets the ability to speak and think. Ink, Blink and Mustard tease Custard for his cowardliness. Moreover, when attacked by the pirate, the mouse strategizes to protect himself.

52. Lamov didn't actually love Natalya but wanted to get married as soon as possible due to his age and poor health. He couldn't afford to wait to find 'real love'. Natalya was 25 years old and unmarried, which was unusual for the era, so she was under a lot of social pressure to get married. Her father describes her as a 'lovesick cat'. When the three of them get Into a quarrel, they insult each other's families and clearly don't hold each other in high regard. Chubukov feels it is a burden to be the father of a 25 year old unmarried daughter and getting Natalya married is a 'weight off his shoulders'. He holds their hands and asks them to kiss each other and agree to get married.

<table>
<tr><td colspan="11">Topic-b: First Flight</td></tr>
</table>

1.

A	(a)	B	(d)	C	(b)	D	(d)	E	(b)

2. (a) **3.** (b) **4.** (c) **5.** (b)

6.

A	(c)	B	(b)	C	(b)	D	(b)	E	(c)

7. Hari was a thief and constantly moved between places. He might have preferred not to make friends to make it easier for him to leave a place.

8. I think when Anil realised that Hari had tried to steal his money, yet was still in the house, he recognised that Hari himself wanted to change and had chosen the better path.

9. No, Anil was not good at managing money. He made money by fits and starts. He would borrow money one week and the next week when he had money, he would lend it. He kept worrying about his next cheque, but as soon as it arrived he would go out and celebrate.

10. Anil has tried to make me a better person by teaching me to read and write but still I have stolen his money. I will go back to Anil and stay with him, just so I can learn to read and write and someday make something of myself Instead of having to steal from others.

11. The greedy man is always In want of more money, so the thought of losing money scares him. The rich man has worked hard to earn his money, and is naturally angry when it is stolen. The poor man is used to being treated unfairly and has accepted loss as a part of his life.

12. Ausable is shown as a fat and sloppy man. One would expect spies to be fitter or muscular, as if they are ready for action at any moment.

I think the author has done this to make the story look more real as compared to glamorous films that are not very realistic.

13. Fowler is a writer who had read descriptions of other secret agents before he met Ausable. He probably wanted to see Ausable because he was going to write a mystery novel involving a secret agent. Meeting a real-life spy would help him create details for his story.

14. Ausable is a good spy because of his presence of mind. Even though Max caught him off-guard at gunpoint, he remained cool and even made up a story about the balcony and the police, which tricked Max into escaping on his own.

15. The price for Griffins freedom was invisibility. He could only escape the consequences of his crimes, if he remained unseen. The London shop assistants would have caught him had he been visible.

16. 'Footprints without Feet' is an adventure story because it details the thrilling escapades of Griffin, an invisible scientist, it describes hard-to-believe events such as his villainous acts in and around London, which he gets away with due to his invisibility.

17. Griffin is disliked by the people around him because he is a violent and dangerous man. He hurts innocent people. For example, he is unable to pay for his stay at Mrs Hall's inn and raises her suspicion about his involvement in the robbery at the clergyman's house. Mrs Hall calls the police to look into the matter. Jaffers, the policeman, tries to arrest Griffin for the robbery, but he attacks and injures him. I feel that In order to reform himself, Griffin can work and earn his living. It would prevent him from robbing others to fulfil his needs.

18. Both Dr. Urquhart and Mr. Weiherer shared ideas with Ebright that helped him to do innovative science experiments or helped him see things in a different way.

19. A person who is competitive 'in a bad sense' will do anything just for the sake of winning, like cheating. Richard Ebright is different because he wants to do the best job that he can do and that makes him competitive.

20. I don't, think the saying 'Jack-of-all-trades, master of none applies to Richard Ebright in the text 'The Making of a Scientist'. Ebright is described as having the same determination for activities like astronomy and collecting coins as he did for collecting butterflies to do his scientific experiments. Further, when Ebright met his social studies teacher, Mr. Weiherer, he was inspired by him and would spend hours on researching for his debates. The text describes him as a 'champion debater. Therefore, even though Ebright had many interests, he was not an average performer in those activities. He showed a deep interest and serious commitment to being very good at them too.